D1451955

THROUGH
THESE DOORS …

THROUGH THESE DOORS ...

The History of the University of Massachusetts Minuteman Marching Band 1863–2003

Kerstin H. Becker

OLD CHAPEL PRESS
Amherst, Massachusetts

LC 2003115896
ISBN 0-9747553-054495

Design by Sally Nichols
Typeset in Berkeley and Shelley Allegro Script

Printed by Sheridan Books, Inc.

To all band members and directors, past and present, be they from the Morris Drum Corps, the Clark Cadet Band, the Aggie Band, the Mass State College Band, the Women's Drill Team, the Redmen Band, the Precisionettes, the Massachusetts Band or the Minuteman Band. Among us, we share nearly 140 years of history and together have created one of the nation's finest college marching bands; And my family.

contents

The Minuteman Marching Band, known far and wide as the Power and Class of New England, stands as an active, living symbol of the University of Massachusetts Amherst campus. This remarkable institution provides an inspirational and visible reflection of the quality and commitment of our students, its performances reflect their talent developed through endless hard work, and its infectious enthusiasm captures everyone fortunate enough to attend its performances.

On the Amherst campus, we mark the end of summer by the sound of band practice, drumbeats echoing through our buildings, announcing the impending arrival of the new academic year. We show up early for our football games to hear a pre-game concert, we stay glued to our seats during half-time to watch the elaborate routines of the show play out, and we stay after the game to hear the post-game concert. The Minuteman Marching Band speaks to all generations, its exceptional award-winning performances capture the campus commitment to achievement, and its energy speaks to the enthusiasm for this place found among our students, faculty, alumni, and friends.

The Band's history is long and distinguished. It spans many generations of students, each one placing its mark on the Band's performances and style. Its history carries with it a tradition of excellence reflected in awards, contests, invitations, and, in truth, a competition to acquire the Band's participation in an endless series of events on and off campus, in Massachusetts and across the nation.

We, who come new to the Amherst campus, learn quickly about the quality of its faculty and staff, the dedication and commitment of its alumni, the high achievement of its students. We find the historic buildings like Old Chapel, the architectural statements and landmarks like the Fine Arts Center and the W.E.B Dubois Library tower, and the science buildings of North campus, but when we look for a clear, living symbol of our student life and their commitment to this campus, it is the Band that captures our attention.

This history of the Pride and the Power of the Minuteman Marching Band serves as a reminder that the quality and achievements of which we are so justly proud rest on the systematic and continuous dedication of generations of students, faculty, staff, and alumni to this campus. This book is indeed a salute to the past, but it is also a promise for the future.

John V. Lombardi
Chancellor

lmost everyone who has seen the University of Massachusetts Minuteman Marching Band's performances will agree that
there is something special about the group. The nationally recognized band is
known for its intensity and for creating exciting, high quality shows.

I had never been part of a marching band before I came to the University
of Massachusetts at Amherst in the fall of 1989. After one season with the
Minuteman Band, I couldn't imagine being involved with a more dedicated
and enthusiastic group of people. I eventually served as a student leader in the
band and, after graduating from the university, began a career as a high school
band director. One of my greatest joys has been seeing my high school students continue their band careers not only as performers with the Minuteman
Band, but also with a number of other outstanding college organizations.

When the opportunity arose to chronicle the history of the Minuteman Band,
I leapt at the chance. The many hours spent in the W. E. B. Du Bois Library and
Special Collections and Archives, searching through newspapers, letters, memos,
and photographs, were rewarding. It was enjoyable to document the band's
growth through the years and to see how the group's advancement paralleled the
development of the university. Few are aware that Massachusetts Agricultural
College began with only a handful of buildings and fewer than sixty students.
Today, the University of Massachusetts at Amherst rests on 1,450 acres and
boasts roughly 23,200 students. The band program, as well, has grown from
eleven members in 1873 to more than 320 members today. Both the university
and its band have a national reputation for excellence and provide outstanding
educations for their students.

Although *Through These Doors* can never be entirely complete, it is none-
theless a fairly comprehensive record of the band's activities from 1863 through
2003. Hopefully its pages will encourage fellow alumni to recall fond memories of their years in the band. It was revealing to interview band members
from across the years, as we realized that time made no difference. No matter
when we were part of the band, we all enjoyed the camaraderie, preparing for
game days, and performing for our audiences.

I have made every effort to ensure that all the names, places, dates, and
events mentioned in this book are accurate. However, as with all historical

records, I found that there were times when references were incomplete, ambiguous, or even contradictory. In such instances, I chose to include the account that seemed the most logical.

I hope that band alumni, directors, parents, friends, and everyone else will enjoy reading *Through These Doors* and learning more about the history of this remarkable organization.

COPY EDITOR
Pamela Wilkinson

PROOF READER
Rosie Pearson

ADDITIONAL PROOF READERS
Lisa Jezowski Roth '95, Colleen Giaimo '00, Lisa Holzer Tohline, Michael Milewski, Steve Robinson '89, Jim Kierstead '92.

DESIGN and TYPESETTING
Sally Nichols

JACKET DESIGN
Ralph Loos

ALUMNI CONTRIBUTORS
Stanley Bozek '38, Harold Hemond '38, Erma (Alvord) Davis '40, John Hilchey '47, Harold Miner '49, Robert Bertram '49, Jack Conlon '49, Tom Fox '49, Bill Mellen '49, George Nickless '52, Arthur Groves '53, Donald Pearse '54, Bob Clowes '60, Richard Glorioso '60, Nancy (Deneault) May '71, Bob Lloyd '78, Jackie Mellen '78, Scott Belgard '78, Bart Newland '81, Liz (MacDonald) Mahoney '81, Jane Bolton '81, Andrea (Roth) Sanna '84, Sue (Boltz) Murphy '86, David Soreff, Chris (Gillette) Connaughton '89, Rob Hammerton '88, Heidi Sarver '86 '88G, Jocelyn (Fein) Steinberg '89, Steve Robinson '89, Joel Gittle '89, James Guidice '90, Mike Jolin '90, Kari (Ewer) Finn '90, Dawn (Delsie) Pence '91, Maureen Foley '91, Beth Ayn Curtis '92, Jim Kierstead '92, Deanna Rutherford '92, Lisa Morrow '93, Sharon Frey '93, Gary Hyman '93, Jason Freedman, Mark Trulson '94, Jillian (Peoples) Ambrose '95, Audrey Carmosino '95, Jill (Richmond) Cayen '95, Chris Brouady '95, Laurie Fabiszewski '95, Jeff Hirsch '96, John Thomson '96, Mikhaela Houston '97, Tanya Carlino '97, Mary Kate Farley '97, Keith Paul '98, Joel Whalen '98, Sanford Jones '98, Rob Luhrs

'99, Kristen Risley '99, David May '99, Timothy Volpe '00, Matt Sexauer '01, Jess Emberley '02, Eric Boehm '02, Carol Graveline '02.

IMAGE SOURCES:
Al Graff, Desiree Meunier, Kerstin Becker, George Nickless, George Parks, John Jenkins, University of Massachusetts Special Collections and Archives, Jill (Richmond) Cayen, Tim Lautzenheiser, Dawn (Delsie) Pence, Frank Becker, Minuteman Band Office, Massachusetts *Index* Yearbook.

SPECIAL THANKS TO:
Stephen Linhart, Tom Range, Sean Smith, Sal Carmosino, Al Graff, Michael Milewski, Steve Robinson, Melissa Watterworth, Helen Perry, Larry Weed, David Hautanen, Ezra Schabas, Thom Hannum, John Jenkins, William Venman, George Parks, University of Massachusetts Special Collections and Archives.

Through These Doors ...

General view of Massachusetts Agricultural College, c. 1886.

THE FOUNDING OF MASS AGGIE
1863–1878

The University of Massachusetts at Amherst had its beginnings on July 2, 1862, when President Abraham Lincoln signed the Morrill Land Grant Act into law. The trustees of Massachusetts Agricultural College (MAC) were incorporated in 1863, and after Northampton, Amherst, Springfield, and Lexington expressed an interest in being home to the new college, the trustees chose Amherst. The school was charged with educating young men in the areas of agriculture and horticulture.

The area chosen for the new college was a truly beautiful one, and the school was placed in "the garden spot of New England," the most picturesque portion of the Connecticut River Valley. Samuel Wheelock Fiske (Amherst College, 1848), writing under the nom de plume Dunn Browne, said of it: "It is just the most beautiful region in the whole world . . . in its fresh spring morning, in its effulgent summer noontide, in its gorgeous autumnal hues, and in its silvery winter moonlight, it surpasses all other most favored climes."

The new college needed a strong leader to see it through the difficult early years. Before the school even opened, two presidents, Henry F. French and

William S. Clark, Henry H. Goodell, Levi Stockbridge, and Charles Goessmann were known as the "Faculty of Four."

Paul Ansel Chadbourne, had resigned. William S. Clark was elected as the third president on August 7, 1867. Clark, a colorful and charismatic individual, was a veteran of the Civil War. During the war, Confederate guns surrounded him and a handful of men from the 21st Massachusetts. Most of his unit was decimated, but Clark was able to escape behind the southern lines. Although reported as killed in action, he sent a reassuring telegram to his family saying, "Still have use for body. Will bring it back in person."

A visionary, Clark worked diligently to bring Massachusetts Agricultural College into existence. The first four school buildings, South College, a boardinghouse, the Botanic Museum, and a chemical laboratory, were constructed by the fall of 1867 and were only barely finished before the first fall term began. Clark also recruited faculty members, picking them from Amherst College professors, local businessmen, and farmers. Among the first professors were Clark, Levi Stockbridge, and Henry H. Goodell. When Charles Goessmann joined the college, the four professors became known as the "Faculty of Four."

The paint was still drying on the buildings when the first freshman class entered on October 2, 1867. By the end of the school year, fifty-six freshmen were enrolled at MAC, and more than one observer considered them "a motley lot." The students had to overcome a number of challenges, including a lack of textbooks and no established curriculum. In addition, the Commonwealth was not convinced of the school's legitimacy, and MAC students were labeled "potato freshmen" by the older and more established colleges. However, Mass Aggie, as the school was often called, persevered. By 1869, student enrollment had grown to 119, and the school was proving its detractors wrong. The college strove to be affordable, and annual expenses for a full year's study, including room and board, were roughly $450.

The agricultural students were active and vibrant. They soon began publishing a yearbook, the *Index*, which first covered the 1869–70 school year. In addition, students played several sports, and the first athletic organizations were a rowing club and the Wilder Base Ball Association. At the time, Mass Aggie's sporting colors were green and white.

Music was always an important part of student life at Mass Aggie, and musical organizations were among the first groups formed on campus. Some of the earliest ensembles were the college choir, the glee club, and an "Association for the Extermination of Bivalves" (bugles), which appeared to be the first unofficial college orchestra.

In 1869, Capt. Henry E. Alvord was appointed as professor of military science and tactics. L. B. Caswell wrote in his book *Brief History of the Massachusetts Agricultural College* that Alvord was the first military officer detailed to give military instruction at an agricultural college. Captain Alvord organized the students into an infantry battalion where they learned regulation drill and skirmishing, as well as the use of sabers, bayonets, small arms, and artillery cannons.

A number of innovations were introduced at MAC through 1870, and the college continued to grow as enrollment climbed to 147 students. Music advanced as well, as students created the first official college orchestra, which joined the choir and glee club as the musical ensembles on campus. In addition, the school's colors became maroon and white.

On July 19, 1871, MAC's "Pioneer Class" of twenty-seven graduated. The people of Amherst took part in the celebration, and during the Commencement exercises, the Springfield Armory Brass Band led the cadet battalion in a torchlight procession from Amherst to President Clark's house. Sen. Justin S. Morrill from Vermont, the man whose vision had brought about the Morrill Land Grant Act, attended the first commencement and was "duly impressed with the fine spectacle." Massachusetts Agricultural College matriculated its first class and gained recognition and respect.

Although MAC's reputation was growing, various forces wanted to turn the school into the agricultural department of an existing college such as Harvard or Amherst. Other private colleges in the Commonwealth doubted Mass Aggie's academic legitimacy, and the Aggies were frequently referred to as "cow college men." However, Massachusetts Agricultural College was more than just a college for farmers. A highlight of the school's early years was the miraculous regatta race of July 21, 1871, where the Aggies, much to everyone's surprise, beat Harvard and Brown. The MAC students were expected to lose handily to the private school students, but as the boats came into view, spectators were heard to exclaim, "Why, it's the damned farmers!" President Clark became so excited that he threw his hat into the air and shouted repeatedly, "We've won! We've won!" This critical victory showed the Commonwealth of Massachusetts that Mass Aggie was not a questionable experiment but a legitimate school with dedicated students. In addition, the country was suddenly aware that there was a Massachusetts Agricultural College, and that "it had a class of students who could compete successfully with students of older institutions of learning." The future looked bright for the young school.

Another example of school rivalry was highlighted in the July 2, 1873, *MAC Alumni Bulletin*. Amherst College students stole one of the Aggie cannons, took it apart, and hid it near their campus, intending to reassemble it and fire off salutes for the Fourth of July. The Aggies formed a plan to get their cannon back. As the Amherst students were assembling the stolen cannon, several Aggies hid in the woods around the Amherst College campus. Although they were spotted, the Amherst students assumed they were classmates, and warned them, "Look out fellows, the Aggies are about." One of the Aggies reportedly replied, "All right, we will!" As the Amherst students were getting ready to fire the cannon, the Aggies rushed out and stuck a rat-tail file into the vent of the cannon, effectively jamming the firing mechanism, and making the cannon inoperable. Their fun spoiled, the Amherst students became so angry that they pushed the cannon into their bonfire and burned off all the woodwork. The Aggies triumphantly returned to campus, and the Amherst students were ordered to pay for damage to the cannon.

The college drum corps, the forerunner of today's Minuteman Marching Band, made its first appearance around 1873, and one of the first photographs of the group was taken at this time. Although the rest of the MAC cadet battalion wore regular army uniforms, the drum corps appeared in civilian dress with black derby hats. The group consisted of eleven members: four snare drummers, two cymbalists, one bass drummer, three fifers, and one drum major. Under the terms of the federal land grant, all Mass Aggie students were required to train in military tactics and drill, and the drum corps was formed to help students stay in step during the infantry drills. The student drummers also performed at the year-end battalion reviews and at other important military functions.

By 1875, as the school continued to gain respect, the cadet battalion received new uniforms. 1st Lt. C. A. L. Totten, 4th Artillery, was appointed to head the military department at Mass Aggie, and he introduced the West Point-style uniform. Soon the students wore gray uniforms with two rows of bright brass buttons that made their shoulders look "wide like a blacksmith." The Aggie battalion and its drum corps, which also received the new uniforms, now looked like proper military school cadets.

LIEUTENANT MORRIS' DRUM CORPS
1878–1889

In the fall of 1878, 1st Lt. Charles Morris, 5th Artillery, became the new military instructor at Massachusetts Agricultural College. Under Morris, the battalion drum corps began to have a life and personality of its own, and by 1879, the group was renamed the Morris Drum Corps in his honor. One of the first student leaders of the corps was Cadet Sgt. Maj. Charles Flint Jr. '81, the "instructor of the drum corps." Flint, originally from Boston, was highly musical and played the flute and cornet. Through his influence, the ten-member Morris Drum Corps was organized, and he also helped organize the college orchestra.

The football program began to grow as well, and the Massachusetts Agricultural College Foot Ball Association was organized in 1878. Unlike modern football, the game was played in the style of English rugby with fifteen men on a side. One of the earliest football games took place on November 22, 1879, and the Aggies, playing at home, beat the Amherst College freshman team 4–0.

Although the school was taking strides forward, there were numerous obstacles to its continued existence. Funding issues have always been a part of the University of Massachusetts, and it was no different for its predecessor. L. B. Caswell wrote that in 1879, the Massachusetts legislature formed a commission to eliminate the school's budget. The commission's 1880 report recommended that all federal money earmarked for Mass Aggie should instead be given to Amherst College, and that the state should abandon any further effort toward maintaining the agricultural college. Although Gov. John Long was in favor of the recommendation, the public strongly rejected the report's suggestions, and the legislature dropped the matter. This attempt to close the college by removing its funding attracted the public's sympathy, and Mass Aggie gained the support of the powerful agricultural community.

For the 1880 school year, Cadet Charles Beach '82 was appointed drum major of the seven-member Morris Drum Corps, and the group played cadences three to four hours a week during the students' required military drill time. Flint was promoted to cadet captain and battalion adjutant, second in command under Lieutenant Morris. A number of musically talented students played in both the drum corps and the college orchestra, and it was common for memberships to overlap. Students played drums for outdoor military drills and wind or string instruments for indoor orchestra rehearsals.

In September, there was excitement as MAC's cadet battalion was invited to participate in Boston's 250th Anniversary Parade. On September 16, the battalion assembled and marched in parade order to the train depot, with the Morris Drum Corps leading the way. After the train ride to Boston, the "lively music of the drum corps" marched the cadets to the barracks. The next day, the battalion paraded in Boston and "received great praise from the press and public for [its] fine appearance." The Aggie cadets, who were cheered along the parade route, received piles of fruit as a sign of appreciation during rest stops. The Boston cadets were especially appreciative of the Aggies and gave them three cheers. This appearance by MAC was highly successful, and the students' military bearing earned them second place among the assembled battalions. After they returned to Amherst, the cadets gave three cheers for Morris before being dismissed.

The football team made great strides as well, and on November 2, its members received uniforms, which were paid for by students and faculty. The uniforms consisted of maroon-and-white caps, white canvas jackets, white canvas pants, and maroon stockings. The students were proud of their good-looking football team.

Music continued to play an important part in the life of the college, and MAC president Levi Stockbridge wrote that the student musical associations were valuable assets to the campus. He felt that the groups, such as the drum corps and orchestra, were successful in unifying the college community and in welcoming friends and other visitors.

Although Morris left MAC in 1881, the Morris Drum Corps carried on his

The Morris Drum Corps and cadet battalion line up for inspection, c.1881.

The 1883 cadet battalion and drum corps on the parade ground.

name. The drum major for the season was Cadet James Paige '82, who in 1891 went on to become professor of veterinary science at MAC and veterinarian for the Hatch Experiment Station. Membership between the six-member drum corps and the college orchestra continued to be interchangeable. That fall, drum corps members George Putnam '85 on flute, Everett Chandler '82 on double bass, and former drum major Charles Beach on cornet played in the seven-member orchestra as well.

During the 1882 school year, Cadet Edward Flint '85 became the new drum major of that year's four-member corps. He was eventually appointed assistant professor of chemistry at MAC in 1893.

By 1883, although an official college band was not yet organized, students continued to have a high interest in instrumental music. The class of 1885 formed its own "1885 Band," and the group included a flute, guitar, cornet, tambourine, piano, trombone, and violin. Putnam, who played flute in the group, was also the president of the Orchestral Association, and Flint, who continued

7

The 1884 cadet battalion and drum corps relax after military exercises.

as drum major of the Morris Drum Corps, played guitar. At the time, a seven-member group was considered a large ensemble, and the college orchestra itself consisted of only three violins, three guitars, one cornet, and two flutes.

In 1884, a major innovation took place as the Morris Drum Corps added fifes to its regular complement of snare drums, bass drum, and cymbals. The fifes allowed the group to become more versatile, since it could now play melodic music as well as military drum cadences. However, not all were pleased with the changes. The following year, the school yearbook's Christmas gift to drum major Richard Duncan '86 was "an ear for music," since he apparently had none.

Construction of one of the campus' most prominent and distinct buildings began in 1884. Money was allocated to build a chapel, and the cornerstone of the "New Stone Chapel" was laid on November 6. The granite for the building, which was also to serve as a library, came from a Pelham quarry that was owned by the college. The beloved future home of the Minuteman Band came into existence. By 1935, the stone chapel became known simply as Old Chapel.

In 1885, Cadet 3rd Sgt. Henry Rideout '87 became the drum major of the eight-member corps, whose instrumentation included three fifes, as well as three snares and one bass drum. Duncan, who was promoted to cadet first lieutenant and Adjutant of the Battalion, continued to lead the orchestra on

Old Chapel was built in 1884 as a dual-purpose chapel-library.

violin. Drum corps fifers Fred Fowler '87, Frederick Brown '87, and James Smith '89 all played flute in the sixteen-member orchestra as well.

On October 8, 1888, the MAC battalion gave an exhibition of its drilling abilities at the Springfield Fair. The students took the train to Springfield and marched to Hampden Park to the "lively music of the drum corps." At the park, the battalion and Morris Drum Corps gave a dress parade performance that was well-received by Gov. Oliver Ames, his staff, and the general audience.

Leader.
EUGENE H. LEHNERT.

Drum Major.
PERLEY E. DAVIS.

EDWIN C. HOWARD	Tuba.
ALBERT F. BURGESS	Trombone.
AMOS H. MASON	2d Alto.
CHARLES H. HIGGINS	Solo Alto.
EUGENE H. LEHNERT	Baritone.
EDWARD O. BAGG	Solo B Flat Cornet
WALTER B. HARPER	Solo B Flat Cornet
GUY A. HUBBARD	B Flat Clarionet.
J. HARRY PUTNAM	Piccolo.
WILLIAM C. BROWN	Snare Drum.
MERLE E. SELLEW	Bass Drum.
JOHN H. JONES	Cymbals.

93

Yearbook listing of the 1892 Clark Cadet Band.

THE CLARK CADET BAND
1889–1899

In 1889, the college cadet battalion was named the Clark Cadets in honor of President Clark, who had died in March 1886. The drum corps, however, continued to be known as the Morris Drum Corps. The first sergeant and chief musician that year was drummer Louis Horner '91, and the ten-member corps consisted of four fifes, four snare drums, one bass drum, and one cymbal.

During the 1889–90 school year, interest in instrumental music reached a new high, and for the first time, an ensemble referred to as the MAC Band appeared in the *Index*. The new band had cornet player Frank Arnold '91 as president, cornet player Homer West '92 as vice president, bass drummer and cymbal player Henry Emerson '92 as secretary-treasurer, and piccolo player Joseph Harry Putnam '94 as the band's leader. The thirteen-member group modeled itself on the highly popular musical ensemble of the time, the British Brass Band. Instrumentation consisted of four cornets, one piccolo, one alto horn, three tenor horns, one baritone horn, one E-flat tuba, one drum, and one bass drummer who doubled on cymbals. Although still under the jurisdiction of the military department, the band was not required to assume martial duties, and it was the Morris Drum Corps that played at mandatory drill rehearsals and other military events.

For the fall of 1890, the drum major for the drum corps was William Ranney '93, and the chief musician was Cadet 1st Sgt. William Fletcher '92. The drum corps' equipment consisted of six drums that were owned by the Commonwealth, as well as two snare drums, four pairs of drumsticks, one bass drum, a bass drum stick and strap, and three fifes that were owned by the college.

Soon the battalion, drum corps, and MAC Band received new uniforms. In October, military instructor Lt. Lester Cornish traded the old gray uniforms for new blue ones with white trim, which looked more like those of the current U.S. Army. Cadet students felt that the blue uniform was a neater and more handsome outfit than the old one, which some thought resembled the uniform worn by "inmates of various Reform Schools."

Artillery practice was mandatory for all students.

While the drum corps played for military drill, the MAC Band began having indoor rehearsals and concerts. An editorial entitled "Our Brass Band" stated that the group met twice a week, and that band members were highly motivated and determined to make the band a credit to Mass Aggie. Apparently, the college as a whole was "indifferent on the subject," as the editorial urged everyone to give the boys in the band a little encouragement, since they had been improving steadily. In addition, listeners were promised they would "surely benefit" from attending the band's performances.

By late October, the band held regular evening rehearsals in the east entry of North College Dormitory. Judging by various editorials in the college paper, one of the group's favorite songs was "America," which the band members rehearsed with great enthusiasm. Although the value of having a college band was recognized, the students had one reservation and asked the band not to practice during study time. However, they enjoyed falling asleep to the sounds of the band playing "Nearer My God to Thee" and hoped that the group would soon rival the drum corps in excellence. By November, students acknowledged that the band had "achieved some measure of improvement," and that a college band was an honor to the institution.

During this time, MAC students discussed the benefits of having women enroll. Women would have a college of their own where they would be looked over by a female principal, and instead of mandatory military drill, they would take calisthenics. Students felt that having a women's dorm and a female administrator would make Mass Aggie more attractive to women and that the young men would benefit from the two evenings each week when they would be allowed to visit the women's dorm.

The band continued to improve. During the winter of 1891, the fourteen-member ensemble had 1st Sgt. and chief musician Eugene Lehnert '93 as the band leader and Perley Davis '94 as the drum major. Band members took part in a variety of college activities, and Lehnert participated in the orchestra while Davis was on the football team. Showing support for the band, the school's newspaper, *Aggie Life*, asked students how many of them had heard the brass band play. If they had not, it was their own fault, since the band had become surprisingly good. The band members met regularly twice a week, and the doors were always open for anyone who wanted to listen.

Although the band made strong progress, in April it lost two members, and the rest of the group was feeling discouraged. However, the college paper wrote that anyone who had heard the band play last term thought it was a success, and that it would do fine this term as well. If those who remained kept up their "splendid enthusiasm," the band would be a credit to the college, despite the loss of a member or two.

Although the Morris Drum Corps had been the military's musical ensemble since 1878, the group was officially disbanded for unknown reasons on April 14, 1891. To compensate for the loss of the drum corps, Lieutenant Cornish filled in as the drummer for the state legislature's yearly visit to view the cadet battalion on May 22. When the drum corps dissolved, the college band stepped in to fill the void, and on June 9, the group performed for Class Day exercises during Commencement Week. It was the first time that the college band played during the graduation ceremonies.

By 1891, the MAC Band took on a new name and became the Clark Cadet Band. The renamed cadet band began serving two functions: providing music for military drill rehearsals and giving indoor concerts. In its first function, the band played at all military drill rehearsals and prominent military ceremonies, including the spring battalion review. In its second role, it began giving outdoor concerts for the college and surrounding communities. Almost all band members played for both the indoor concert and outdoor drills, except for the drum major, who appeared to be only used for military functions. The band soon became an indispensable college organization, and students felt that the battalion looked much sharper when it was enhanced by the band's spirited music. Cadets found it was almost impossible to imagine marching drill without the band playing.

In the spring of 1892, due to changes in military regulation, the battalion was expected to parade and drill daily. Before, military drill was limited to three times a week, but now, the cadet band provided music each day. Military drill was a requirement for all Mass Aggie students, and Frank Prentice Rand provided a fanciful description in his book, *Yesterdays at Massachusetts*

State College: "On clear commencement days the college boys will still parade, they will be carefree, keeping in step with the band, executing their maneuvers, with dreamy eyes, confident of their own and their country's destiny. And parents and sisters and sweethearts will thrill to the sights. And the flag of the nation will float proudly above."

As the Clark Cadet Band's reputation spread, it began to give more off-campus performances and was invited to provide music for Amherst College's mock convention in March. Due to the band's growing popularity, the college community decided to build a bandstand for the group. The April 27, 1892, edition of *Aggie Life* alerted readers to the soon-to-be bandstand and suggested that band music would shortly "add its charms" to student life at Mass Aggie.

In warmer months, the band gave concerts in the bandstand.

The bandstand was completed in May at a cost of $125 with twenty-five cents left over, which band members generously donated to the football association. The new bandstand stood near South College and Chapel, and the fourteen-foot-high wooden structure was considered an ornament to which the college could point to "with pride." The townspeople looked forward to the grand opening, and students considered the bandstand "neat and tasty." The faculty generously provided several incandescent lights to illuminate the bandstand, and during the warmer months, there were open-air evening concerts once a week. It was generally believed that the concerts would bring much-needed publicity to the college, and students felt that weekly band concerts were a step in the right direction toward making their college life "brighter and happier."

The Amherst community appreciated the band as well and asked it to furnish music for the town's 1892 Memorial Day celebration. Since the group had considerable experience leading battalion reviews and parades, many felt it was a solid match, and the band and two volunteer companies of Clark Cadets led the May 30 Memorial Day procession.

On June 7, the band was photographed, which was somewhat unusual since photography at the time was not widespread. It was a memorable event, and the *Index* humorously commented that band member and cornet player Homer West '92 accidentally broke one of the photographic plates. The band closed its season on June 10 by playing at a Republican Party celebration after the presidential salute was fired.

The band's reputation continued to grow on and off-campus, as the group shouldered the responsibilities of being one of the college's musical ambassadors. In the review of the year, the Clark Cadet Band was acknowledged as having upheld the college's reputation for musical ability.

In the fall of 1892, Lehnert continued as band leader and was promoted to cadet first lieutenant in charge of the band. Lehnert, who eventually joined the MAC faculty, was also the orchestra manager, and Davis returned as the group's drum major.

The cadet band had a number of engagements that season. On September 28, it provided music for the county fair, and in October, the group gave outdoor concerts in the bandstand for the college and local communities. In November, the band furnished music when the Democratic clubs of the town of Amherst, Amherst College, and Mass Aggie celebrated the election of Grover Cleveland. The band played at a Democratic rally on November 17, and by the end of the month, the bandstand was repainted. In December, the group also received new band music, which is significant in that there was not a great deal of money generally available and represented an investment in the band's future.

When the weather turned warmer in May 1893, the overworked and worn-out students looked forward to the beginning of the Clark Cadet Band's outdoor concert season. "Music hath charms to soothe," they quoted, showing support and encouraging the band members. Due to the success of the previous year's Memorial Day ceremonies, the band was again invited to provide music for the event.

By the fall of 1893, the band program was on solid footing. Although Eugene Lehnert, one of the band's strong leaders, had graduated, Cadet 1st Lt. Joseph Harry Putnam took his place. Davis continued as drum major, and the band leader position now outranked that of drum major. Band members continued their involvement with other school activities, which was possible because of the small size of the agricultural college. Putnam was quarterback of the college football team and played flute in

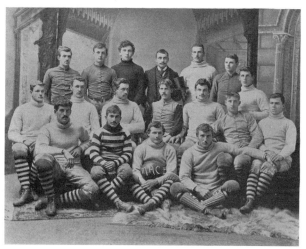

The 1892 MAC Aggie football team.

Three band leaders from 1893: Joseph H. Putnam, far left; Walter Harper, far right; Eugene Lehnert, second from right.

The 1893–94 cadet battalion and Clark Cadet Band on the parade field.

The drill hall was used for military drill as well as band rehearsals.

Students playing hockey on the Campus Pond.

A 1901 classroom in the Campus Pond. In the background are the bandstand, South College, and North College.

the orchestra. Various other band members were also on the football team, including Charles Higgins '94, an alto horn player and football tackle.

Although the twelve-member band lost a few players with their graduation, it gained a number of freshmen to compensate. Visitors were encouraged to look in on the ensemble during its rehearsals in the drill hall to see how good it was. The band rehearsed faithfully to present excellent music for spring, when parades and reviews were daily features for the cadets.

A new campus landmark came into being that fall. The Campus Pond was first a brook that flowed downhill, east of Butterfield Dorm, making the middle of campus a marsh. In 1890, students began digging and created a small pool of water. In 1892, construction on the pond dam began, and there was hope that in the future the pond could be enlarged and used for winter sports. By 1893, the dam was complete, and in the following years, students skated and played a version of ice hockey called "polo" on the artificial pond.

Massachusetts Agricultural College continued to gain national recognition. The *Index* wrote that in 1894, MAC's battalion was celebrated for its excellence, and it was noted that not all schools had the distinction of having a military department.

The battalion and its band had another change in uniforms, as white military trousers appeared in April 1894. The cadet band's new look consisted of blue tops with white pants, and the drum major had the added distinction of wearing a tall, bearskin-style hat. This marked the first year that the band's drum major wore a uniform distinctly different from the regular cadets and officers.

In the fall of 1894, the band's leadership structure changed to include a student military commander, William Brown '95, whose title was First Lieutenant Commanding the Band. The band's first sergeant and new band leader was Walter Harper '96 and the new drum major was Asa Kinney '96. Harper, a "chemical genius from Wakefield," was known for playing his cornet, leading the college orchestra, and talking too much. Kinney was praised in the *Index* yearbook as being a great storyteller, and as drum major of the battalion, he was considered the "observed of all observers." Apparently, with his towering form, a noble and "firmly set head crowned with masses of flaxen hair and a roman nose," Kinney had "comprehensive knowledge of everything," and his peers held him in high regard, with a little tongue-in-cheek humor. The band ended its season by performing at Class Day on June 18, 1895.

In the fall of 1895, Harper continued as leader of the fourteen-member Clark Cadet Band, and the new drum major was Charles I. Goessmann '97, son of professor Charles Goessmann. A highlight for the year was the cadet battalion's attendance at the birthday exercises of General Joseph Hooker in Hadley.

During this time, Massachusetts Agricultural College continued to come under fire as people questioned the legitimacy of educating farmers. Mass Aggie endured sarcasm from the press, and even students felt that the "Agricultural" portion of the name drove potential freshmen away, since many were more interested in liberal arts subjects than in agriculture.

In June 1896, the Clark Cadet Band ended its season by performing at Class Day and the military review during Commencement. The group also gave a concert for the college on June 3.

After a number of successful years, the band fell on hard times in the fall of 1896. 1st Lt. William Wright, head of the military department, wrote that a band was not formed due to lack of musical talent and experience among the students. Since the battalion needed music to accompany its drills, he remedied the situation by creating a trumpet and drum corps and purchased new instruments for the group.

On March 7, 1897, the new drums and bugles arrived for the revitalized drum corps, which consisted of six drummers and six buglers. To provide the group with necessary instruction, Lieutenant Wright aside two hours for rehearsal time each day. However, *Aggie Life* reported that the buglers enthusiastically played their new instruments at all hours of the day,

The Clark Cadet Band and cadet battalion by South College, c.1894.

The 1894 Clark Cadet Band by Old Chapel.

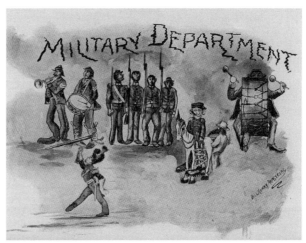

A humorous yearbook drawing of the 1899 military department.

17

and the outdoor music became a distraction to students who needed to study. The students requested that the group's rehearsal time be confined to the established hours, and after the issue was resolved, the students acknowledged that the drum and bugle corps was improving.

For the fall of 1897, drums and bugles continued to be the instruments of choice for the military department. Alfred Gile '00 was the corps' cadet corporal and drum major, Cpl. Warner Crowell '00 was the chief drummer, and Cpl. Arthur Frost '00 was the chief trumpeter. Drum corps members continued to play on the college football team: Crowell was a halfback and Gile a fullback.

MAC Avenue and view of the drill hall, Old Chapel, and South College.

Wright wrote that the drummers were efficient and interested in their work, but that the buglers of the trumpet corps were not up to a proper standard, owing to lack of professional instruction. He recommended that a drum and trumpet teacher be hired to give music instruction once a week during the winter term. It was the first time that the college considered hiring a music instructor for the military band program. However, due to the outbreak of the Spanish-American War, a professional instructor was not secured until later.

In 1898, the war began to influence life at MAC, and students left to enlist in the army. The MAC military department was suspended indefinitely when Lieutenant Wright rejoined his army regiment in April, and with the war drawing away resources, it was not possible to find a qualified military instructor for the MAC battalion. Military drill at the college ceased, and the drum corps was dissolved as well. In what was to be a general historical trend of the college, whenever war broke out, the cadet battalion and college band, which were under the military's jurisdiction, disbanded as students joined the war effort.

Although the band was defunct, Mass Aggie students continued to be musically active. In June 1899, the banjo club, one of the few remaining instrumental groups on campus, provided music for the Class Day ceremonies. In addition, students played in the orchestra and sang in the choir. When the war ended, students returned to campus, and nearly two years had passed without military drill and band music at the school.

GROWTH AND PROGRESS
1900–1911

*I*n January 1900, Capt. John Anderson became the new military instructor at Massachusetts Agricultural College. He had served as an officer during the Civil War and was on duty for thirty years in the active army before retiring to Belchertown. With Anderson's support and encouragement, the band was revitalized and became a more established college organization. By the fall of 1900, the Clark Cadet Band was almost back to its former glory, under the energetic leadership of band leader and Cadet 1st Sgt. Myron West '03. It was West who had convinced Anderson to come to MAC to reorganize the cadet battalion.

Throughout the history of the marching band program at the college, a number of army officers recognized that bands were an indispensable part of the military department, and that a musical marching unit was critical to the proper functioning of a military unit's esprit de corps. Anderson wrote, "The value of a good band to the military department, in fact, to the whole college, cannot be overestimated." Without the work of these officers, the cadet band would not have had the stability it needed to grow. Anderson's support and

The cadet battalion and Clark Cadet Band by South College, c. 1900.

belief in the band was invaluable, and he went to great lengths to ensure that his band was a success. In a variety of ways, the band moved away from being a strictly military ensemble during Anderson's tenure and came closer to being a more modern college band.

Anderson set the stage for hiring the band's first professional director, and the October 10 edition of *Aggie Life* reported that William Day from Greenfield was brought in as the cadet band's new instructor. He taught the band for two hours a week, and the college paid for his salary as well as the band's new music. Although Day was not a faculty or staff member, he was the band's first official, nonstudent band director.

In order to encourage more practice, Anderson excused band members from all other military exercises and drills and apparently turned the military period into rehearsal time for band members. He also recommended that the college give the band every possible encouragement, including a small appropriation for distinctive trimmings for its uniforms. At the time, the band wore blue army uniforms with blue caps, white gloves, and dark pants with a white stripe down the leg. Band members also purchased their own instruments and planned to pay them off in quarterly installments.

On October 11, the newly reorganized sixteen-member Clark Cadet Band had its first rehearsal in the drill hall. With Anderson's support, West had remustered the band, two-thirds of whose members were freshmen, and returned the group to its prewar brass band configuration. In addition to Day's instruction, the band received another three hours of rehearsal time with West, who also composed music for the ensemble. The cadet band resumed its former military duties and played for drill, which took place three hours a week. Later in the month, the battalion participated in a Republican parade in Northampton, and the new band performed admirably.

"THE NEW BAND."

What are those various noises
   Coming from the drill hall room?
They are strange and rancorous-awful!
   And they fill my heart with gloom
As I walk along the campus,
   Or, upon my window seat
Try to study, try to figure
   Try my problems hard to meet.

There's a rip-a roar-a rattle,
  A toot-a snarl-a bang;
A wail both long and woeful,
  A scraping and a whang.
And then a welcome silence,
  All too short it proves to be,
Then again the air is fractured.
  Are the furies in high glee?

Furies! Nonsense, my poor student,
  Knowest not what we have here?
'Tis a band-you'd scarce believe it,
  Yes, a band which does not fear.
It's practicing to play well
  In a far and distant day;
meantime you must have patience
  Or else must run away.

"TO THE M.A.C. BAND."

Where's the music that is half so grand
As the wailings of the Aggie Band?
Must we listen to the tune (?) they play?
I can hear them from afar,
Now a crashing, now a jar,
And I fear they're coming nearer,
For they practice night and day.
   Oh, listen to the band,
   How terribly they play;
   "There's no poorer in the land,"
   Hear everybody say.
   Oh, listen to the band,
   Will it never, never cease?
No, a shout of "Here they come,"
And a banging of the drum,
   Shows it's useless to expect a minute's peace.
   How the students and the poor Profs. run,
They are in a hurry, every one.
Crowds are flocking for some distant land,
  And they tear along the street
  Muttering maledictions sweet,
For there's fearful, awful discord in the music of
  our band.

The humorous poems above appeared in the yearbook and were written shortly after the band reorganized in October 1900.

The spring of 1901 was a busy time for the band. On March 4, the group had its first grand march in the drill hall, and the galleries were crowded with spectators. On March 7, the band held its first public parade, which was proclaimed a grand success, and on May 8, it gave a well-received evening concert. Besides giving several concerts in the bandstand, the band also had two performances out of town.

The cadet band's activities soon caught the attention of members of the state legislature in Boston. When State Senator Gardner reviewed the MAC battalion in the spring of 1901, he was so pleased with the band's performance

MAC students and cannons by Old Chapel.

The 1901 Clark Cadet Band, led by Myron West, on the back steps of Old Chapel. West is the seated cornetist, second from right.

that upon his return to Boston, he introduced a bill that would appropriate four hundred dollars to benefit the band. The bill easily passed both houses, and the cadet band found itself the recipient of a generous legislative gift.

Although the band had been rehearsing for a relatively short time, its improvement was evident, and by Commencement, the Clark Cadet Band was praised as one of the "brightest and attractive features" of the college. In addition, the newly restructured MAC cadet battalion was almost back to its former glory.

In the fall of 1901, in recognition for his work in rebuilding the cadet battalion, Anderson was promoted to the rank of major. West continued as the band's leader, and Charles Halligan '03 was the new drum major. The growing cadet band made up a large percentage of the student body, and out of 125 students in the military department, twenty-two of them were in the band.

The Clark Cadet Band, which was by now also known as "The College Band," continued to excel through the fall. Of the money from the state legislature, $350 was used to purchase new instruments, which was appropriate because some of the band members were having a difficult time paying for their instruments.

Major Anderson felt that the legislature's financial gesture helped place the band on solid footing by making it a more permanent organization. He expressed his gratitude to the legislators and said that all students were grateful for their generous financial support. The college invested money for equipment, and band members were motivated to work for a better future.

The college football program also made great strides, and in September, James Halligan, who had been captain of the 1899 football team, became the first full-time football coach in the school's history. In October, after a spectacular win over Wesleyan, the uniformed cadet band led the entire college in columns of two to the center of Amherst, where the student body waited for the football team to return on the Northampton trolley. After the students circled Amherst Common, the proprietor of the Amherst House invited the band to occupy the piazza, where it gave a short but enjoyable concert. Mrs. Stearns, daughter of President Clark, presented the band with twenty-five dollars as a token of her appreciation for its fine work. After the team arrived, the students marched back to campus and celebrated with a roaring bonfire and a six-gun salute. The cadet band then generously gave Mrs. Stearns' money to the football team, and the students gave Mrs. Stearns a rousing cheer. Following a cannon salute, the celebration ended. The band and the cannon were important elements of a successful celebration, as they kept students cheerful and in good spirit. Students proudly noted that not all colleges could boast having both a band and a cannon.

In November, after the Aggie football team beat rival Amherst, students formed a parade behind the team's carriage and marched through the streets, yelling and cheering. Later in the evening, there was a rally, after which the band formed up and, with students, alumni, and the football team, marched downtown and around the Common. The parade stopped in front of the Amherst House, where the band gave a concert while the students danced around the square. Afterward, the parade returned to campus where the celebration ended around a large bonfire. The 1901 MAC football team was one of the most successful in early school history and boasted a record of 9–1.

The band also had a strong fall season and excelled in supporting the football team while encouraging school spirit. In addition, the Massachusetts General Court recognized the band's excellence and continued its support by appropriating an additional two hundred dollars.

Starting on the evening of April 25, 1902, the band gave a series of concerts in the bandstand. The hour-long programs included marches and serenades such as "The Washington Post," "The Stars and Stripes Forever," and "Moonlight Fancies Waltzes."

In May, the band played for an exhibition drill in the drill hall. Afterward, the group gave a concert and occupied a decorated stage at the north end of the hall, opening the program with "Medley Overture" by Beyer. There was an additional concert on May 23, 1902, and music included the "Clark Cadet March," "Overture, Jolly Students," and "The Merry American March." The

The 1902 MAC Battalion and Clark Cadet Band in formation by Chapel.

band's leader, Myron West, was featured as cornet soloist during "In the Sacramento Valley." Students remarked that the band, under West's leadership, had developed "into a very credible state of perfection."

In the fall of 1902, West was promoted to first lieutenant and Halligan continued as the band's drum major. The multi-talented West was also the editor-in-chief of the *College Signal*, the new name for the school's newspaper. Innovations included new drills for the battalion and its band, as well as new regulation U.S. Army caps for their uniforms. The college band also traveled off-campus to perform for the October 7 Belchertown cattle show.

Anderson wrote that the band did excellent work under West, and he felt that the group could be permanently organized and maintained if it had proper support and encouragement. At the time, it was on secure footing, although funds were needed for one or two new instruments to replace those owned by students who were graduating. In addition, Anderson requested an additional appropriation of seventy-five dollars to fund band music and equipment repairs.

An exciting event took place in December 1902, as "Sons of Old Massachusetts," written by Howard Knight '02, made its first appearance. This song served as Massachusetts Agricultural College's unofficial alma mater for many years, until "When Twilight Shadows Deepen" became the official school song in 1962.

Assisted by C. M. Kinney, an organist from Northampton, the cadet band gave a concert at the North Amherst Church on February 27, 1903. The program was presented with enthusiasm, and the performers were highly praised. The band also gave a concert at Belchertown Town Hall, which included a banjo solo, "The Star-Spangled Banner," and the march "Blaze Away."

The band gave three concerts in May, and after the May 13 performance, some less-than-pleased listeners wrote that the music had been "murdered" by the band. Nonplussed, the band members ended their year by playing at the Class Day program in June and gave an open-air concert for the thirty-third Commencement on June 15. Myron West, who had been responsible for the creation of the vigorous and impressive cadet band, graduated, and Arthur Peck '04 was named as the new band leader.

When the college opened in the fall of 1903, prospects for the cadet band's season were dimmed because neither Peck nor one of the drummers returned to school. However, the band was fortunate to find three players from the freshman class who were experienced musicians and bolstered the group's membership. In addition, Frank Waugh, a professor of landscape architecture, stepped in to help the band in various ways. Waugh, who also played flute with the group, assisted with directing and running rehearsals in his spare time. He was the first faculty member to serve as the group's unofficial band director.

By November, Peck returned to school and took over the band's student leadership. Although students had worried that the band would not be as good as the previous year's due to the graduation of two of its strongest players, there was nothing now "to warrant such a pessimistic view."

Since band funds were limited, Waugh provided the students with new music. To secure additional funding, Anderson wrote in his annual military department report that Peck was doing good work and that the band merited all the appropriations it had received in the past. He requested that $150 be given for the current year for two or three more instruments, new music, and other equipment. However, the band's growth throughout the previous years had stabilized, and the generosity of the state legislature leveled off, as well.

In May 1904, the open-air band concerts, which were popular in past years, resumed under the baton of Waugh. When Levi Stockbridge died that month, the Clark Cadets, headed by the college band, acted as an honor guard and accompanied the procession to the North Hadley Cemetery. Stockbridge, one of the legendary "Faculty of Four," had been recruited by President Clark to bring the Massachusetts Agricultural College into existence.

Cadet 1st Lt. C. Sheldon Holcomb '05 was the chief musician and band leader for the fall of 1904. The previous school year, he had played in the band and had also won an "M" as a member of the varsity football team. The band's membership stayed steady at twenty-two members, with Norman Ingham '05 serving as the new drum major.

The 1904 Clark Cadet Band, here posed by Chapel, resumed giving outdoor concerts in the bandstand.

The cadet band continued to perform at off-campus ceremonies for the college. When MAC's president Henry Hill Goodell, another of the "Faculty of Four," died, the funeral was held on April 27, 1905. With draped colors and a muffled drum, the uniformed college band and battalion led the cemetery procession. The band also gave two concerts in April, and Holcomb was credited with working hard to develop a good band.

In a note of appreciation to one of the most effective early supporters of the college band, the class of 1907 dedicated its *Index* to Major Anderson, "Honored as a soldier, respected as an instructor, and esteemed as a sincere friend." Without Anderson's support, the Clark Cadet Band would not have received the solid footing it needed to grow and mature into a strong musical ensemble.

A major change occurred at Mass Aggie as more and more women began attending classes. Rand wrote in *Yesterdays at Massachusetts State College* that in 1905, for the first time, two women graduated with bachelor's degrees and another with a master's of science. Before this, a woman had enrolled in 1875, but was not part of the regular college; the class of 1896 also had a woman student, but only for a short time.

In the fall of 1905, Capt. George Martin, 18th Infantry, replaced Anderson as the professor of military science. Like Anderson, Martin felt that a band was an asset to the military department, and with his support, $109 was appropriated for new band instruments. Cadet 1st Lt. Stanley Rogers '06, chief musician and solo B-flat cornet player, led the college band. At the time, the student band leader was often referred to as the group's chief musician. Since there was a demand among students, Rogers also organized a fourteen-member college orchestra.

The Clark Cadet Band was one of the most successful musical groups on campus. The September 1905 *Alumni Bulletin* reported that the college musical organizations, with the exception of the cadet band, had showed little activity in recent years, which was a shame, since there was good vocal and instrumental musical talent at the college. However, in later years, the glee club and orchestra grew in size while the cadet band diminished.

In October, Martin excused band members from military drill, and those students used the time to rehearse music and work on their technique. Showing additional support, Martin wrote that Rogers was a good band leader, and that the group deserved all the funding it had received. Through the winter, one of the band's new duties was to provide music for *Butts Manual*, a compilation of military drills for the battalion.

In March 1906, the College Musical Association, traditionally comprising the college orchestra, the mandolin club, and the glee club, gave a concert at South Hadley Falls. For the first time, the college band was included as part of the Musical Association, presumably because Rogers ran both the band and the orchestra. All groups played well and received generous applause. The band played various marches, and due to the favorable response and audience request, gave an encore at the end of the concert. The concert ended with the singing of "Sons of Old Massachusetts."

In early June, the band gave a concert on the balcony of Draper Hall. Although the weather was threatening and there was not a large audience, students still enjoyed the music, since the band could be heard across campus.

In the fall of 1906, the student band leader and chief musician was Capt. George Chapman '07, a trombone player. Frederick Cutter '07 was the drum major, and the college band consisted of four drums, four cornets, four horns, three clarinets, three trombones, and one tuba. Martin oversaw the hiring of an experienced band leader, T. V. Short from Springfield, to lead band rehearsals for two hours a week. Short, like William Day before him, was not a member of the faculty or staff but served as an independent consultant hired to direct the band. Martin wrote that the college band, under Short's leadership, made wonderful improvements.

On September 21, a new college tradition, the freshman-sophomore rope pull, was introduced on campus. A three-hundred-foot rope was stretched across the pond, and fifty-one men on each side took hold. Five minutes later, as a crowd of five hundred students and townspeople watched, the sophomores of 1909 dragged the rope and the freshmen through the murky water and out the other side. The rope pull was considered a milder replacement for the old midnight campus rush, where the sophomores forced the freshmen to parade around in their pajamas.

The band continued to excel during the spring semester. In May 1907, it gave two concerts in two weeks, which were well attended by both students and local residents. The band, in conjunction with the glee club and orchestra, also played at the Musical Association's musicale, closing the concert with an overture.

The year 1907 marked the fortieth anniversary of the opening of Massachusetts Agricultural College. Despite various trials and tribulations, the school

The 1906 Clark Cadet Band received professional instruction from T. V. Short.

The freshman-sophomore rope pull tradition started in 1906.

The 1907 Cadet Band and Battalion mark the college's fortieth anniversary.

South East, from South Dormitory, M. A. C. Amherst, Mass.

Old Chapel with bandstand in lower left corner. Varsity field is shown on the right.

had reached an important milestone. To celebrate this momentous event, the shell from the 1871 regatta race, at which the Aggies had beaten the Harvard and Brown boats, was taken from the drill hall to the North College trophy room. On October 4, the Clark Cadet Band, led by student band leader Cadet Capt. Kenneth Gillett '08 and drum major Roy Cutting '08, headed up the long procession of students and alumni. The new trophy room was dedicated, and the shell was given a place of honor. The students ended the ceremony by singing "Sons of Old Massachusetts."

On December 11, 1907, the band gave one of the first documented concerts in its future home in Chapel. During the winter months, the band played for callisthenic drills and gave a number of enjoyable concerts.

In the fall of 1908, although it had lost a few members to graduation, the band was in excellent shape and had Cadet Sgt. Raymond Whitney '11 as the new band leader and solo cornet player. The group had grown to twenty-nine members.

An editorial in the November 25, 1908, *College Signal* stated that the college band and its leader Whitney deserved credit for the progress they were making. The band, which was almost entirely made up of freshmen, had already surpassed expectations and possessed "the right sort of spirit." The writer noted that often the band was troubled by the same problem that hampered the athletic teams—both existed in cycles. Once every four years the college had a winning team and a winning band, but after that, the athletic teams and the band slumped, because the essentials of teamwork graduated with the veteran players and the groups had to start all over again. It was easy to recruit new band members and players but more difficult to create a functioning unit out of them. Nevertheless, the college band strove to put together a solid program each year.

A fledgling music department emerged that fall. Edgar Ashley, the newly appointed German instructor, began giving a History and Interpretation of Music class, where he played works from Handel and Grieg on the piano. It was the first time music classes were listed in the school's course catalog. Ashley, arguably the school's first music instructor, was a skilled musician and over the years gave a variety of concerts for the college. During the 1909 school year, 350 students enrolled at MAC, and the school's musical ensembles experienced a period of strong growth. In addition to the college band, musically talented students could join the glee club, the orchestra, and the mandolin club.

Throughout the spring of 1909, the band continued to represent MAC off-campus. On May 31, the students traveled to North Hadley and gave a well-received concert. Newly promoted Cadet Capt. Whitney continued as band leader for the fall of 1909, and James Adams '11 was the new drum major of the twenty-eight member college band.

In January 1910, the band, under the direction of Short, rendered a "striking program" in Chapel during the college's Assembly Hour. Students applauded enthusiastically after each selection, and their interest was "so intense that it was quite difficult for Mr. Short to bring the concert to a close." The band played "The American Musician" march, a waltz called "American Students," and a serenade entitled "Sweet Thoughts." The concert ended with the "M.A.C. Medley," a mix of various college songs arranged for the college band by Short.

During 1909, 350 students enrolled at MAC, boosting the band and battalion.

The band was now officially part of the extracurricular Musical Association, which included the orchestra and the glee club. On March 9, the association held a concert in Chapel, where Whitney gave a cornet solo during "American Cadet Polka." The band gave a third concert in Chapel on May 11. Conducted by Short, the program included "Boccaccio," "Sunny South," "Old Gray Bonnet," and ended with the crowd pleasing "M.A.C. Medley."

On Memorial Day, the band played in Sunderland for the local post of the Grand Army of the Republic. It also performed at Amherst's Memorial Day ceremonies and marched into town. After the procession to the cemetery, the battalion gave a review and the band played a short concert.

For the fall of 1910, Whitney returned in his third year as the group's student leader, and the band grew to thirty-five members. It was a large band at the time, considering there were only 434 students enrolled at MAC.

In September, the college took steps to formalize music instruction and hired Edward Sumner from Worcester to teach the student body how to sing. Each Friday, the noon Assembly Hour in Chapel was turned over to Sumner, and the students rehearsed the college's songs. Sumner also took over direction of the musical clubs and instructed the mandolin club, the orchestra, and the glee club through the year. However, Sumner was not a faculty or staff member and, like Day and Short, was thought of as more of a "coach."

The college band continued its musical support of the football team throughout the fall. There was an impromptu rally before the November 12 MAC-Springfield Training School football game, and Sumner, the band, and other students paraded around the football field, sparking enthusiasm for the upcoming game. Although the Aggies played well, they lost 15–3.

Old Chapel on a snowy day.

Student victory celebrations in those days seemed to include burning down college buildings. Unfortunately, on May 25, 1911, after beating the Tufts baseball team 8–3, the celebrating Aggies burned down the bandstand. The band had been giving weekly concerts there since the 1890s, and the bandstand had also been used for Class Day events.

After the destruction of the bandstand, the Clark Cadet Band lost some of its momentum and began to fade. The previously popular bandstand concerts were not re-created, and student interest in the band waned. Instead, undergraduates began playing in the Combined Musical Clubs, and these groups became the school's newest musical ambassadors, taking over the band's public relations work in the local and surrounding communities.

THE BAND FADES
1911–1920

Over the next few years, there is little mention of the Clark Cadet Band or its adventures. However, although local appearances were limited, the band continued to play for military drills and the end-of-year military reviews. The band was no longer considered an extracurricular activity, and it returned to its military roots.

Before professional band directors were hired at the college, it was mainly student interest that determined which activities grew or faltered. A strong band was often the result of an enthusiastic student band leader who organized the group, recruited members, and scheduled engagements. In addition, it helped greatly to have faculty members, especially military department instructors, who felt that a vibrant band was an asset to the college. In the years when student leadership was not particularly strong, other musical groups flourished as musicians chose to play in those groups instead of in the band. Nevertheless, a number of dedicated students still joined the band.

In the fall of 1911, Cadet 1st Lt. Frank Gray '12 became the band leader, and Fred Griggs '13 was third in command as the band's principal musician.

The 1913 Clark Cadet Band shows the final changeover from the older blue to the newer olive-drab uniforms.

Second in command was Cadet Sgt. Lewis Drury '13, a "wonderful wind-bag for his diminutive size," who, when not asleep in the library, was off playing his horn. Drury, the drum major, was voted most musical among his classmates.

The May 7, 1912, *College Signal* reported that the MAC battalion held a mock battle in the village of Cushman. Two companies held the railroad bridge, and the remaining four companies, supported by the music of the cadet band, attacked. Although various "dead" soldiers remained in the action, the event was declared a draw.

In the fall of 1912, Cadet Capt. Fred Griggs became the new band leader, and John Hutchinson '14 was the drum major. Griggs, nicknamed "Frederick the Great," went on to compose the school's current alma mater, "When Twilight Shadows Deepen." He was best known as the author and composer of college songs, and the *Index* predicted that he was destined to be a future president or, at the very least, a band director.

There was an important uniform change in October, as most of the cadet battalion received the new olive-drab uniforms of the U.S. Army. However, all of the upperclassmen and most of the officers continued to wear their blue single-button jackets and blue caps. Consequently, band photos show the twenty-six-member cadet band with three-quarters of its group in blue and one-quarter in olive drab, which made for an interesting mix.

For the first time, several college musical ensembles spent spring vacation giving concerts throughout the Northeast. In March 1913, the musical clubs, which consisted of the orchestra, mandolin club, and glee club, entertained audiences from Massachusetts to New Jersey and across New York State. The tour was a tremendous public relations success, and cities and towns asked the clubs to return for the following year. The fame of the creative and spirited MAC musical ensembles spread to areas far beyond Amherst, and the school received a great deal of positive attention.

Although the cadet band was not as active as the musical clubs were, it nevertheless played an important role in recruiting efforts for Massachusetts Agricultural College. For a number of years, potential freshmen visited and toured the college campus on High School Day. In May, the band performed at the sixth annual High School Day, as the cadet battalion paraded for the visitors. Although it was bitingly cold, visiting children were thrilled to see cadets marching by to the band's music. The band ended its year with a performance at the Class Sing and gave a concert for the June 1913 Commencement ceremonies.

In the fall of 1913, due to the enthusiasm and effort of band leader and Cadet Capt. Munroe Tarbell '14, the twenty-six-member band was revitalized. Tarbell was also credited with leading the band in its "passionate support" of the football team.

Before Goodell Library was built, Chapel served as the college's library.

Another strong leader was Ralph Tower '15, the band's chief musician, who played "all kinds of instruments" and performed not only with the college band but also with the musical clubs. The battalion pictures show most of the band now wearing the olive-drab uniform, although four of the upperclassmen still wore the old blue uniform. The year 1913 marked one of the last years that the college band was officially listed as "The Clark Cadet Band" in the yearbook.

The band played an important part when the student body gave a rousing send-off to the football team for the September 27 Dartmouth game. Due to President Kenyon Butterfield's enthusiasm, bonfires and parades became fashionable on campus, and the football team began to live up to the school's new motto of "Boost Old Aggie." In addition, the band rehearsed diligently and wanted to do its best to raise morale at the Tufts game. Captain Tarbell promised real music from the band and held "secret rehearsals" to bring band members up to speed.

Although the band expected to be ready with performable music by the end of October, there was a setback when Tarbell contracted mumps and had to leave school. However, band members were relieved when he recovered and returned to campus on October 28. By October 30, the band regrouped and performed at the Democratic rally in Amherst Town Hall.

Chapel was always a popular place for the college band to rehearse. In the December 2, 1913, edition of the *College Signal*, an alumnus wrote that the band was respected by the students and greatly appreciated by the military authorities. It did an excellent job of adding spirit to athletic games, and even the veterans accepted the band as a substitute for the old fife and drum corps on Memorial Day. Although he noted that the band was an asset to the college, this writer requested that it no longer practice in Chapel, since playing its favorite piece, "Alexander's Ragtime Band," distracted students who wanted to study. The Chapel library was overcrowded, and he felt the band should vacate the building and rehearse in either the drill hall or the dining hall. Although the band did not rehearse exclusively in Chapel until later, it was one of the group's first rehearsal and performance spaces.

As early as 1908, students had envisioned having an enclosed athletic field with a large cheering section that would cause the Amherst hills to "echo and reecho with [their] songs and cheers." In April 1914, students were excited when work commenced on the long-awaited athletic field. Under the direction of a professional landscaper, the classes of 1914, 1915, 1916, and 1917 each pledged five hours of labor per student to drain and grade the new Alumni Football Field.

In May, in light of the political turmoil with Mexico, the MAC drill companies formed up and marched into Amherst to show the college's strength and enthusiasm. Between speeches, the band played a number of selections, and one of the cadet companies fired volleys. After the rally, the crowd cheered for Wilson's policies and for Capt. George Martin, who was elected honorary colonel of any regiment that would be mustered out of MAC. Headed by the band, the companies marched once around Amherst Common and returned to the drill hall on campus.

In the fall of 1914, newly promoted Cadet 1st Lt. Ralph Tower became the band leader. The band and battalion uniforms were modified, and flat army caps replaced the peaked caps. The twenty-member band also had Raymond Cushing as one of its drummers. The talented Cushing was cited in the *Index* as being known for his ability to "make the drum talk, walk, lie down, play dead, jump through a hoop, make it call him papa and feed it out of his hand."

The musical clubs continued their public relations work for the college and traveled to the Boston area in January 1915, under the direction of the glee club's coach, John Bland. After giving a number of concerts, the musical clubs brought positive attention to Massachusetts Agricultural College.

For the fall of 1915, the band leader was Cadet Capt. Raymond Cushing, the chief musician was Ray Swift '18, and the chief trumpeter was Cadet Capt. Edward Boyer '16. The new Alumni Field was used for the first time that fall and was located where the Whitmore Administration Building stands today. The field was formally dedicated during the MAC-Colby game on October 9, 1915, when the Aggies beat Colby 26–0. Now the Aggies had a "real" college field, and spirit at the school ran at an all-time high. Students and band members often held rallies for the team and traveled with the players to away games. With the new field in place, a new era of Massachusetts football commenced.

In October, the team was given a send-off for the MAC-Worcester Polytechnic game, and the band was commended for the way in which it kept the straggling line of students in step long enough to reach Amherst Common. The Aggies won 27–0.

The band achieved a milestone when it traveled to its first away game on October 30 against Tufts. A number of Aggie students attended the game, and fifteen cents of each student's $3.15 train fare went to pay for the band's trip expenses. The students chartered a train, and the "Tufts Special" left Amherst at 7:50 on Saturday morning and returned to campus on Sunday evening. The

During World War I, an infantry ROTC unit was established on campus.

game ended in a 14–14 tie and was one of the most exciting contests ever seen on the Tufts field, as MAC came back from almost certain defeat.

As the band increased its support of the football team, the musical clubs increased their publicity work for MAC. By May 1916, the musical clubs were firmly established as the musical ambassadors of Mass Aggie and performed at Commencement ceremonies in place of the band.

The *Index* editors often wrote humorous short stories about various band members. When one thought of chief musician Ray Swift, one immediately thought of music. He played any and all "species of instrument from the bass drum to the flute, and could get away with it." The cornet was his specialty, while the others were merely "thrown in for the sake of variety." Swift went on to become the band leader. Theodore Mitchell '18 was also in the band and had acquired a reputation for blowing his cornet, which, surprisingly, few held against him. Herbert McRae '18 was quiet most of the time, but made "so much strange noise on the alto horn" that some of his fellow students suspected he was having a "wee nip of dry scotch" on the side.

The lightheartedness of the *Index* soon turned serious, as the United States entered World War I in 1917. There were a variety of changes at MAC, and the war in Europe had a profound impact on enrollment. In April, an infantry ROTC unit was established at the college, and by the fall of 1917, barely any men were left on campus, since most had enlisted or been drafted.

Bayonet practice outside Old Chapel.

Even with declining student numbers, bits and pieces of the Mass Aggie Band remained. A military bugle corps came into existence, presumably to bolster the small numbers of the cadet band, and band members included Charles Dunbar '19 who joined the musical groups with "a rattle and roll of drums." His main occupation at Mass Aggie was playing drums in the musical clubs, band, and orchestra.

On April 19, 1918, the two hundred-member MAC battalion was invited to march in Northampton's Liberty Loan Demonstration and Parade. The MAC Cadet Band also marched and led its division, and all were credited for giving a fine appearance in the 4,000-person parade.

During the war, various scheduling changes were implemented at the college, and the fall 1918 semester started late in September. By October, MAC had taken on the aspect of a military camp, as a Student Army Training Corps (SATC) unit was established on campus. The college band and other musical groups were disbanded, although a college orchestra tried valiantly to start up.

When World War I ended, the SATC demobilized. A large number of students were expected for the spring of 1919, and Massachusetts Agricultural College planned to return to prewar standards. In the flurry of activity that accompanied the start of the spring semester, various sports and clubs that had been dormant were re-activated. The military department was transformed as well, and in January, the cadet battalion was absorbed into the ROTC.

However, a longtime fixture of the school did not survive the war, and by the fall of 1919, the Clark Cadet Band was defunct. Students wrote that the Clark Cadet Band was famous, good, and well loved, but had faded out of existence, and *Index* editorials lamented the loss of the band. The band had earned a great reputation and was in demand not only for college functions but also for events in neighboring towns and cities. The cadet band faded away, and it was not until the following spring that a college band was re-created on campus.

ALUMNI REVIVE THE BAND
1920–1927

By April 1920, Mass Aggie's Alumni Association, which had become an established and recognized group, felt it was time to create new traditions. It proposed to hold a parade at the end of each school year, where all alumni classes would dress up and march to the final college baseball game. Since a band was needed for such a parade and because the Aggie army no longer had a band, something had to be done. The alumni took matters into their own hands and set out to recruit a band. Students agreed with the alumni and felt that a volunteer group like the band was also an important part of athletic games. The band had been entertaining at halftimes, and the "zip and whim" it inspired caused the fans to cheer louder for the team. The band was greatly responsible for pushing teams to victory. Extensive recruiting efforts paid off, and for the June 19, 1920, Vermont baseball game, a newly formed Aggie fife and drum corps led the Alumni Parade from North College to the baseball game at Alumni Field. Following Commencement, the first stone was laid for Memorial Hall on June 20, to honor veterans of World War I.

By the fall of 1920, 833 students were enrolled at MAC, and the band was

The cadet band was revitalized in the 1920s.

getting back into the swing of things under the leadership of Ray Swift. By October, twenty-two men reported for the first band rehearsal in the Social Union Room in North College. To entice students to join the band and attend rehearsals, that year, for the first time, each band member received one college credit per term for participating in the group. Since the band was still under the jurisdiction of the military department, which prohibited women from being cadets, women were not allowed to join until later.

The revitalized band was known as "The Aggie Band," and the group's instrumentation consisted of five trumpets, four clarinets, three trombones, two saxophones, three alto horns, three drums, one baritone horn, and one bass horn. The military department provided instruments for those who did not have their own, and Swift rehearsed the band frequently in order to have a "top-notch group in shape" for the October 30 New Hampshire game. Students hoped that the band would regain "its previous stature as an important college organization." Swift's efforts were successful, and at the game, the band gave a solid showing and received praise for its successful reorganization. The football team continued to grow as well, and on October 2, picked up its hundredth win in school history, defeating Connecticut 28–0.

On November 13, after six hundred students took the train to Springfield, the band led the student body to the MAC-Springfield football game. Although the Aggies lost 28–7, they paraded back to the train in good cheer, blocking traffic and singing happily. Students felt that the college spirit was improving and that a great deal more "pep" was seen than in previous years.

The military department underwent additional changes, and in the fall, the infantry ROTC became a horse cavalry unit. Cavalry tactics replaced infantry

A 1920s cadet band parades in front of the drill hall.

basics for juniors and seniors, although freshmen and sophomores were still required to take infantry. Although students were sometimes less than fond of infantry drill, they greatly enjoyed riding horses during cavalry drill.

For the Amherst baseball game on June 11, 1921, the Aggie Band led the Alumni Parade, which was made memorable by the "band, costumes, and pep." After the game, the band gave a concert as part of the college's Semi-Centennial Commencement. A lawn festival was part of the celebration, as tents were pitched by Chapel and electric lights and Japanese lanterns were hung along the roadside. In addition, for the first time in many years, the band played at the Commencement exercises.

By the fall of 1921, there was interest in having a large and well-organized college band. Recruiting ads ran in various issues of the school's newspaper, urging all men who could play an instrument to come to the 4:30 p.m. Friday rehearsals in the North College Social Union Room. The band wanted to play at the Tufts game, but until more men joined, the group's activities were limited.

Apparently the recruiting drive worked. In December, after a successful marching season, band members created a basketball band to play for home games, one of the earliest incarnations of the modern-day Minuteman Hoop Band. At this time, entertainment at basketball halftimes consisted of students singing Aggie songs, and all were encouraged to bring their songbooks and join in. Basketball games were played in the drill hall, and halftime allowed the students to learn the less-familiar college songs.

In April 1922, the ROTC freshman class formed a drum and bugle corps under the leadership of drum major John Nylen '25. The group, which consisted of six buglers, three snare drummers, and one bass drummer, rehearsed three mornings a week and was recognized for its rapid progress. This year marked one of the few during which the college band did not play for the spring military review or other military events.

President Butterfield was an active supporter of the band and asked Cavalry Maj. Frederick E. Shnyder if the U.S. Army would issue sets of band instruments to the college. He also wondered if it was possible for band members to rehearse during the hours reserved for military instruction. In October 1922, Shnyder sent a memo to Butterfield stating that sets of band instruments could only be issued to senior units of four hundred or more, but that it was possible to permit band rehearsal during the military period. Although the band did not receive new instruments, it was allowed to rehearse during military time and, as in previous years, band members were exempt from drill.

The college band held a rehearsal in North College on October 25, and although all band members were encouraged to be present, only twelve students attended. After more recruiting through *Massachusetts Collegian* articles and the warning that if more men did not come to rehearsal, it would be impossible for the band to play at the Tufts game, seventeen men attended the next meeting. The band leaders admitted that seventeen students represented a better showing than before. However, it was still not as good as could be expected; there were at least thirty-five men in college who played instruments, and every one of them should be in the band.

In spite of some recruiting issues, the November 15, 1922, *Massachusetts Collegian* reported that a highly successful Tag Day was organized to raise money for the college band to go to the Tufts game. Twenty students sold seven hundred red ribbons to students and faculty members, which brought in one hundred dollars and allowed the band to travel to the November 18 game. 163 students, including the football team and the band, took a specially chartered train to Tufts. Bostonians in North Station were amazed when the MAC Special pulled in, and they wondered if the fine band they saw was the West Point Band or that of the Salvation Army. At the football game, Tufts won for the first time in four years by a score of 9–6, although the Aggies backed their team to the limit. On the train trip back, the band split into various groups and kept things lively, playing music for the rest of the students in each of the cars.

The band resumed playing for the military department in the spring of 1923. When 250 members of the state legislature visited for Massachusetts Agricultural College's May 4 military review, the corps of cadets put on an exhibition of drilling and horsemanship. The visitors were most impressed by the school's spirit, and the college band played a large role in the day's success with its "splendid work" during the review. The troops were aligned and disciplined, the spectators applauded long and hard, and the school made a good impression. One of the assembly speakers went so far as to say that MAC was "the finest agricultural college in the world."

The review came at a good time, since the state legislature was debating

The college band carried on its military duties during the 1920s.

The 1923–24 ROTC Band.

whether a public state college was needed in the Commonwealth of Massachusetts. State Senate President Frank G. Allen said that, if such an institution was needed, "Where could we find a greater beginning than here" in Amherst? In addition, Speaker of the House R. Loring Young prophesied a brilliant future for Massachusetts Agricultural College. The positive sentiment and successful military reviews went a long way to ensuring that when the time came for Massachusetts to have a public state school, it would be placed in Amherst at the site of President Clark's agricultural college.

In the fall of 1923, the band kept up its military commitments, although not much mention was made of its other activities. The college orchestra was revitalized under the guidance of William Davis, professor of botany, a former band leader at the University of Illinois. The college band was mentioned again on January 10, 1924, when Cadet Sgt. Emery Loud was detached from Troop A and became the band's new drum major. In the spring, Davis, a professional clarinetist who also performed with the Northampton American Legion Band, assumed the role of unofficial band director. The band performed at the May ROTC inspection, and the band members were commended on their fine appearance.

In the fall of 1924, the band was under the command of Sgt. Everett Pyle '27. Students continued to give financial support to the band, and for many years, the group existed and traveled mainly because of the generosity of fellow students. In November, a collection was taken up after Chapel Assembly in order to send the college band to the November 22 Tufts game. The students raised enough to meet more than half the expenses, and the band was able to make the trip. However, more stable funding for the college band was still many years away.

Although finances were volatile, the band continued to make steady progress. Pleased alumni wrote that there was a "real band" at the November 1 MAC-Amherst game, the best that had been seen in some time. The band paraded well, sounded good, and provided an "inspiring spectacle" at the game. Observers felt the band was getting better and better each year, with improvements in music, songs, and cheers. The band ended its season on June 13, 1925, and gave a concert for Alumni Day before leading the Alumni Parade to the MAC-Connecticut Agricultural College baseball game.

In the fall of 1925, the Aggie Band traveled to the October 17 Massachusetts-Connecticut football game in Storrs, where MAC won 13–0. After hearing Connecticut's band, the Massachusetts students voiced their appreciation of the MAC Band. Apparently, the Conn Aggie Band had been organized the day before the game, and band members had differences of opinion regarding what key the music was in. For the November 4 MAC-Amherst game, after the Aggies lost 27–0, the *Massachusetts Collegian* ran a story with the humorous headline, "Chief feature of the game? Our Band." During this time, the athletic teams at Mass Aggie often carried the nickname "Agates," chiefly for variety and because students felt being called "Aggies" was becoming tiresome.

By the middle of November, the MAC Band was acknowledged as one of the stars on campus. As an incentive for students to attend the rally for the November 21 Tufts game, the *Massachusetts Collegian* advertised in big block letters, "The Band Will Be There." In addition, the band led the rally parade from fraternity row to Stockbridge Hall, after which seven hundred students attended the energetic rally.

The Student Senate was supportive of the college band, and since a majority of the college community wanted to have the group present at the Tufts game, the Senate collected the needed funds. At the game, the Agates won the day 6–4, and the band provided spirited entertainment.

In 1926, the band played for the ROTC commissioning exercises, and photos show band members in the military's olive-drab uniforms. The band wore the military dress only during specific military events, such as drills, reviews, and ceremonies. During football season, students made do with matching civilian attire, such as maroon sweaters, white shirts, and black pants.

The Massachusetts Agricultural College held its first Homecoming in the fall of 1926. On October 30, over three hundred alumni returned to campus and enjoyed lunch before cheering at the Massachusetts-Amherst College game. Although the Agates fought bravely, they were defeated 21–7 by the heavier and more experienced Amherst team. The alumni concluded the day with an evening dance.

The cadet band in 1926. The group soon underwent tremendous growth.

In November, a Tag Day was organized to help send the college band to Tufts with the general student cheering section, and tags were on sale for fifteen cents each. Without such active campus support, the band would not have been able to support the football program successfully.

Capt. Edwin Miles Sumner, a strong advocate, friend, and future director of the MAC Band, joined the military department in October 1926. Before long, his efforts would take the college band to new heights, and the next few years marked one of the most prolific periods of growth in the band's history.

The band was a critical component of the year-end military review, which took place on Varsity Field between Old Chapel, South College, and the drill hall. Photo taken c. 1916.

The 1927 cadet band forms an M on the parade ground, with South College in the background.

CAPTAIN SUMNER'S LEGACY
1927–1934

Starting in the spring 1927 semester, the military department took an active role in sponsoring the college band program. In January, the department, in its *Massachusetts Collegian* "Military Notes" section, started an extensive recruiting campaign to bolster the band's ranks. The band needed more men, and anyone who was interested was encouraged to contact the military office. Men who were not in the military program were welcome to join the band, especially juniors and seniors who had opted out of military training and those who played a band instrument of any sort.

The military department also added new instruments and equipment to its band, and in late January, an order was placed for twenty-eight new instruments. By February, more students had joined and the requisition for the band instruments had been approved. With the new equipment, the military department wrote that MAC would soon have one of the best-outfitted bands in the East. In March, the new instruments arrived, and they were a beautiful set. Band leaders felt that if the students played up to the standards of their new instruments, the college would have a fine band that all would be proud of.

Captain Edwin Miles Sumner

Edwin Miles Sumner, originally from Boston, was born in 1888. He was a 1923 graduate of the Fort Riley Cavalry School and served in the Second U. S. Cavalry in World War I. Sumner joined the Massachusetts State College military department in 1926.

In addition to his military duties, Sumner became the director for the college band and wrote "Fight Massachusetts," as well as the march "Massachusetts State College." Sumner was greatly honored when the Class of 1933 dedicated its yearbook to him: "To Captain Edward Miles Sumner, because of his genial and kindly interest in the student body, because of his part in the new spirit of the college, because of his cheerful and capable organization and direction of a new college band."

Sumner's contribution to the band program was invaluable, and it was mainly through his efforts that the Mass State College Band became a recognized academic college activity.

Edwin Sumner brought the college band to new heights.

The band's rehearsal space in North College was also reorganized. Students set about turning the band instrument storage room into a music library, so that the music could be systematically arranged and organized. When work on the band room was done, there was space for each new instrument and storage for all the band's music, and the group had a pleasant rehearsal area.

By April, the band rehearsed three days a week, meeting Mondays, Wednesdays, and Fridays from eleven to noon. In addition, new music and well-known marches were ordered. By the end of the spring semester, the band had benefited greatly from the military department's dedicated support and was well on its way to becoming a permanent and recognized college ensemble.

The military department's recruiting efforts continued into the fall semester. In the October 5, 1927, *Massachusetts Collegian*, Captain Sumner and Professor Davis extended a cordial invitation to all band musicians to join the college band, and membership soon grew to thirty. A number of the new band members were highly talented, and the group was quickly able to play many of the previous year's marches.

The music department, although not yet officially established, continued its steady growth, as well. Stowell Goding, the newly appointed instructor in

The 1927 cadet band leads the military review.

French, took over teaching Edgar Ashley's three music history and appreciation classes.

On October 28, the college band and more than six hundred college officials and delegates took part in the Inaugural Parade for the college's new president, Roscoe Wilfred Thatcher. The college community thanked the ROTC for its splendid showing and commended the band for its strong support.

Aggie spirit and band music were obvious at the November 18 mass meeting in Stockbridge Hall, where there was "real pep" shown. "Real honest-to-goodness Aggie spirit" was displayed, and "plenty of yelling, a few good songs, and the band" helped enliven the rally. Boosting morale, the *Massachusetts Collegian* wrote that the football team and the "famous band" were going to the November 19 Tufts game, and that all students should go along to cheer, as well.

At the MAC-Tufts game the next day, both Tufts and Mass Aggie were well represented by their bands. The halftime show had the Tufts Band forming a "T" and the Aggie Band forming an "M," after which the bands combined and played various songs under the direction of the Tufts drum major. Football fans felt that the music was enjoyable and that the show was an effective and efficient use of halftime. During the second half of the game, outweighed by twenty pounds per man, the young Massachusetts Agates nevertheless put up a heroic struggle before going down 32–6.

For the fall of 1928, the college band was bolstered by a strong cornet section headed by David Nason '31 and George Flood '31, both members of the previous year's band. In addition to a large saxophone section, nine "excellent freshmen" joined as well, and Sumner predicted a brilliant year for the band.

The music department continued to progress, as well. Goding paired with Miles Cubbon, an assistant professor in the agronomy department, and the two men taught the first music ensemble class. The class was formed to teach students to play music in a laboratory setting, and the professors hoped to eventually maintain a full orchestra.

Sumner continued his work with the band, and in October, he requisitioned the U.S. War Department for new pieces of music for the group. In addition, he went to Boston to look at new band literature and chose some of the latest published marches and popular music pieces.

That fall, the band was excited by the prospect of going to Boston. On November 16, fifty MAC alumni gathered at the Boston Chamber of Commerce to welcome the team and coaches for the Tufts game. The thirty-five-piece Aggie Band opened the rally, and after a buffet luncheon was served, the football team appeared amidst music and cheers. The next day, despite a hard fought game, the Agates again lost to Tufts 32–6.

In January 1929, the band moved out of North College and into its new rehearsal area in Grinnell Arena. In March, the group played at the school's interscholastic basketball tournament, and here the innovation of having the band rehearse three times a week showed "splendid results."

Highlights for the fall 1929 band season included a rally in Stockbridge Hall for the October 5 Bowdoin game. The *Massachusetts Collegian* reported that the college band was an "outstanding feature in the meeting" and played "stirring music between the speeches."

In February 1930, Sumner took sole leadership of the college band and devoted time and effort to its development. Before this, he and Davis shared responsibility for directing the band. Soon the group began playing more popular music and specially written arrangements, and for concerts, Sumner invited vocal quartets, as well as banjo and accordion accompaniment to enhance the overall musical presentation. In addition, Sumner's band provided music at basketball games. Since Sumner's overall goal was to create a permanent band made up of volunteers that was not associated with the military department, he began searching for a dependable student band leader who would take charge of the college band.

The fall of 1930 was an exciting season for the band, and on October 31, "Pershing's Own," the U.S. Army Band, gave a concert on campus. Sumner had the honor of conducting the famous group as they premiered his new march for the college, "Fight Massachusetts." The march gained instant acceptance, since "the tune was catchy with great opportunity for harmony in singing, and the words were appropriate and fit the music."

Sumner wrote "Fight Massachusetts" to give MAC a "snappy marching song" that would inspire the football team to fight. He dedicated the march to the 1930 football team and had a friend of his, Hendrick Shelton, band director of the Seventh Field Artillery Band at Fort Ethan Allen, arrange the piece for the college band. The song had its gridiron premiere at the November 1, 1930, Massachusetts-Amherst College football game, and the headlines read

School Songs

Looking to give Massachusetts a new fight song, Captain Edwin Sumner wrote this march in the spring of 1930.

"FIGHT MASSACHUSETTS"

Fight, fight Massachusetts,
Fight, fight every play,
Fight, fight for a touchdown,
Fight all your might today.

Fight down the field Massachusetts,
The stars and the stripes will gleam,
Fight, Fight for old Bay State,
Fight for the team, team, team.

On November 28, 1962, this song became the official alma mater of UMass. It was written by Fred Griggs '13.

"WHEN TWILIGHT SHADOWS DEEPEN"

When twilight shadows deepen
and the study hour draws nigh,
When shades of night are falling
and the evening breezes sigh,
'Tis then we love to gather
'Neath the pale moon's sil'very spell,
And lift our hearts and voices,
in the songs we love so well.

Chorus:
Sons of old Massachusetts,
Devoted daughters true:
Bay State, ol' Bay State,
We'll give our best to you.
Thee, our Alma Mater,
We'll cherish for all time.
Should auld acquaintance be forgot,
Massachusetts, yours and mine.

The chorus above was modified from this original chorus.

Sons of old Massachusetts,
Devoted sons and true,
Bay State, my Bay State,
We'll give our best to you.
Thee, our Alma Mater,
We'll cherish for all time,
Should auld acquaintance be forgot,
Massachusetts, yours and mine.

From 1902 until 1962, this song was the school's unofficial alma mater.

"SONS OF OLD MASSACHUSETTS"

Bay State's loyal sons are we;
In her praise our song shall be,
Till we make the welkin ring,
With our chorus as we sing,
With the tribute that we bring.
Holyoke's hills prolong the strain,
Echoing to our glad refrain,
And the gentle winds proclaim
Far and near thy peerless fame,
Praising e'er thine honored name:
Massachusetts.

Chorus:
Loyal sons of old Massachusetts,
Faithful, sturdy sons and true,
To our grand old Alma Mater,
Let our song resound anew.
Cheer, boys, cheer for old Massachusetts,
Give our college three times three;
Sons forever of the old Bay State,
Loyal sons, loyal sons are we.

This current Minuteman Band fight song was written by Jerry Bilik in 1964.

"ROLL DOWN THE FIELD"

Roll down the field, take that ball,
Give your all, never yield.
Let's roll up the score,
Let the foe really know what we're here for.
Let's crash through the line and
Show them how to fight, fight, fight,
Yes until victory's sealed,
Massachusetts roll down the field.

In 2003, George Parks modified the "Roll Down the Field" lyrics, making the song more flexible for use at a variety of sporting events.

Cheer for UMass, show them strength,
Show them power and class.
Let's cheer for the past,
Minutemen, they had pride, guts, and glory.
So cheer, Massachusetts,
Show them how to fight, fight, fight,
And with fierce loyalty,
Massachusetts, we cheer for thee.

A wintry scene from the new Massachusetts State College.

"New Song Has Pep and Fire to Suit a Football Fight." Unfortunately, the Aggies lost the day 22–6.

"Good old Mass Aggie" was slated for a major transformation in the spring of 1931. State legislators felt that the Commonwealth of Massachusetts should have a public state college, and on March 26, Gov. Joseph Ely signed the bill that transformed Mass Aggie into Massachusetts State College. On April 15, Dean William Machmer made the official announcement, and the bells of Chapel rang as the new state college students sang "Sons of Old Massachusetts" in celebration. One of the band's first performances as the Massachusetts State College Band occurred on May 2, when it gave a concert for High School Day in the newly opened physical education building. The band concert was one of the day's highlights.

Curry Hicks, head of the physical education department, wrote that there was a new spirit on campus and that many were immensely excited about the rebirth of the agricultural college as a full-fledged state college. Students held their heads high, and no one neglected an opportunity to mention that he belonged to Massachusetts State College. Hicks attributed part of this new esprit de corps to the name change but also to the best college band in years. With new songs and new marches, the band's success was a tribute to Sumner, who, as leader of the band, author of "Fight Massachusetts," and true friend of the college, had endeared himself to the whole student body. In addition, Sumner was one of the leaders who had "fostered the awakening of the country and state" to the existence of Massachusetts State College.

Sumner's "Fight Massachusetts" continued to gain accolades and ended up in the repertoire of "Pershing's Own." The U.S. Army Band broadcast the song over the radio and played it on numerous occasions in Washington, D.C. Various distinguished listeners enjoyed the march, including the president of the United States.

On June 6, the college band played for Mount Holyoke College's Alumnae Day. Music for the concert included marching and football songs, as well as classical music and the ever-popular "Fight Massachusetts." The event was a great success, and Mount Holyoke College hired the band for the following year, as well.

The Mass State College Band continued to perform for military department functions. However, beginning in the early 1930s, band members no longer wore the army uniforms for military drills and reviews, and instead wore white flannel pants, dark shoes, and a maroon sweater over a white shirt and tie. Sumner wanted to keep the band separate from the military department, and during his tenure as band director, the group was listed as a student-run organization.

In the 1930s, the college band no longer wore the army's olive-drab uniform for military duties.

In October 1931, Sumner felt that prospects for a high-ranking band were bright, and he was confident that he could turn out a strong thirty-five- or forty-piece group. Since the band did not have auditions, the only requirement for membership was a student's ability to play a band instrument. After a rally and game in November, students wrote, "We are proud of the band after both of its performances. Try and compare it to some of the former bands which formerly represented the college and what a difference is noted both from quality and quantity." Many applauded the group for its appearance and vitality, and the band was considered a credit to Massachusetts State College.

On January 21, 1932, the forty-six-member Mass State College Band made its radio debut over WBZ, Springfield. The band played "Fight Massachusetts," "The Stars and Stripes Forever," and "Hail Purdue" in honor of Mass State's football coach Mel Taube. The broadcast, which included jazz band numbers as well as xylophone and accordion solos, ended with "Sons of Old Massachusetts." Alumni across the state heard the broadcast and were thrilled. "When Mass State College finally crashed the radio it did so with a bang. It was grand. Boy were you good," wrote Charles Cox '30. "It did my heart good to hear such a fine program put over by the College," wrote Ray Griffin '27. It was rumored that immediately following the highly successful concert, which was broadcast from Springfield's Butterfly Ballroom, several band members vanished into the restroom. When the ballroom opened for business, they reappeared and quietly gained free admission to the dance.

The band performs at halftime during a 1930s game against Rensselaer.

After a number of strong years under Sumner, the band was granted legitimacy as a permanent and indispensable campus organization. On March 28, 1932, the Massachusetts State College Band was voted in as an official academic activity by the Academic Activities Board. The band gained the financial and administrative support it had long sought and was now in all respects a "real" college band. The Academics Board also recognized the need for a student band leader and manager, and arrangements were made to appoint two students to the positions. Band members also received academic credit, an important recruiting and retention tool, based on attendance at rehearsals. In addition, for away games where at least three hundred Mass State students were expected to attend, the board agreed to furnish transportation for the college band.

The decision to admit the band as an academic activity officially severed the group from the military department. Now two bands existed on campus: the football band, which performed at athletic events, and the ROTC Band, which continued to play for military reviews. However, the two bands shared many of the same members and were essentially the same ensemble. The Academics Board decided to address the matter of football band uniforms later, so students continued to wear their maroon sweaters and white pants. For military events, the band members later wore "boots and breeches," as drum major Robert Bertram '49 referred to the army uniforms.

By the fall of 1932, Massachusetts State College was growing, and 919 students had registered for the fall semester. After Sumner was transferred to Kansas, the Academic Activities Board appointed an undergraduate student, Grant "Chic" Dunham '34, as the new college band leader. Dunham, Sumner's assistant, had led the ROTC Band during the previous year and received training in Benjamin Teel's Boston Band. He also composed various pieces that were played over the radio, one of which was the new Mass State College football song, "Statonia." In a show of support, Sumner wrote Dunham from Kansas, saying that the forty-member MSC Band was much stronger than the Kansas University groups. Dunham was assisted by band manager Ralph Henry '34. Henry was considered a master of several instruments and an artist on the cello, having played for several years as a staff musician in the WNAC studio in Boston.

In early fall, the band held marching rehearsals in the gymnasium, which had since become known as "the Cage," as marching on the field during half-time shows was something that had not been attempted by the MSC Band for several years. Drum major John Veerling '35, an accomplished trombonist who saw service in Europe with an American Legion band, and Sam Snow '35 helped write drill for the new field maneuvers. Since most students did not own their instruments, the band loaned out bass horns, alto horns, clarinets, mellophones, and percussion equipment.

In preparation for the October 22 MSC-Worcester Polytechnic Institute game, Mass State held a cheering and singing rehearsal for the student body, since student enthusiasm at football games was lacking. For the rehearsal, the band played Dunham's arrangements of the "Victory March" and "Fight Massachusetts." At the game the next day, the band was applauded for playing "Victory March," which was one of the students' favorite pieces. Apparently, the improved cheering bolstered the team's playing, and MSC defeated Worcester 25–0.

In the spring of 1933, a number of difficulties arose within the band. After members of the Academics Board and the band leadership met, Henry requested that a new student leader be found to replace Dunham. The Academics Board agreed and recommended that an official and accredited vote should take place for the new student band leader. In addition, band instruments had gone missing, and the board wanted better accounting for college equipment. Apparently, questions over the band's student leadership resulted in additional changes. Although the band had been an academic activity in the fall of 1932, the policy was reversed in the spring. In a memo dated April 3, 1933, from the Academics Board to ROTC Colonel Charles Romeyn, the band was again placed under the jurisdiction of the military department.

Dunham ended up leaving the band. A supportive band member wrote in the May 1933 *Alumni Bulletin* that Captain Sumner left a "mighty good band and a mighty good band leader" in Dunham. Sumner also left a balance in the

Professor William Davis, seated third from right, and the 1933 college band.

treasury, and the band spent the money, some of it unwisely. Dunham did great work with the college band, and everyone was proud of the group and wanted to be a part of it. Now that Sumner and Dunham had left the band, the writer was not sure what the future of the Mass State College Band would be, but acknowledged that it had had a good year.

In the fall of 1933, after being absent from the band for a number of years, Professor Davis took over the responsibilities of technical coach and director of the college band. In addition, Herbert Warfel, professor of zoology and a former member of the 110-strong University of Oklahoma Band, offered his services and played bass horn with the MSC Band. Although there was still no officially appointed band director, a diverse group of faculty members and students maintained the Mass State College Band.

There were a number of talented instrumentalists in the incoming freshman class, and at the first rehearsal, Davis stated that the band showed promise of being a first-class organization. Band members who attended rehearsals promptly and regularly received academic credit, which counted toward medals awarded for excellence in extracurricular activities. At the time, the band rehearsed every Thursday at 7:30 p.m. in Memorial Hall, and Davis promised that the rehearsals would end promptly at 9, so that students had time for their studies, as well.

The band had its fall debut in the October 6 Inaugural Parade for the college's new president, Hugh Potter Baker. With the Mass State College Band leading the way, the parade proceeded from Memorial Hall to Stockbridge Hall. Governor Ely, various state and local officials, delegates, and presidents from seventy-eight collegiate institutions took part in the parade and added to the ceremony.

In November, the Mass State Band members took a bold stance and went on strike after learning that the Connecticut State Band had been charged admission for the October 14 Massachusetts-Connecticut football game. Outraged at the unsportsmanlike treatment of the Connecticut Band, the MSC Band refused to play at the later Amherst game or at any other events unless guest bands were exempted from charges. Henry expressed the feelings of the MSC Band and said, "Such a charge [the admission fee] was unfair and not calculated to foster friendly intercollegiate relationships." He went on to say that it was the custom at all colleges to admit visiting college bands for free, so there was no reason to charge the Connecticut Band. The issue was soon resolved, as the Athletic Advisory Board voted to allow free admission to any band. Visiting band members would only have to pay the ten-cent amusement tax. When the strike was settled near the end of November, and the Connecticut Band's bill was waived, the MSC Band agreed to play at the Tufts game. Curry Hicks said he was glad that the matter was over and added that the band was an important factor in college activities. Henry regretted the inconvenience of the band's strike, but felt that it was important to insist that visiting bands be treated fairly.

After a successful period of growth, the Mass State College Band was poised to take a tremendous step forward in its evolution.

THE SNAPPY
MAROON-AND-WHITE BAND
1934–1942

Efforts to formalize the Mass State College band program crystallized in the fall of 1934. This year marked the forty-fifth anniversary of the band's founding, dating back to 1889–90 and the cadet band under Eugene Lehnert. In addition, the band was again removed from the military department and re-absorbed into Academic Activities. Dean Machmer voiced his support, saying, "In Academic Activities, we point with pride to the excellent work of the college band."

In September, Massachusetts State College took a major musical step forward and appointed its first official faculty instructor of music, Frank Stratton. Stratton graduated from MIT in 1929 and received a master's of music from the Eastman School of Music, after which he was assistant professor of music at Phillips Academy. At MSC, he was placed in charge of directing all the college's ensembles, which included the band, the men's and women's glee clubs, and the orchestra. The French instructor, Stowell Goding, continued to teach music history and appreciation, and Stratton taught harmony and mod-

ern music classes. Stratton took an interest in the band and soon announced that a professional band leader would be hired to train and direct it.

Strong student band leadership was also in place, and Sam Snow '35, the band's leader and manager, wanted nothing less than a fully equipped and uniformed college band. He took his first steps toward that goal by starting a recruitment drive in September. Snow felt it was unacceptable that of the nearly one thousand men at MSC there were only fourteen currently in the band. In addition, the band was not taken as seriously as it should be. Every college needed a group that would play at football games, special events, basketball games, graduations, and Convocations. "A college band was a vital and indeed necessary campus organization," wrote Snow, adding that the time was right to create a strong band. He asked the college community, "How much longer would students and friends of MSC smile sadly when asked about the band? We have had good bands in the past at this college, and we undergraduates are now ready to make a crack band." All that was missing were excited and dedicated band members.

Recruiting was one of the main challenges for the band program. Stanley Bozek '38 recalled that students usually joined because band membership exempted them from mandatory freshman and sophomore military drill. First- and second-year students could opt out of military training by joining the group, but reaching their junior year, some students elected to drop band. To help with recruiting and retention, Snow argued that college academic credit should be given to all band members, and that a twenty-five-cent tax on the student population would put a greatly needed $250 into the band treasury.

In October, a major innovation took place when the college hired John Jenney, a professional band director, to rehearse and drill the band twice a week. Jenney, a former member of Sousa's and Pryor's bands, was the manager of the band instrument division for the Conn Instrument Company in Hartford. He was not a member of the MSC faculty or staff and was hired to direct ten band rehearsals.

In addition, the band received new instruments, and Colonel Romeyn echoed Snow, suggesting that military credit should be given for band participation. The Student Senate also stated that it was prepared to use student funds to buy the needed band uniforms if the band members were organized enough to use them wisely.

Although the band credit and uniform questions were unresolved for the moment, the re-energized Massachusetts State College Band appeared at both the October 27 Worcester Tech game and the November 3 Amherst game. Next, the bolstered ranks of the twenty-five-member band went to Tufts for the November 24 game. Spectators felt the band's playing was good, and it earned a good deal of praise for the halftime performances. Having a professional like Jenney rehearse the band brought about tremendous improve-

Sam Snow brought about a uniformed college band.

Charles B. Farnum

Charles B. Farnum was the first long-term band director at Massachusetts State College. A professional band director from Holyoke, Farnum was a brass instrument specialist, particularly on the trombone and baritone. He also managed the American Legion Band in Northampton.

Farnum, a concert band director, was not part of the Mass State College staff and was hired as an independent contractor. He worked with the college band from 1935 until 1942 and provided much-needed stability for the band program. A highly disciplined and organized band director, Farnum was also a generous and caring man. Stan Bozek recalled that Farnum was married, and his wife was disabled. Since she could not walk from the car to the bleachers, on game days Farnum drove their car and left it under the goal post, so that his wife could watch the action from there.

Farnum continued his professional work off-campus and directed a number of ensembles, including a Symphonic Band at a Holyoke Soldier's Memorial Concert on January 27, 1939. He died unexpectedly on November 3, 1954.

ments, and the band ended its successful fall season with a concert at the Athletic Insignia Convocation on December 13, where letters were awarded to fall athletes.

After Jenney's fall contract expired, Snow took over directing the band and both men were applauded for their effective leadership. Interest among the band members ran high, and although there was currently only one rehearsal a week, the students eagerly wanted two. The band continued to grow throughout the year, and the *Alumni Bulletin* stated, "This year's thirty-five piece band is perhaps the best in history." In January 1935, Snow was commended for successfully reviving the college band. In addition to his work in rehearsing and leading the band, he had more than doubled the group's membership.

The band took another step forward in its evolution when the next professional band director, Charles B. Farnum, was hired in February 1935. The college band had many leaders and directors before Farnum, but they were students, military officers doubling as band leaders, professionals hired for a few semesters, or college faculty members volunteering their time. Although not part of the faculty or staff, Farnum was the band's director until 1942 and provided stable and dedicated leadership. Farnum, a highly talented trombonist and concert conductor, came to campus and ran one rehearsal a week. Under

him, the band's style and musicality improved noticeably. When Farnum was not on campus, the group rehearsed under the direction of the student band leader, Snow.

At the Combined Musical Clubs Concert on March 15, Stratton conducted the men's and women's glee clubs and the orchestra, and Farnum and Snow directed the college band. The band, which opened the concert and played "The Stars and Stripes Forever," was well-received, and Farnum was praised for all he had accomplished in his six weeks at Mass State. Music critic Paul Williams reviewed the concert and wrote that the band's balance was good and that band members followed their directors' gestures, exuding a strong sense of confidence. "Congratulations, Band!" wrote the *Massachusetts Collegian*.

Snow's next project was to raise enough money to buy new uniforms for the band. By late spring, he had succeeded, and the *Massachusetts Collegian's* front-page headline read, "Maroon and White Band Soon to Be a Reality." A contract was signed with D. Klein and Brothers of Philadelphia to provide the first uniforms for the Mass State College Band. In less than six months, Snow and the Student Senate had raised $1,000 for the new band uniforms. Since the band was not supported by the student activity tax, the uniform money came from other sources, such as the alumni, the Athletic Advisory Board, and the Student Senate. Thirty-seven uniforms were ordered, and it was the first time in the band's history that the group had its own, nonmilitary outfits.

In April, Snow paraded into the Alumni Office dressed in the new maroon-and-white uniform. It consisted of long maroon trousers with a white stripe, a wide white garrison belt, a maroon coat with white piping on the pockets and a major's knot on each sleeve, and a maroon cap with two white bands. Snow was proud of the new good-looking uniform, and alumni felt that the boys would present a neat appearance when they led the parade to the spring ball game.

Around this time, Massachusetts State College decided it was time to have a fully supported college band, and vitally needed financial support appeared from various campus sources. One of the main reasons that the band, unlike other campus groups, struggled for so long was that it was not supported by the student activity tax. However, when the group received new uniforms, students were more willing to support the group with their tax money.

On Sunday, May 19, 1935, the MSC Band made its first uniformed public appearance, when it presented a two-hour Mother's Day Concert on the front lawn of Memorial Hall. The program, conducted by Farnum and Snow, featured a variety of soloists, and the band's feature number was "Home Sweet Home the World Over." The band ended its season with a concert in Memorial Hall after the Alumni Day luncheon. Snow conducted the band and was awarded the Conspicuous Service Trophy for his part in the group's revitalization.

With the growth of musical interest on campus, President Baker, a great friend of the band, laid the foundations for a stronger music program. In addi-

The 1935–36 MSC Band displays its first nonmilitary uniforms. Charles Farnum stands far left in a white band director's uniform, while drum major Stan Bozek appears far right.

tion, Baker restored the fifty-cents-per-student tax to support the college band. The tax had previously subsidized the band, and the collected money provided for coaching, trips, replacements in equipment, and other necessary expenditures. His support was invaluable to the growth of the college band program.

For the fall of 1935, the forty-five-member band was one of the largest in the school's history. Farnum directed the music rehearsals, which took place on Thursday evenings in Memorial Hall. The band members learned their marching skills from military department instructors such as Lt. Col. Horace Aplington, and drill rehearsals took place on Fridays at 4:30 p.m. on the practice field. Snow returned to campus to pursue graduate work in landscape architecture, and a new position, graduate student band leader, was created for him. Stanley Bozek, the new drum major, won the post because he could throw the twirling baton, which "amazed Snow to no end." Bozek specialized in catching the baton behind his back and thrilled audiences as the school's first baton-twirling drum major.

At the time, Memorial Hall was a highly popular meeting place. Band music was often heard from the second floor, and it seemed as if the campus' energy was focused on that building. Since the band rehearsed in the evenings, students enjoyed listening to the music on their way to the library. Evenings at the college were pleasant, with the campus illuminated by lights and band music drifting by in the darkness. In later years, a similar mystique surrounded Old Chapel, the Minuteman Band's home.

The MSC Band performs during halftime in the fall of 1937, while the drum major watches for his baton.

Although the MSC Band experienced unprecedented growth and support, questions remained as to whether it was an academic or a military activity. At a meeting on October 3, Frank Prentice Rand, the head of the Academics Board, wanted to return the group to the military's jurisdiction, but President Baker disagreed, saying that he was strongly in favor of continuing the band as an academic activity. Despite the disagreement, it was one of the first times that officials discussed the college band's administration, and band operating policies were set. Stratton was held responsible for coaching and supervising the use of army and college instruments and uniforms. The Academics Board collected the student tax, and the band manager had access to the college funds but needed written authorization to spend the money. In addition, Stratton and the student manager were responsible for awarding band credits to deserving members, which was subject to approval by the Academics Board. Baker continued advocating for the band program and secured funding, credits, and other necessities for the group. With his strong support, the band found itself on solid footing for many years to come.

A *Massachusetts Collegian* editorial congratulated the band on its first appearance of the year at the October 5 Bowdoin game. Mass State now had a band that was the equal of any rival school. Band members' and directors' efforts were obvious and the result was "truly spectacular." The editors hoped that this was only the beginning and that the group would eventually be one of the best in the country.

The MSC Band's busy season continued with the Amherst game on November 2, where it performed special drills and numbers. On November 5, the band played a major role in the Alumni Night radio broadcast. The show, broadcast from Springfield's Hotel Kimball, served to bring alumni together to talk about old friends and classmates. The broadcast was aired on WBZ, WBZA, and W1XK in conjunction with alumni meetings throughout the country. The band played music throughout and signed off with "Sons of Old Massachusetts." The show was an artistic success and a source of joy, pride, and inspiration to the hundreds of alumni in the radio audience. Listening alumni wrote, "Three cheers for the band!"

After the successful radio performance, Snow secured funding to attend the Northeastern away game on November 9, the band's first away game with its new uniforms. The band members played the same show they had at Amherst, with special drills to delight the audience.

On December 13, the band was invited to present a concert as part of the college's Bay State Review. The well-received performance took place in the Student Union, and the band opened the program with the "Alda Overture." Other student skits and musical numbers filled out the evening.

The band also played at the dedication for the new Goodell Library, at the Insignia Convocation, and during the Combined Musical Clubs Concert. The January 1936 *Alumni Bulletin* stated that one needed only to hear and see the MSC Band to understand why the student body was so proud of it. Bozek was praised as the sharp drum major and baton twirler at the front of the band: although not as good as the Clarke Sisters who led the Barnum & Bailey Band, this was to be expected because Bozek was only a sophomore.

Stan Bozek demonstrates his baton twirling skills.

In January, the MSC Band filled its musical ambassador role and traveled to Hartford, Connecticut, giving a concert at the Neuro-Psychiatric Institute. In addition, since the military department was not fielding an ROTC Band for the spring review, the college band resumed its former military duties and learned the review drills.

In March, the MSC Band played at the Western Massachusetts High School Basketball Tournament, gave a concert in the Cage for a recreation conference, and played a program of old-time college songs for Convocation. The Mother's Day Spring Concert, the highlight of the year, was widely enjoyed.

In June, for the annual spring review, the battalion lined up in front of Old Chapel, and the MSC Band led the entire procession to the football field. On the field, the ROTC students paraded to the music of the band, which was allowed to wear its maroon-and-white uniforms instead of changing into the army's olive-drab. The military department appreciated the effort, and Lieutenant Colonel Aplington wrote a letter thanking the group for its work at the review. Although not all band members were members of ROTC, they still "cheerfully turned out for our spring review. Naturally the presence of the Band

The Mass State College Band leads the end-of-year military review.

at our ceremonies [is] of vital importance, for the ceremonies are built around the band." He thanked Snow, Bozek, and "all the men in Maroon and White."

Music continued to grow at Massachusetts State College. In the June 1936 *Alumni Bulletin*, Clark Thayer '13 wrote a letter to Fred Griggs, saying that there was an upsurge in musical interest among the Mass State students. One reason was that for two years Stratton, a full-time instructor in music, had been working with various musical groups. Another reason was that the college band had also changed for the better since Thayer's undergraduate days, when the main reason for playing in the band was to take three years of required military training in the easiest manner possible. Now that the band was no longer affiliated with the military department, it was a great deal better. More students were interested in joining the band, which was also stronger because it had a professional band director. Thayer concluded that music at the college was improving and had bright prospects for the future.

By the fall of 1936, the band was an established and supported campus organization. Farnum returned as director and, over the summer, had toured as the featured trombone soloist with various bands in New England. Recruiting paid off as fifty men turned out to audition; with the increased membership, the band planned to buy several new uniforms.

In September, the band was organized into two different groups: one group for football games and another for concerts. This split was created to give students a chance to play fall sports and then join the band during the winter term.

A typical halftime show for the fall consisted of the band taking the field playing its favorite march, "On Wisconsin." Football fans were often amazed at the band's "sensational" antics, since it was unheard of to march onto the field under the goalpost, with a baton-twirling drum major in front. The band members, then as now, showed great enthusiasm for being in the band. One day, Farnum was late getting to Amherst for rehearsal. Instead of waiting for the band director, the students took matters into their own hands and rehearsed under the enthusiastic leadership of Ralph Gates '37 and Bob Spiller '37.

In October, the MSC Band gave a short concert for the State Federation of Women's Clubs and played at the dedication of the women's athletic field, which was located west of the Cage. There was plenty of "good yelling" to cheer the team on to victory for the October 17 Rhode Island State game, and the band was commended for appearing at halftime and putting on a good showing despite the mud.

One of the highlights for the fall was the MSC Band's trip to the November 7, 1936, Coast Guard Academy game in New London, Connecticut. The band traveled to the night game, where it combined with the Coast Guard's band for a parade from the New London city center to campus. The two groups created a sixty-piece massed band, and Bozek led the combined musicians for the one-and-a-quarter-mile parade. Afterward, the band ate with the Coast Guard cadets in the Academy mess hall and performed in a joint concert. MSC lost 7–6 in a close game.

The band's January 1937 concert season began with a performance at the Alumni Broadcast. The group also gave a concert at Convocation on February 25, where it performed novelty pieces such as a trumpet trio. The concert ended with Farnum's arrangement of the alma mater and included "Grand Fantasie—Home Sweet Home the World Over," with ten dancing women dressed in outfits representing England, Germany, China, and Russia. The band also performed at the Bay State Review in February.

The 1937 MSC Band in playing formation outside Memorial Hall.

The band's budget was limited to one new instrument a year, so in March, the Student Senate purchased eight new uniforms for the group. The previous year, the band had bought a sousaphone. This year, the band purchased a larger bass drum with a white shell and maroon rims and painted the college name on both heads. Band members were pleased with the new bass drum, which was far superior to the old one. The previous bass drum was so antiquated that it rattled every time it was hit, and the heads could not be tuned to each other.

Farnum coached the band while students ran the band programs' day-to-day logistics.

Drum majors Alberta Johnson, Stan Bozek, and Erma Alvord. Johnson and Alvord were the first women to join the college band.

The MSC Band gave an additional radio broadcast on March 18, although only twenty-five band members were able to perform due to the lack of studio space. The band played "National Emblem March" before closing the well-received broadcast with the alma mater.

The climax of the band's season was the May concert on the Memorial Hall lawn, where various band members were featured as soloists. For Alumni Day on June 12, the group gave a short outdoor concert before leading the Alumni Parade to the ball game.

In the fall of 1937, Conrad and Harold Hemond '38, twin brothers, were the band's co-managers, and Major Leo Connor of the military department taught the band its drills. The group acquired a chime as well, and the Maroon and White Band planned to have forty on the field, due to the influx of a large number of freshmen.

That fall saw a major innovation for the college band, and in a break with precedent, Bozek, in his third and final year as drum major, added two female drum majors. He recalled, "It was a peachy idea to have assistant drum majors who were coeds." It was the first time that women were allowed to be part of the Mass State College Band, and even then, women were allowed to serve only as drum majors and not as regular band members. Although the band was considered a member of Academic Activities, it also maintained connections with the military department, which did not allow women to join its ranks.

The new drum majors, Erma Alvord '40 and Alberta Johnson '40, conducted the band, which allowed Bozek to devote his time to twirling, at which he was rated one of the best of all the New England college band leaders. Erma (Alvord) Davis recalled merrily that although freed from his conducting responsibilities, "Poor Stan had to put up with us." The appearance of a woman as a drum major gave the Maroon and White Band a unique distinction among eastern college bands.

As with all major changes, there was controversy, and the campus was soon locked in intense debates over how long the new drum majors' skirts should be. Bozek felt that skirts down to the knee would be appropriate, but Edna Skinner, the dean of women, required that the skirts be ankle length. In the end, the new drum majors wore the regular band coats, but with medium-length white skirts underneath.

On October 28, the college band performed at the Alumni Night radio broadcast. Trumpet player Vernon Coutu performed "Aire Vaire," and the band played "Under the Double Eagle March," "When Twilight Shadows

The 1937–38 MSC Band was one of the most successful in school history.

Deepen," and "Victory March." After the band's radio concert, appreciative alumni sent letters praising the performance. According to Emily Smith '25, the group sounded so good that she thought it was a professional band. Harold Caldwell '16 wrote, "The band's performance was very high class—especially that of the cornetist," and Barbara Bradley '36 added, "Vernon Coutu can certainly play the trumpet. And how well the band does sound!"

The women drum majors soon gained acceptance, and Alvord received an ovation for her performance at the October 30 Amherst game. She also played with the band at the November 12 Bay State Review, where she was the featured chime soloist in "Sweet Evening Bells." The band opened the evening with a few lively selections, and the *Massachusetts Collegian* later reported that the group continued to surprise and please everyone with its steady and continued improvement. Both the Bay State Review Concert and the November 13 Dad's Day Concert played to full audiences in Bowker Auditorium.

For the November 13 Dad's Day game, the MSC Band played host to the Rensselaer Band, and both groups, numbering seventy, combined for the half-time show. The idea of combining bands had worked so well at the Coast Guard game that the managers of the MSC Band decided to do the same with the RPI Band.

President Baker continued his strong support of the band and wrote, "We all have the interest of our fine band at heart. The band has become a great asset on the campus and it has been very well handled." He pledged that the administration would "do everything possible to further its right operation and development."

By the end of the football season, it was widely acknowledged that the band had completed its most successful season ever. In January 1938, due to the group's increased popularity, students voted to raise the activities tax and to give additional funding to the band. The band received an additional twenty-five cents from every student enrolled at MSC and was able to purchase new instruments, uniforms, and music.

A new discipline characterized the 1938–39 MSC Band.

On February 24, the band, conducted by Farnum and Harold Hemond, gave a concert for Convocation. Alvord played a solo on the chimes, Coutu had a trumpet solo, and Conrad Hemond gave a bass horn solo. Bozek had been expected to spin his baton during one of the numbers, but the day before he had lost his grip on the heavy stick, and the weighted end had hit him in the face, cracked his nose, and given him "a beautiful black eye."

During the winter, the band appeared at the Winter Carnival and gave a concert for the Western Massachusetts High School Basketball Tournament. On April 1, the group, conducted by Farnum, gave a concert for 2,500 people in the Springfield Municipal Auditorium at a benefit for the Springfield Unemployment Fund. Band manager Conrad Hemond thanked the band for its "hearty cooperation" during the concert. Such "inspiring spirit" made it easier for the managers to continue building the fine band that everyone was so proud of. On April 9, the band members adopted a Band Constitution, which set guidelines for band operating policies and defined student officer positions. The constitution completed the formal reorganization process that was started in 1933.

By the fall of 1938, students felt that there was a new discipline in the Mass State College Band, and that "smart uniforms clothe the spirit which has been so characteristic of the reorganized band." Alvord continued as drum major, and Joseph Paul '39 took over as band manager. The band's increasing excellence was attributed not only to strong leadership and willing instrumentalists, but also to new instruments, new musical arrangements, and tailor-made uniforms for the female drum majors. Recruiting became less of a challenge, since freshmen and sophomores were allowed to substitute band for military drill during the first half of the fall semester. In addition, during ROTC season, band members were excused from the mandatory drill.

After Stratton left MSC, the music department gained a new instructor when Doric Alviani, the "musical bombshell," arrived on campus that fall. He soon had students singing as never before, and in later years, took over directing the college band. At the time, Alviani and French professor Goding were the entire music faculty, and Memorial Hall became the department's headquarters. Although the band room was on the basement level, the MSC Band also rehearsed on the second-floor auditorium stage.

Typical halftime shows that fall consisted of the Maroon and White Band marching in formation up the center of the football field. After the drum major twirled a baton and gave a whistle blast, the band formed a large "M" and played "Sons of Old Massachusetts." The October 1938 *Alumni Bulletin* noted that the band was going full blast, "bigger and better than ever before." The band also traveled to the October 29 Amherst College game and contributed a "bright bit to the pageantry."

On December 15, the band gave a special Christmas Concert in Stockbridge Hall in recognition of five years of "brilliant and steady" advancement. It was considered one of the band's best concerts ever, and audience members referred to the group as a "well-oiled machine." Although the technical precision of the performance alone deserved praise, the band's spirit and enthusiasm had the crowd waving programs and stamping feet in time to the music. The highlight was the band's medley of "Five Favorite Yule Tide Songs," which had the audience singing along with gusto. During the program, a tribute was held for Sam Snow, now a landscape architect in Arizona's Coronado National Forest. He was called to the front of the stage and was presented with a scroll that read: "Massachusetts State College Band honors Mr. Samuel P. Snow. On this occasion of the fifth anniversary of the reorganization of the Massachusetts State College Band we, the officers and members, extend to you our sincere appreciation for the part you have had in assuring the continued success of our organization." Then Snow was given the baton, and he conducted the band for his favorite march, "Men of Harlech." It was a memorable night for all.

During the spring of 1939, the MSC Band played at the March 23 Convocation, and Farnum was

A fall 1938 halftime performance.

The band forms an M for Massachusetts.

A baton-twirling drum major leads the band onto the field.

Erma Alvord, one of the first female drum majors.

The band began marching more letter-based drill patterns for halftime performances in the fall of 1939.

praised for his work with the band. He "produced results worthy of a Sousa," and his efforts raised the band's musical excellence.

The first Alumni Band made its appearance in June, when Conrad Hemond arranged for former band members to return for Alumni Day. The July 1939 *Alumni Bulletin* reported that the plan was a success, and alumni and undergraduate band members combined to play a concert on the Memorial Hall lawn. Afterward, Alvord, the "smart-looking drum major" who was "resplendent in a new white uniform with plenty of gold braid," marched at the head of the Alumni Parade, and it was the first time anyone could recall that a woman led the procession to the Commencement ball game.

For the fall of 1939, the forty-member band added "real zest" to its marching formations, which made it a hit with the students. Over the next few years, the band began marching more letter-based drill patterns and spelled words on the field. Band manager Douglas Cowling '40 was applauded for his work in keeping the band organized, and he, assistant manager Al Eldridge '42, and drum major Dave Eskin were also credited with the band's sharp drill formations. Students were pleased with the strong leadership and crisp football drills that resulted in the "snappy" marching group. The MSC Band captured that elusive and magical quality called "oomph," which was essential in creating strong school spirit and played a necessary part in the color of college sports.

On October 12, the band performed at the dedication ceremonies for the new Calvin Coolidge Memorial Bridge, which connected Northampton to Hadley. The ceremonies were overseen by U.S. Sen. David Walsh and Gov. Leverett Saltonstall.

The night before the November 4 Amherst game, the band led a torchlight parade along fraternity row. The parade ended at a rally, where a bonfire, fireworks, cheers, songs, and speeches greeted the students. For halftime the next day, the band amazed the audience and formed an "M," "JEFF" for the Lord Jeffs of Amherst College, and "STATE" for cheering MSC fans.

In the fall of 1940, the band was the bright spot of college activities and was "pleasing both to the ear and to the eye." Students felt that the Mass State College Band looked and sounded good and added to the college's reputation and fame. The group demonstrated its marching skills by forming such drills as "TECH," "HI DAD," and "MSC" at the Worcester Polytechnic game. Eldridge took over as the student manager, and band members credited him with enthusiasm and an insistence on hard work. Drum majorettes Marion Avery '42 and Jean Carlisle '42 were praised for their spirited performances throughout the fall as well.

The band played a holiday concert at the Veteran's Hospital in Leeds, Massachusetts on December 11. The group also gave its annual Christmas Concert on December 16 in Bowker Auditorium, where it performed a variety of classical, semi-classical, and novelty numbers. Favorite band music that year included "McNamara's Band," "Saber and Spurs," and "Columbia Polka."

In the fall of 1941, the MSC Band became known as "the instigator of spirited student support at football games" and often proved to be the backbone of the cheering section. Football fans enjoyed seeing the band with its "pretty drum majorettes and its expert marching formations." At the Tufts game, the band amazed everyone by spelling out a new formation of "YEA TEAM," one letter after the other.

On December 15, the choir, a brass quartet, and most of the student body sang Christmas carols on the snow-covered lawn between Old Chapel and Memorial Hall. The concert was broadcast over the radio and ended with music played on the chapel's chime.

At the Christmas Concert in Bowker on December 17, the band presented a patriotic program, which included the "Over There Medley" of World War I songs. By audience request, the band repeated the popular march "Saber and Spurs" from the previous year, featuring trumpets, drums, and drum majorettes. The program closed with "The Star-Spangled Banner."

When the United States entered World War II after the attack on Pearl Harbor, Massachusetts State College joined the war effort, and President Baker created an accelerated program of course work for the spring 1942 semester. Semesters were shortened, and all male students were required to take part in a physical fitness curriculum.

In January, there was great excitement because the MSC Band received a new glockenspiel. The glockenspiel and its new player, Henry Martin '43, were officially unveiled at the February 26 Convocation Concert during Goldman's "Chimes of Liberty." In addition, the band played a medley of light and clas-

The MSC Band marches past Memorial Hall after a football game.

The 1941 Mother's Day concert on the Memorial Hall lawn.

Band members relax after halftime of the 1941 Dad's Day game.

Gloria Maynard '45 leads the MSC Band onto the field in the fall of 1941.

Chapter Eight

Leo Moreau '44 gives a trumpet solo.

sical pieces, and the drum majorettes put on a twirling display.

To further the development of college bands in the Northeast, MSC student band leader Al Eldridge created the New England Intercollegiate Band Association. Eleven schools, including MSC, Boston University, Tufts, Connecticut, Northeastern, and Boston College, sent their bands to the festival, which was held in April 1942 at Boston University.

The MSC Band also gave a concert at the April Insignia Convocation, where students were awarded medals for college service and academic excellence. For his work with the band, Eldridge received a diamond chip and was awarded a Massachusetts State College Conspicuous Service Award.

On May 3, although the college was functioning under an accelerated program, the band gave its

Outdoor concerts, like this one from 1942, were highly popular.

Mother's Day Concert on the Memorial Hall lawn. It was the first time that students were able to persuade Farnum to play a solo with the band, and he performed a trombone piece entitled "Satellite." In addition, highly popular trumpet players Bob Radway '47 and Leo Moreau '44 appeared together in a duet called "Friendly Rivals." In a moment of foreshadowing, the *Massachusetts Collegian* headline read "Eldridge Conducts Last Band Concert." Not only was it his last concert, but also the full MSC Band's last performance until after the war.

Al Eldridge leads the MSC Band.

Since the semesters were shortened, graduation exercises were held in May instead of June, and due to the accelerated program, members of the band weren't available to play for the May 16 Alumni Day Parade. However, music department instructor Doric Alviani, various alumni, and undergraduates found an assortment of drums and cymbals and "rattled away at the head of the procession," creating a makeshift band.

Over the summer, Captain Farnum resigned from Mass State College, presumably to join his army unit. His innovations and musical discipline as the first long-term band director created a seasoned and well-polished band and provided the group with invaluable stability.

Doric Alviani revitalized music at Massachusetts State College.

TRANSITIONS
1942–1950

*I*n the fall of 1942, Doric Alviani became the new director of the Mass State College Band and was the first faculty member to officially assume that role. An enthusiastic teacher, he single-handedly kept the music program running at Mass State during the war. Alviani was a colorful character, yet underneath lay a strong current of seriousness and a sincere love for music. The 1939 yearbook was dedicated to Alviani, thanking him for teaching the students how to sing and "for causing the rebirth of the most beautiful of all traditions, the music of the college."

During Alviani's tenure, the college band functioned as a year-long ensemble and was no longer split into a football band and a concert band. John Hilchey was the band's student manager, and Robert Bertram was the student leader and drum major. Alviani rehearsed the band, made sure it was prepared, and let students run the show on game days.

In a major break from tradition, due to the war in Europe and the loss of male band members, the MSC Band also began to admit women into its general ranks. Although this caused controversy, it was decided that it was better

Doric Alviani

Doric Alviani was born on October 8, 1913, in Fall River, Massachusetts. After graduating from Salem High School in 1930, he attended Boston University and received a bachelor's degree in music in 1937.

In September 1938, Alviani was appointed as the instructor in music at Massachusetts State College. He was eventually involved in nearly all aspects of music on campus, including the marching band, the Music Theater Guild, the University Chorale, and the glee clubs. Fletcher Prouty '41 recalled that when Alviani arrived at Mass State College, music was low on the list of activities. In fact, it was all but non-existent, except for band. Then came Alviani, who, in short order, scheduled auditions in Memorial Hall and began reorganizing the men's and women's glee clubs.

Alviani, the "gentle hurricane," dominated Mass State College, and his mission was to create a comprehensive music department. When he first arrived on campus, he immediately became known for his enthusiasm, drive, and personality. He was hired to coach the glee clubs and orchestra, and students responded to his magnetic leadership, flocking to the vocal ensembles. A mercurial man, he nevertheless had the ability to inspire students and could be easily recognized from afar by his ever-present raccoon coat. Jackie Mellen, a member of Alviani's band, recalled that the last time she saw him was when, true to form, he was "bombing down the road in a red convertible."

Although more a chorale and musical director than a band director, Alviani twice took over leading the college band and was a strong advocate for the band pro-

Doric Alviani was also known as the "musical bombshell."

gram. He also formed the women's drill team in 1946, and over the years, the Precisionettes grew into a highly respected marching ensemble. In 1948, Alviani became the first chair of the fine arts department, and in 1956, he became the head of the new music department. Helen Perry was hired by Alviani in 1958 to be the department's new secretary. The interview was brief. Alviani asked her if she needed a job. Perry replied she did. Alviani said, "Well, I need a secretary," and Perry was hired on the spot.

Alviani continued as a professor of music and was named an honorary alumnus of the university in 1984. He passed away in June 1996, at the age of 82.

to let women into the band than to have a small, weak group. The women, who wore the same uniforms as the men, handled the emergency, showing "male skeptics that girls had a place in a college band, even behind a bass drum."

The band traveled to two away games and paraded to the Amherst football game, where it put on a spectacular show that even the Amherst crowd appreciated. Showing its patriotism, the band also played "Anchors Aweigh" when a group of WAVES were taking their seats. Fans felt the band was doing a good

Women made a strong showing in the MSC Band, due to the small number of male musicians during World War II.

job and the *Massachusetts Collegian* wrote, "More power to the bandsmen." The band also traveled to the Tufts game on November 14, and although band members did their best to cheer on Mass State, they could add very little, as it was an icy cold day, and their instruments literally froze.

In mid-October, the cadet corps began having Wednesday afternoon retreats, and the band and cadets formed up in front of Memorial Hall. Throughout the retreat, the band played several marches, and its main military duty during the fall was to play the national anthem as the flag was lowered in front of the drill hall.

The MSC Band's theme for the year was "Music for Morale," and the annual Christmas Concert on December 19, 1942, opened with the "Army Air Corps March." Additional music included "American Patrol" and "The Stars and Stripes Forever," and Alviani also arranged medleys such as "Praise the Lord and Pass the Ammunition" and "Yankee Medley." The concert was a "splendid performance," and Alviani and the band were congratulated as they were called back for encore after encore. The *Massachusetts Collegian* wrote, "Well Done Bandsmen!"

By December, women had gained acceptance as regular band members. The *Alumni Bulletin* stated that after all these years, women now played in the band, and they did it well, as the band was a good one.

When the Enlisted Reserve Corps was called to duty in the spring semester of 1943, the college band disbanded, because now there were not enough male or female musicians left attending MSC to fill the band's ranks. However, dur-

Harry Silver, 58th CTD, displays instruments donated to the college by the community.

ing World War II, Mass State College played host to a number of Army Air Corps cadets, many of whom brought their musical talents with them. Starting in February 1943, six hundred cadets of the 58th College Training Detachment (CTD) were quartered in Lewis and Thatcher Halls. The cadets of the "Singing 58th" livened up the campus with songs such as "Up We Go, Into the Wild Blue Yonder" on the way to classes, as the remaining female students watched with great interest. From then until May 1944, nearly 2,400 Army Air cadets received training at Mass State College. Although college activities were not suspended, the school became largely a military cadet and women's school.

Although the MSC Band was dissolved, there was no lack of interest in instrumental music, and other bands sprang up in its place. On May 1, 1943, the "58th College Training Detachment at Massachusetts State College Band" gave a Guest Night Concert as part of the school's fifth annual Music Week Festival. The 58th CTD Band played the "Guest Overture" and ended the concert by combining with the men's and women's glee clubs for "The Star-Spangled Banner."

In September 1943, another band was created on campus as two women, one Stockbridge student, and various 58th CTD cadets joined to create a new cadet-student band. By October, the twelve-member band, directed by Air Cadet Carl Globesky, had been rehearsing for a month. The cadets made use of the college band instruments and practiced frequently. The cadet band gave a number of informal concerts regularly and thanked Barbara Beals '47, who joined the band and played trumpet with it. Another instrumental group on campus at the time was the Sinfonietta, a twenty-one-member full symphonic orchestra, conducted by Alviani. In addition, a number of MSC women formed a brass band to welcome classmates who were returning from the war.

In the fall of 1944, Alviani created a variety of vocal and orchestral ensembles and invited guest soloists to give concerts. In addition, Alviani, who had a fine baritone voice, sang in chamber concerts. Under his direction, the seventy-one-member glee club was also

The ROTC Band outside Stockbridge Hall, c. 1943.

Although the MSC Band was disbanded, the ROTC Band and 58th CTD Band operated during the war.

Robert Bertram, center, and the 1946–47 MSC Band.

The revitalized MSC Band, drill team, buglers, and drum corps perform during halftime in the fall of 1946.

active, giving Christmas concerts in Old Chapel and traveling extensively throughout the local area.

When the war ended, the college band was slowly remustered in September 1945. The G.I. Bill allowed millions of military men to attend college across the country, and the influx of veterans on campus was a monumental event. Although a large number of veterans returned to Massachusetts State College, they were not anxious to get into uniform and march, and the MSC Band was subsequently small.

Alviani, newly promoted to assistant professor of music, wrote that after the war, conditions for the band were strange. On the one hand, there were a number of excellent G.I. musicians who had little time or interest in formation marching practice. On the other hand, large numbers of women were enrolling as students at MSC and were eager to march and to be part of the band. As a result, Alviani's vision for the new college band grew to include forty instrumentalists augmented by a women's drill team.

In May 1946, the band launched a recruiting drive in the *Massachusetts Collegian*: "Wanted: Alviani wants 40 men and 40 girls for his band project." Alviani also advertised for one drum major, three twirlers, and six buglers. With a number of "skeptical pioneers," "fancy drummers," and "fanfare buglers," the women's drill team was started. Alviani wrote that during the band's difficult postwar years, it was able to stay in place on the field while the drill team marched formations to the music.

In the fall of 1946, Robert Bertram, the band's drum major before the war, resumed his former position, and the drill team was directed by drillmaster Wally Kallaugher '49. Rounding out the new band's student leadership was Alvin Alkon '49 as manager.

The MSC Band came back to life and, under Alviani, again became an active and versatile campus group. The drill team received new uniforms, which consisted of white sweaters, white shoes, and dark skirts, and the women buglers wore dark uniforms with white socks, shoes, and belts. The regular band members resumed wearing the maroon-and-white uniforms from before the war.

Alviani's band project takes the field for halftime.

The band rehearsed in Memorial Hall and in the drill hall for marching practice. Rehearsals were somewhat sporadic depending on whether it was a game week, and alumni recalled that it was impressive how good the band was because the students had limited rehearsal time. The group's repertoire expanded to include new music, and it began playing highly popular Glenn Miller songs and favorites such as "Little Brown Jug." In addition, various band members restored the prewar tradition of sneaking into Old Chapel and ringing the chapel bells after a football victory. Although Old Chapel was often kept locked, band members were not deterred in their efforts to celebrate a hard-fought gridiron success.

Alviani held tryouts for the drill team, also known as "Band Aides" and "Bandettes," in early October and looked for twelve additional male instrumentalists to fill out the band. During the fall, the diverse ensemble, consisting of instrumentalists, drill team members, buglers, twirlers, and a female drum corps, all marched for halftime performances.

John Hilchey, a band member who joined the armed forces during the war, returned to campus as part of the class of 1947. Since the band had only forty members, it was difficult to write drill more complex than a few letters or simple shapes. He came up with a humorous show concept, and the band performed his drill for the Dad's Day game. For halftime, the band members first played to the visiting stands. Then Bertram fired his pistol into the air, and the MSC Band appeared to fall apart. The drummers played a conga beat, some band members ran toward the home stands, and others wandered aimlessly around the field, looking lost. The football fans, not knowing what was happening, began to boo the band. After the band, herded together by trumpeter Leo Moreau, reformed in front of the home stands, Bertram fired his pistol again, and the students lay down on the field and formed the words "HI DADS!" The football fans "fell over dead" and, realizing they had been had, applauded loudly for the band. Hilchey recalled the band never received as much applause as it did that day.

The band and drill team also appeared at the November 2 Homecoming game against Vermont, where their "snappy maneuvers, stirring marches and a touch of swing" won applause from the 3,000-member audience. Featured drills included a sharply executed "V" for Vermont and "M" for Mass State, and MSC won the day 28–20.

The drill team caused a "riot" at the 1946 Tufts game.

The band also appeared at the November 16 Mass State-Tufts game where, according to the *Boston Post*, the drill team's appearance caused a mild riot on the Tufts campus. The Tufts Band was not allowed to have a woman drum majorette perform with it, because the dean of women felt it was not an established New England custom. When the MSC Band showed up with three female drum majorettes and the sixty-woman drill team, the Tufts Jumbos were amazed and dismayed and petitioned the dean to revoke the "no drum majorette" edict. The *Massachusetts Collegian* smiled and added that perhaps next year Tufts would have at least "one female form divine in the bandwagon."

A long-running tradition ended that fall as the Massachusetts State and Amherst College football teams met for the last time on November 20. Fittingly, the game ended in a 7–7 tie.

In the spring of 1947, the MSC Band played in the Mass State Combined Glee Clubs Concert, performing "In a Persian Market," "Full Moon and Empty Arms," and "American Patrol." The concert ended with the band and glee clubs performing "Sons of Old Massachusetts." On February 13, the glee clubs and band, directed by Alviani, presented "Snowman's Frolic" in Stockbridge Hall and opened the annual campus Winter Carnival. On February 28, the band played at the Hatfield Music Festival, performing "Saber and Spurs" and "American Patrol."

Hilchey, who went on to work for NASA on Werner Von Braun's team, recalled that the "Saber and Spurs" march was highly popular, since several band members were also in the ROTC horse cavalry. For a concert in Bowker Auditorium, the drummers and Alviani, who was open to all new ideas and

The 1981 Minuteman Band on the steps of the Capitol Building in Washington, D. C.

The Minuteman Band prepares to step off.

The 1959 Precisionettes and Redmen Band.

Block M for pregame.

Part of the 1963 Massachusetts Band drumline.

A Massachusetts Band bass drummer performs during halftime in 1963.

The 1953 Precisionettes take the field.

Part of the 1994 Minuteman Band.

President Bill Clinton greets Minuteman Band members.

The Pearl Corporation began sponsoring the UMass drumline in 1986.

The Alumni and Minuteman Bands combine for halftime during Homecoming 1997.

Trombones from the 1988 Minuteman Band form the point of the M during pregame.

The Minuteman Band performs at the 2002 Freshman Convocation.

A closeup of Minuteman Band trumpet players.

2003 Minuteman Band trumpet players.

Next page: The 1959 Redmen Band and Precisionettes.

Saxophonist Rob Graff smiles through the crowd of band members.

Students make lifelong friends in the Minuteman Band.

Metawampe drum major Richard Draper as the university's athletic icon.

Metawampe and a band member review halftime music in the fall of 1959.

The Minuteman Band unveils the university's new logo.

The Minuteman Band and military department share a long history together.

The 2002 band gives its traditional Faneuil Hall concert in Boston.

The 1981 Minuteman Band passes in review for President Ronald Reagan.

Closeup of a Minuteman Band trombonist.

The band plays "Fight Massachusetts" as the team enters the stadium.

Closeup of a Massachusetts Band bass drummer.

Closeup of a Minuteman Band colorguard member.

University Herald Walter Chesnut opens Commencement while George Parks looks on.

George Parks as drum major of the Reading Buccaneers.

Parks' enthusiastic style carried over to the Minuteman Band.

Parks leads marching rehearsal at Band Camp 1977.

The 1994 Minuteman Band outside its home, Old Chapel.

"would try anything once," decided to create a memorable performance. Before the trumpeting section of the march, the band added a street beat, and the drummers marched onto the stage playing on long Civil War-style snare drums. The audience, among them the World War II former Marine football team, was amazed, and when the whole band joined in during the trumpeting section, the audience cheered loudly, stood up, and sang along for the rest of the march. It was a command performance, and the band brought down the house.

A major transformation soon took place at Massachusetts State College, and the new University of Massachusetts came into being on the very land that was cleared by Clark and Stockbridge in 1867 to create Massachusetts Agricultural College. However, many state leaders had hoped that the Commonwealth's public university would be centered around Harvard University or in Boston, and not everyone was pleased with the location of the new state university. The military department also underwent transformation when the horse cavalry was replaced by armored tank cavalry. The loss of the cavalry horses, which lent a romantic air to the cozy campus, had a profound effect on the school and neatly severed the remaining ties to Mass Aggie days. It was the end of an era.

On April 20, 1947, while the Old Chapel bells chimed, students and faculty held a rally to celebrate the new university. On May 7 the university bill was signed into law, and the Old Chapel bell chimed out "Happy Birthday to You!" The University of Massachusetts at Amherst soon experienced unprecedented growth.

The seal of the University of Massachusetts.

The new "U of M Band," led by Bertram, performed at the ROTC spring military review on May 17, as the ROTC "staged a snappy review to the martial airs of the University Band." Gov. Robert Bradford and various state senators and representatives were on hand to honor the new university, among them those who had introduced the name change into the legislature. Some legislators, who were on campus for the first time, appreciated the school's beauty as well as the friendly students. They were greeted by a varied and colorful program, which included band music, a military review, and a parade, and left feeling impressed with the new university.

In September 1947, enrollment hit a historic high of 2,400, with another 1,800 students enrolled at the temporary Fort Devens campus. In addition, the Yankee Conference football league began operating and pitted Massachusetts against such teams as Maine, New Hampshire, and Rhode Island.

For the fall, Bertram was the band's student leader, and Jack Conlon '49 was the drum major. The new University Band, which included both the band and the drill team, continued to give sharp halftime performances. Throughout the fall, the band played marches and other music while the drill team executed letters and drill formations. Alviani said, "The drill team and band act as a unit. The band plays the music; the girls form the lettering. As a unit, each part contributes something to the color of the game. Together they represent the University."

In October, due to scheduling conflicts, the band was placed under the

HOL-YOKE'S HILLS PRO-LONG THE STRAIN, ECHO-ING   TO   OUR   GLAD   RE -   FRAIN,   AND THE

Robert Bertram leads the drill team onto the field.

MAKE THE WEL-KIN RING, WITH A CHO-RUS AS WE SING, WITH A TRI-BUTE THAT   WE   BRING .

The band and drill team form an M for halftime in the fall of 1947.

jurisdiction of the military department, and the drill team was supervised by the women's athletic department. This enabled band rehearsal to take the place of military drill for men and physical education class for women. The new rules applied only to freshmen and sophomores, since juniors and seniors were already exempt from the requirements.

A favorite band tradition started in the fall. Although the band and drill team planned to go to the Springfield away game, the game was cancelled due to rain. The University Band found itself with extra funding, and a "Band and Drill Team Banquet" was organized instead. The banquet was a success, and the tradition continues to the present day.

On November 17, the band, also referred to as the "UM Band," combined with the chorus and chorale to present "Songs of Christmas," which was broad-

Twirlers parade onto the field in the late 1940s.

cast over WHYN. Members of the band played in the brass choir and accompanied the singers on various carols, including "O Come All Ye Faithful," "Joy to the World," and "O Holy Night." In early December, the band's brass section also played carols in downtown Amherst.

During the winter, most of the band members played in specialized groups such as the brass choir. When the UM Band regrouped for the spring semester of 1948, manager John Weidhaas '49 and Bertram conducted the band at various ROTC events. The spring concert concluded the band's activities for the year.

In the fall of 1948, Ezra Schabas was hired to run the university band program, and for the first time, the music department's official faculty grew to two. Alviani turned his attention to vocal music and conducted the University Chorale, a well-loved and respected group that functioned as the university's musical ambassadors.

Schabas restructured the band and created a traditional all-male marching unit. The band also changed its look and no longer wore the maroon-and-white uniforms of earlier years. The group's new uniforms consisted of white sweaters with maroon music lyres emblazoned on them, maroon pants with a white stripe, and black shoes. The drill team wore gray blazers, gray skirts, white shoes and socks, and white gloves.

For the first time, the cheerleaders were placed under the direction of the fine arts department and were considered part of the band program. Since the founding of Mass Aggie, only men had served as cheerleaders. However, this year, women were added and performed as "special cheerleaders." In addition, the Metawampe drum major rapidly became the new university's mascot, and after George Burgess' and Alviani's successful mascot campaign, the university adopted the nickname "Redmen" for its athletic teams.

Ezra Schabas

Ezra Schabas became the new band director at the University of Massachusetts in the fall of 1948. Prior to his appointment, he was in the Army for three years as a member of an Army Air Force Band in Europe. He played with several New York City symphonic orchestras and jazz bands and also taught music at a boys' school in Tarrytown, New York.

Schabas, who received a bachelor's degree in music from Juilliard and a master's degree in music from Columbia University, was hired as a full time assistant in music at the University of Massachusetts. He worked with the UMass Band for two years.

A former principal at Canada's Royal Conservatory of Music, Schabas went on to be co-founder and first general director of the National Youth Orchestra of Canada. His publications on Sir Ernest MacMillan and the Canadian Opera Company are considered to be definitive works. Schabas received Canada's highest honor for lifetime achievement and was appointed to the Order of Canada in 2001.

Ezra Schabas formed the University Concert Band.

Throughout the fall, the band and the drill team provided a variety of music for football games. Since the audience enjoyed the halftime programs, the band began performing its first pregame show as well. The show consisted of a "new and tremendous pregame fanfare" that announced the entrance of the football team onto Alumni Field and ended only when the players reached the bench. The band continued adding innovations, and Schabas declared, "Your Massachusetts Band will be one of the best in New England next fall!"

At the Holidays of Music festival, the band gave a concert on November 23 in Bowker Auditorium. The ten-day series of musical events, the school's first music festival since the war, was a complete success and far exceeded everyone's expectations. Schabas gave a recital of clarinet solos and performed in a jazz concert as part of a student and faculty sextet. The festival ended with the Amherst College Band and UM Band giving a joint concert. Before Christmas vacation, the band's brass ensemble played carols on the Amherst Common and in Memorial Hall.

Schabas also separated the band into two groups: a marching band for the fall football games and a concert band for more formal, sit-down concerts. After the football season, Schabas directed the newly established University Concert

Band, which was made up of men and women. He also created the school's first jazz band, the fifteen-member University Dance Band.

The new concert band was a hit, and the February 10, 1949, *Massachusetts Collegian* reported, "Huge Audience Cheers New UM Concert Band." The audience enjoyed the spirited music of the sixty-piece group, as it performed "Rhapsody in Rumba," "Pavanne," and Glenn Miller's jazz arrangement of "Song of the Volga Boatman." Schabas declared that the band was truly on the road to success and acknowledged the hard work of the student administrative staff as the reason for the band's excellence.

Due to the excitement surrounding the band program, more students began to join, and in March, Schabas requested additional uniforms for the fall. Alviani agreed and recommended the purchase of ten new sweaters with emblems and ten maroon trousers with a white stripe. More uniform blouses were also requested, which allowed the concert band to have its own uniform for winter and spring concerts. The concert band began giving performances at local high schools and soon became an effective musical ambassador for the university.

"Mothers Enjoy Band Concert" was the headline as guests attended a Sunday afternoon pops concert in the "good old style" on Memorial Hall lawn. Schabas and several student conductors led the band and presented a balanced musical program that drew enthusiastic applause from over 1,000 appreciative listeners.

The UM Band also continued its affiliation with the military department. At the spring review, Schabas directed the ROTC Band, which was commended for having "served efficiently throughout the year." The ROTC Band was made up of military personnel and regular marching band members. In an arrangement with ROTC's Colonel Richard Evans, men were excused from mandatory drill as long as the band played at the spring review or on other special occasions that the military requested.

In the fall of 1949, the band grew to forty members, all men, under the leadership of marching band director Robert Bertram. Since the band was considered a

Jack Conlon '49 leads the UMass Band in the fall of 1948.

ROTC drum major George Nickless '52. Band members often played in both the ROTC Band and the marching band.

FORMATION at UNIV. of MASS.
AMHERST, MASS.

The band plays while the drill team spells GO in the fall of 1949.

student-run organization, Schabas served as the group's faculty adviser and, like the coaches before him, was not directly involved in running the marching band. Students ran all aspects of the band program, including writing drill and directing music rehearsals.

Supplemented by the fifty-member women's drill team, the band played an active part in encouraging school spirit at football games and rallies. The ninety-member band, drill team, and cheerleaders took part in the "Beat Norwich" torchlight parade, which was led by female cheerleaders who rode on the military department's tanks. At Bowker Auditorium, Schabas conducted the band as it played a medley of school songs, and the reorganized cheerleaders, who now officially included women, led the rally.

That fall, the band and drill team worked more closely together than they had before. Drillmaster Doug Footit '50 added, "The difference between drilling girls and Marines is that with females there's a lot of talking in the ranks, but no curse words." The drill team, known as "The Gray Ladies" because of the color of its uniform, was the only women's marching squad in the East. Schabas added that women would be allowed to join the marching band if there was enough interest.

For the October 22 UMass-Rochester Homecoming game, the band and drill team were the highlight of the day with their exhibition of music and precision drilling, as over one hundred students spelled out "HI GRADS" to welcome the alumni back to campus. In addition, the drill team formed a large "R," and the highlight of the show occurred when the drill team spelled "FIGHT" and the band spelled "UM."

For the November 5 UMass-Springfield College away game, the two schools combined their groups and nearly two hundred band members performed for pregame. The UMass and Springfield bands played in unison and marched from opposite end zones to the 50 yard line, flanked by the two squads of the UMass drill team. At center field, the bands played "The Star-Spangled Banner" while the drill team saluted. During halftime, the UMass groups played first. The drill team formed a large revolving wheel, while the band filed inside the wheel and revolved the other way to the tune of "Here We Go Round the Mulberry Bush." The UMass performers then paid tribute to Springfield by forming an "S" and a "C" while playing "The Old Gray Mare." Springfield College's band and its thirty-two-man singing drill team then performed "Faith of Our Fathers," after spelling out a greeting to visiting fathers for the Dad's Day game. Although UMass lost to Springfield 22–0, both groups' performances were appreciated by football fans.

On November 22, the music department's third annual banquet in honor of the University Band, which included the marching band, drill team, concert band, and cheerleaders, was held at the Drake Hotel. Nearly 150 students attended and were treated to steak dinners, after which they watched color movies of halftime shows from the 1948 and 1949 Homecoming Weekends. Wally Kallaugher, Doug Footit, and Robert Bertram were awarded for their outstanding work with the drill team and marching band, and the banquet ended with a dance.

The concert band gave its annual Mother's Day Concert on May 7, 1950. Despite a high wind that played havoc with the audience's hats and the band's music, the concert was pleasant and well-received. Music included jazz pieces, marches, and the audience favorite "Some Enchanted Evening."

After a successful tenure as band director, Schabas resigned to become director of public relations and artist management at Toronto's Royal Conservatory of Music. After his resignation in the spring of 1950, Alviani took over supervision of the band program, and student director Robert Bertram was chosen to act as coordinator.

Torchlight parades were a tradition before home football games.

THE REDMEN BAND
AND THE PRECISIONETTES
1950–1963

*I*n the fall of 1950, Joseph Contino was hired as band director at the University of Massachusetts. Under Contino, the band broke away from the old traditions and began marching with a wider range of musical selections. Donald Pearse '54 recalled that at the time, the band was much like other student-run organizations on campus. There were no scholarships, participation was strictly voluntary, and the band averaged thirty-five to forty members. The music was rehearsed and polished, but the band's primary function was to provide rhythm for the drill team, which was the main attraction. Contino stepped into this arena full of "effervescence, exuberance, and vitality."

For the first time since World War II, both the marching band and concert band opened its ranks to women. Contino said that the bands were "planning a vigorous program in both marching and concert bands with a view towards more extensive student participation." He added that it therefore no longer made sense to deny women the right to be in the band.

Women made a fine showing with the band at the UMass-Bates game on September 30, which the Redmen won 26–0. A dozen women "infiltrated the

Joseph Contino

Joseph Contino, here conducting at Homecoming 1966, led the University Bands from 1950–1963.

Joseph Contino was born on October 20, 1922, and grew up in Conneaut, Ohio, where he was a member of the high school's top band. He served in the Army's Glider Artillery from 1942 to 1945 and received a Bronze Star for his efforts during the Battle of the Bulge. He was also the survivor of a torpedoed troop ship on its way to the D-Day invasion of Normandy.

After graduating from Oberlin Conservatory in 1949, Contino received a master's degree from Columbia Teacher's College. He was appointed as an instructor of music at the University of Massachusetts in September 1950. Contino directed the marching band, drill team, youth orchestra, and the instrumental music program and was also a member of the faculty woodwind quintet.

Under his direction, the University Bands reached new heights. The Redmen Band and Precisionettes entertained audiences at football games, and the University Concert Band won wide acclaim during its spring tours. In 1954, President Jean Paul Mather presented Contino with the University's Distinguished Teaching Award for his service to the school.

Contino's ability as a conductor, performer, adjudicator, and clinician won him warm praise and extended his reputation throughout New England. He was devoted to teaching and was known for his musicality and integrity. Contino died on June 30, 2000, at the age of 77.

ranks" of the once all-male band and played everything from clarinets and drums to baritone horns and glockenspiel. Despite the outraged uproar of a few diehards, the twelve women were welcomed into the group, and their musical ability and "feminine charms" were indisputable.

After years of use, the Metawampe drum major uniform was worn-out and falling apart at the seams. The university's senior honorary societies, Isogon and Adelphia, saved the day and, despite their low treasuries, bought the band's drum major a new outfit. In November, Metawampe's new headdress arrived. It was made by Chief Red Cloud from Thompsonville, Connecticut and had the distinction of being the first headdress to leave the tribe.

In February 1951, a statue honoring Metawampe was unveiled on the Old Chapel lawn. After a concert on the Chapel chimes, the band played the alma mater, and President Ralph A. Van Meter accepted the statue, which was to serve as the focal point for athletic rallies and other student meetings. However, although Metawampe was a distinguished Native American chief, his statue was small, and students had a hard time taking it seriously. Over the years, the statue was involved in various college pranks and once ended up submerged in the Campus Pond.

Although the marching band was growing in size and experience, students felt that it lacked in certain areas. In the March 27 *Massachusetts Collegian*, band publicity director Bruce Fox '54 wrote a letter to the editor, reprimanding students for making negative remarks about the group. Fox challenged the students to join the band if they played an instrument to boost up the numbers or, if they did not, to support the band at rallies or other functions.

After nearly eighty years, the long relationship between the college band and the military department ended. After this, the band no longer participated in the spring reviews, and the director of the University Band was no longer the default ROTC Band director. Instead, the school's Army ROTC Band took over the UMass Band's former duties.

In the fall of 1951, Contino implemented strict

The band and drill team form a UM in the fall of 1950.

The 1951 Redmen Band and drill team step off for pregame.

Redmen Band members continued to play in the 1956–57 ROTC Band.

A closeup of the 1951 band trombones.

The 1951 twirlers perform during halftime.

The 1952 Redmen Band.

musical standards and required all students to pass an audition in order to join the band. Fox added that the band program was "building something new and different—numerically, mechanically, and musically." The band added twice as many drum majorettes as before, and Bill McBane '58 became the band's new Metawampe drum major. The band, which was now referred to as the "Redmen Band," had strong camaraderie, and Contino was a cheerleader, a teacher, and a friend. Due to his efforts, the Redmen Band was a special place to be.

As Contino tightened standards, students found that there were consequences for their misdeeds. That fall, Pearse missed two band rehearsals, and Contino suspended him from performing at one of the games. Pearse learned a valuable lesson, and it was the last time he missed a commitment. In later years, he became a lieutenant colonel in the U.S. Air Force.

Soon, the fifty-member marching band was recognized as a bigger success than ever before, and Contino received praise for his fine work with the group. The band members were commended for their "distinguished service in the field of rally pep and school spirit," and the drill team became known as "The Pride of the U of M."

Due to hazardous traffic conditions created by Columbus Day travelers, the Amherst police did not allow the usual rally, which included tanks, torches, the band, and hordes of yelling students, to take place for the October 13 Williams game. Instead, a new Bonfire Band Concert was held near Memorial Hall, where the band played school songs and popular numbers by the light of the fire.

For the May 4, 1952, Parent's Day Concert, the concert band broke with tradition and moved the performance into Bowker Auditorium. The concert, which in past years was held on the Memorial Hall lawn or the Student Union Terrace, was enjoyed as the highlight of Parent's Weekend.

During the fall of 1952, the fifty-member Redmen Band performed hesitation steps, waltz steps, and executed rapid flank movements while playing the latest hit songs. The band also played a greater vari-

The Metawampe Drum Major

One of the Redmen Band's favorite traditions during the 1950s and 1960s was the Metawampe drum major. Metawampe, a Native American chief, was first mentioned in 1674, when he and other members of his tribe sold a tract of land north of Mount Toby to the white settlers.

The band's drum majors first began wearing the Native American uniform in 1949, and two of the earliest students to play the role were Robert Bertram '49 and Jack Conlon '49. The Metawampe drum major, one of the school's icons, led the band to the football field and cheered on students during evening bonfires and football rallies. The tradition continued until 1963, when Metawampe and the band drum major positions were separated. Metawampe continued on as the school's mascot until the 1970s, when the university teams became the Minutemen.

Metawampe continued as a band tradition until 1963.

ety of music, and halftime shows included "rapid-fire" letter changes and animated designs. Under Contino, quality improved and the band presented "a snappier type of field marching style."

Since the band was without a drum major at the beginning of the semester, Contino picked Pearse to be the new Metawampe. However, the Metawampe uniform was made for a six-foot-tall drum major, and all of the previous wearers had been "strapping specimens." Pearse was five foot seven and "135 pounds soaking wet," and the band had no funds to alter his new uniform. Responding to emergency tailoring needs, the drum majorettes, armed with boxes of straight pins, kept the pants and sleeves from dragging, and the latest drum major took his place at the head of the Redmen Band. Although Pearse felt that he was not all that imposing, he was proud to be the latest Metawampe.

Recruiting continued to be one of the Redmen Band's main goals. Pearse wrote in the *Massachusetts Collegian* that contrary to popular belief, the band was a student-run organization, and faculty supervision was kept to a minimum. Although the band had a limited budget, the group wanted to grow and needed more support from the student body and instrumental musicians.

The fall marked the Redmen football team and band's first appearance on TV, when they were seen nationwide on WBZ during the November 15

The Women's Drill Team
and the Precisionettes

The Precisionettes were known for their crisp attention to detail. Shown here is the 1961 team.

In the spring of 1946, Doric Alviani created the women's drill team. Initially made up of twenty-four women, the drill team became enormously popular, and in later years, nearly two hundred women auditioned for fewer than thirty openings. University women competed to be in the ensemble, since it presented them with the opportunity to perform at football games as part of a highly trained marching unit.

The drill team was renamed the Precisionettes in the spring of 1953, and throughout the 1950s and 1960s, the Precisionettes were the highlight of halftime shows and performed detailed drill maneuvers. The Redmen Band provided the musical accompaniment, and fans enjoyed seeing the drill team's sharp marching abilities. The Precisionettes numbered sixty women, with forty-eight regular performers and twelve alternates.

With the transformation of the marching band program in 1963, the Precisionettes were absorbed into the ROTC program and functioned as a military ensemble. The group performed at the military department's fall and spring reviews and marched in Homecoming parades. In September 1970, after the Student Senate cut the Precisionettes' funding completely, the proud history of the women's drill team came to an end.

UMass-Tufts game. The halftime show featured a bow, which was formed by the band, and an arrow, which was composed of cheerleaders and the drill team. As the drummers played, the bowstring moved back and fired the arrow, which exploded into letters. The performance ended with the drill team spelling out "TUFTS" during a salute. After the university group's performance, Tufts' band gave an exhibition, and UMass won the day 32–0.

For the October 1952 Homecoming Weekend, instead of playing the usual marching music, the band performed popular music such as "Down Yonder,"

"Botch-A-Me," and "Far-away Places," a dance number complete with a special waltz step.

In the spring of 1953, in recognition of their fine marching abilities and military bearing, the women's drill team was renamed "The Precisionettes." The group was highly popular, and since competition was keen, it was common for two hundred women to audition for roughly twenty-five open drill team spots. Basic training for the drill team consisted of learning the elements of posture, cadence, and pace; memorizing routines; and responding to commands.

Contino stated that a bright future was ahead for the Redmen Band and the Precisionettes. A larger student staff was added, and drill routines for both groups grew more complex. At the time, students served as announcers, technicians, photographers, movie camera operators, and administrative personnel for the band program. In addition, the head of the athletic department, Warren P. McGuirk, was supportive of the band and allocated $1,000 to cover traveling expenses to away football games.

After twelve years of constant use, the band's white lyre sweaters were nearing the end of their lifespan. After Pearse met with the Student Senate and explained the band's critical need for new uniforms, the Senate appropriated the necessary money. Students were supportive, and John Miller, a member of the Student Senate, added, "If the University Band does not represent the student body, what other organization does?"

There was great excitement when the Redmen Band received sixty sharp maroon-and-white uniforms. The new maroon coats had white buttons and white trim on the collar, sleeve, and pockets, and the rest of the uniform consisted of maroon pants with white stripes and white buck shoes. Designed as a dual-purpose outfit, the uniform also functioned as formal dress for the concert band. The Precisionettes had a new look as well, and their new gray-and-white uniforms, which the students had made themselves, complemented the band's maroon. New uniforms always attracted attention and newspaper coverage, which often led students and football fans to

The 1953 Redmen Band and its new, maroon uniforms.

The Redmen Band received support from the Student Senate.

give more support to the band program. With the band's new look, its transformation from a post-World War II ensemble into a more modern college marching band was complete. An enthusiastic band director, new uniforms, and revitalized standards all propelled the Redmen Marching Band and Precisionettes forward.

There were additional changes at the University of Massachusetts when the fine arts department was split into the Departments of Music and Art, and university trustees recognized the first music major program. The new music department, with its headquarters in Memorial Hall, supervised all extracurricular programs in music and theater, as well as instrumental and vocal groups. Alviani became the first head of the new department, which at the time boasted a fine faculty of two: Alviani, director of vocal music, and Contino, director of instrumental music. Alviani's duties included directing all campus choirs, as well as producing numerous musicals, operettas, and sinfoniettas. Contino directed the University Concert Band, the Redmen Marching Band, Precisionettes, and various other campus instrumental ensembles.

In the fall of 1953, membership standards for the extracurricular Redmen Band were kept high, and students were allowed to join only if they maintained their grades. In addition, all band members were required to memorize their music as well as their individual marching formations. In the days before drill charts, students sat in a classroom and learned their marching drill from Contino, who drew the formations on a chalkboard.

During the football season, Contino and the Precisionettes' drillmaster held weekly planning sessions, where they created the drill formations for the weekend's game. The Redmen Band and Precisionettes rehearsed separately on Mondays through Wednesdays, from 5 to 6 p.m. On Thursdays and Fridays, the two groups came together and rehearsed the show for the Saturday game. On the field, fifty band members joined forty-eight Precisionettes for a

Before drill charts, band members learned their steps from a chalkboard.

Contino, Metawampe, and Thomas Picard, the Precisionettes' drillmaster, confer.

combined performing ensemble of ninety-eight students. It was one of the largest groups in the school's history, and music for halftime shows that fall included "When the Saints Go Marching In" and "On the Warpath." The Redmen Band also traveled to Pittsfield to perform in the city's Halloween celebration.

Contino continued to receive praise for the direction the band was taking, and the group was acknowledged as "a huge success." To encourage band member retention, the band also implemented a new award, which was given after a student was in the ensemble for two years. The award consisted of a gold-plated lyre with an interlocked UM in maroon relief and was presented at the annual fall banquet.

For basketball season, a newly formed pep band started under the leadership of band manager Don Hanson '56. The group of twenty musicians played at the home basketball games and traveled to the UMass-Clark game in Worcester. The pep band also played at UMass' annual Winter Carnival.

On March 31, 1954, the University of Massachusetts honored musical theater greats Richard Rodgers and Oscar Hammerstein at a special Convocation. The concert band performed music from *Carousel*, *The King and I*, and *Me and Juliet*. Gov. Christian Herter presented Rodgers and Hammerstein with honorary doctorates, and the band played a moving rendition of "You'll Never Walk Alone" as the audience and University Chorale sang along. The ceremony ended with "The March of the Siamese Children" from *The King and I*.

Ever since the creation of Massachusetts Agricultural College in 1863, its students had to contend with condescending attitudes from private school students. In the early years, Harvard College argued that Mass Aggie should be its agricultural department, and the university regularly endured attempts to reduce its funding and operating budget. Charting the growth and development of the university in his book *The University of Massachusetts; A History of One Hundred Years*, Harold Whiting Cary wrote that the large number of private colleges in

The 1953 band, twirlers, and Precisionettes form a UM.

Highlights from the fall 1953 football season with Donald Pearse '54 as Metawampe in the bottom left

Spring Tour

The University Concert Band became the university's musical ambassador.

In 1954, the popular University Concert Band started the Spring Tour tradition. In 1955, in its second Spring Tour, the concert band traveled for three days and performed for more than 4,500 people at evening concerts and high school assemblies. The band won high praise wherever it appeared and was a highly effective musical ambassador for the university. For a number of years, the group toured throughout the Commonwealth and surrounding states, giving concerts for thousands of alumni, high school students, and members of civic organizations.

In the 1960s, the University Symphony Band began undertaking the Spring Tour. In later years, the symphony band tours were abandoned, and the Minuteman Band became a new musical ambassador for the university.

Massachusetts prohibited the faster development of the state's public university. However, UMass soon had its day in the sun.

In the fall of 1954, the Redmen faced Harvard for a football game on October 2. Harvard's school paper gleefully predicted UMass' complete destruction and wrote that the "cow college" from western Massachusetts should not even bother coming east. It was the fourth meeting in the history of the schools, and Harvard had won the previous three games with shutouts.

"Operation Harvard" commenced as a two hundred-vehicle UMass motorcade, with President Jean Paul Mather in the lead, made the trip to the game. After the bus ride, Pearse recalled that the band and drill team were ready to dazzle the "massive" crowd. At the time, Harvard's band consisted of an informal group of musicians who did not wear uniforms and did not march on the field. By comparison, the UMass Band looked like a "Super Bowl halftime production" and proved that it knew more than "just milking cows." Along with the band and drill team, the cheerleaders yelled themselves hoarse during the tightest moments of the game. In a lashing, pelting rainstorm, coach Charlie O'Rourke's Redmen finally overcame the odds and stunned Harvard 13–7. The stadium went wild. The following day, newspaper headlines read, "Redmen Warwhoop Heard from Amherst to Boston." In terms of football, Massachusetts State College had finally become the University of Massachusetts. The Boston newspapers added that the UMass football team won the game, and the UMass Band won the halftime show.

The Precisionettes continued to excel as well, and Contino was given credit for the "snappy appearance" of the drill team. Lois Bain Steel '57 said Contino imposed a height standard for the women and arranged for the Precisionettes to have uniforms custom made by an Amherst tailor. "Beautiful fabric," recalled Steel, "one hundred percent wool. When it rained we smelled just like a flock of sheep." Yet on the football field, in their saddle oxfords and white gloves, the Precisionettes were audience favorites when they formed a giant "M" and did a "ripple salute." When the football season ended, the concert band presented its Christmas Concert and played such pieces as "American Folk Rhapsody," "Sleigh Ride," and "Barnum and Bailey's Favorite."

For the fall of 1955, the fifty-member Redmen Band maintained its reputation for excellence and performed with the Precisionettes at football games. Although another motorcade made its way to Harvard for a game on October 1, there was no salvation that year as UMass fell 60–6. However, the band and drill team won praise as they formed a maroon-

H is for Harvard, Victory is for us.

The 1955 twirlers smile for the camera.

The 1957 Precisionettes salute crisply.

A halftime performance in the fall of 1955.

The 1955 Redmen Band and Precisionettes perform at Harvard Stadium.

The Precisionettes celebrated their tenth anniversary in 1956.

and-gray "UM" on the field. In a surprising musical tribute, the Harvard Band honored the Redmen Band by playing a medley of UMass songs during its half-time show.

By the spring of 1956, the thirty-seven-member concert band was one of the campus' top musical groups. A typical spring semester schedule had the band performing at the annual Winter Concert in February, taking a four-day tour during spring break, and giving an outdoor pops concert in May. At this time, the concert band outshone the marching band in importance and stature.

Although Contino's groups were traveling widely and gaining accolades, students did not receive academic credit for being in the band. Since the marching band was composed mainly of freshmen and sophomores, Alviani, chair of the music department, felt that giving academic credit would encourage juniors and seniors to stay in the group. The band also continued to suffer from sporadic funding, and although the Athletic Council supplemented its budget with money for away games, that funding was neither regular nor predictable.

In the fall of 1956, the Redmen Band continued to function as a show band, and the group began to gain a reputation as one of New England's finest precision marching bands. That year, the Precisionettes celebrated the tenth anniversary of the women's drill team. On September 29, the band, cheerleaders, and Precisionettes traveled to Boston for a pregame rally at the Boston University Field. Although the Redmen played well, they lost 19–6.

After UMass was beaten 71–6 by UConn at the October 13 Homecoming game, editorials speculated that whereas eliminating the UMass football program was possible, it was unacceptable because it would also mean dissolving the Precisionettes, the cheerleaders, and the Redmen Band. When asked to recall one memorable marching band experience, Contino described the UConn game, where a seventy-year-old alumnus of the band came up with his instrument and asked to play with the Redmen Band. He joined in with the youngsters and had a great time.

By the fall of 1957, the Redmen Band, like the Harvard Band, was run more as a fun-and-games pep band. During this time, Contino started focusing more of his energy on the concert band, which began rehearsing in the fall to prepare for a longer annual Spring Tour. The concert band was by now the university's musical ambassador. Although most Redmen Marching Band members were also in the concert band, by the end of the 1950s, membership in the concert band had more prestige. By February 1958, the concert band, with forty-eight members, was the largest in the group's history and received praise for its outstanding interpretation of various musical pieces.

Starting in 1958, the Redmen Marching Band and University Concert Band began to develop along independent lines with independent staff leadership. Contino felt that this would enable the Redmen Band to grow in stature and accomplishment and to take its place alongside other New England college groups. He also merged the Redmen Band and Precisionettes and created a one-hundred-member unit called "The University Bands."

In the fall of 1958, the Redmen Band received new uniforms. The outfits consisted of silver-gray jackets with maroon details and white buttons, a white citation cord, a maroon "M" on the chest, gray pants with a maroon-and-white stripe, and gray military hats. The band soon had the nickname of "The Gray Ghosts," as the drill team had earlier been known as "The Gray Ladies." With its fast entrance onto the field, the band was a fitting musical complement to the sharp maneuvers of the Precisionettes.

Another instrumental music group on campus at the time was the University Dance Band, which had gained a reputation as one of the finest campus swing bands. Directed by Bob Clowes '60, it was supervised by the music department, which allowed the band to be student-run.

Contino created a new award system that encouraged excellence among band members. Students were awarded points for being in the band program and received a pin after 25 points, a pin guard for 50

A closeup of the fall 1957 Precisionettes.

Trumpets herald the arrival of the band's new uniforms in 1958.

The 1958–59 Redmen Band displays its new, silver uniforms.

The traditional M is formed for pregame.

Redmen Band members cheer on the football team in the fall of 1958.

Richard Draper '60 as Metawampe.

points, and a trophy cup for 120 points. Participation in the marching band was worth 13 points, and the dance band and concert band were each worth 15 points. In the days before band membership merited academic credit, the point system was an invaluable aid for maintaining participation in the band program.

Financial difficulties soon arose for the band. Since the Student Senate controlled the University Bands' finances, band directors sometimes found that they did not have the flexibility needed to run the program as they saw fit. In a fit of passion, after the Senate eliminated $472 for Precisionettes sweaters and additional funding to send him to a national conference in Chicago, Contino considered resigning as the university's band director in May 1959, saying, "I am planning to drop my band activities." He felt the Senate failed to recognize the quality of the groups that were involved, and he would resign unless he was given a reasonable degree of control over the bands' budget.

Contino's students supported him and went to the school administration to try to find a solution. Band manager Dick Draper '60 and Precisionettes drillmaster Don Witkoski '60 told officials that the band could not function without Contino as band director. Draper bluntly said that the program "can't get along without him," and added that the Senate did not realize that the band program gathered more favorable publicity for the university than any other program on campus. A faculty director was critical to its success. Provost Shannon McCune responded that there was no need for a faculty member to direct the marching band and drill team. He wrote that the two groups should be able to stand and march on their own two feet without direct faculty assistance. Although there were disagreements regarding the need for a faculty band director, Contino returned on the assumption that a financial resolution with the Student Senate was being worked out.

After these difficulties in the spring, controversy continued to follow Contino and the Redmen Band into the fall of 1959. "No UMass Band to Play" was the *Massachusetts Collegian* headline for the September 19 UMass-Maine game. Due to administrative difficulties, the Redmen Band and Precisionettes found they were unable to attend and perform at the football game. For the game, the Hadley High School Band took their place and played on the field during halftime.

There were two main issues to resolve. The first centered on the earlier disagreement regarding the need for a band director. Faculty members were not allowed to participate directly in student activities such as the band and Precisionettes, so Contino's role as the band's director exceeded the limits of involvement. The second issue hinged on the recurring theme of the band's funding. Contino was in favor of a new system to fund the band, saying that the Student Senate had too much control over funds and in essence manipulated the organizations it funded.

The 1958 Redmen Band and Precisionettes form a UM.

The fall was a difficult time for the University of Massachusetts. In addition to the traditional lack of funding, President Mather had just resigned. At halftime during the September 26 Harvard game, which the Redmen Band and Precisionettes did not attend, the Redmen were losing in a shut-out. For halftime, the Harvard Band entertained fans by highlighting UMass' troubles, and the group's drill spelled out "no dough," "no pres," "no band," "no booze," and "no score." To complete the ridicule, the Harvard Band ended its show by playing "I've Got Plenty of Nothing." After the performance, a group of UMass students, one of them wearing a Native American headdress, marched onto the field and valiantly played "Fight Massachusetts," which silenced the Harvard Band and raised the UMass fans' spirits. Although the UMass team had a valiant late rally, the Redmen lost 36–22.

A 1959 Redmen Band member with the new uniform overlay.

Shortly thereafter, various administrative issues were resolved, and the Redmen Band and Precisionettes took part in the Friday night football rally before the October 3 Delaware game. Both groups reappeared for the game the next day. At the time, Delaware was thought of as the number one small-college team in the nation, and UMass was sorely outclassed in what was widely considered a "suicide game." After a heroic effort, the Redmen fell 42–12. However, fans were relieved to see the one

The concert band performs at the December 1959 Rockefeller Center tree-lighting ceremony.

hundred-member Redmen Band and Precisionettes, who, in their bright red-and-black uniforms, were "a welcome sight at the game." The Redmen Band also modified its look and received new overlays for its maroon-and-gray uniforms. Instead of the maroon M, band members now sported a multicolored Native American chief's head.

At the October 17 Homecoming game against Rhode Island, the band and drill team's performance added the "one bright note to the otherwise dreary day." Since the band was not at the Harvard game, the Senate also reappropriated $863 and sent the groups to the October 24 Northeastern game.

The highlight of the season was the concert band's December trip to New York City to perform at the lighting of the Rockefeller Center Christmas tree. On December 10, the band and the Statesmen, a male octet, gave a half-hour program for the Rockefeller Center audience. During the lighting ceremony, the band accompanied the Radio City Choristers and played three pieces: "Season's Greetings," "Joy to the World" when the seventy-nine-foot Norway spruce had its 4,050 lights turned on, and "O Come All Ye Faithful" to close the program. The spruce tree was a gift from the Commonwealth of Massachusetts to the Rockefeller Center, and the tree-lighting ceremony, officiated by Massachusetts' governor Foster Furcolo, was seen live by millions on NBC.

During Contino's tenure, a number of musical ensembles grew. In 1950, there were twenty-five students in the concert band, and the group gave two concerts a year. In 1954, the concert band took its first Spring Tour, and by 1959, the band had fifty members, took an annual tour around the state, played three annual concerts and an annual pops concert, and had several off-campus performances each year. The drill team also came a long way, from its founding, when no one had uniforms, to the sixty-woman Precisionettes that was well known and loved for its marching crispness.

The growth and success of the Redmen Band was attributed directly to band members' enthusiasm, and Contino felt that students had to have real drive and intensity to be in the University Bands. The group was invited to march in more parades than ever before, which showed the state's growing awareness of the band's existence. Membership in the group was considered both "hard work and hard fun," and if a student had abundant school spirit and enthusiasm, he would be a "successful Redmen Bandsman."

Contino attributed the growth of the programs to self-determination, that is, letting the groups function as needed without restraining them. In the past few years, he added, there had been attempts to stop them, and that until these ended, the controversy of who controlled the University Bands program would continue.

The fall of 1960 was an active season for the University Bands. On October 1, UMass beat Harvard 27–12, and the *Boston Globe* ran the headline, "Harvard Band Loses, Too!" At halftime, the Redmen Band and Precisionettes successfully stole the show from the Harvard Band, and fans felt that Harvard's band looked "ridiculous" running around on the field for every new formation, while the UMass Band maneuvered into much more difficult formations in an orderly fashion. The writer said that the UMass students were proud of the way they were represented at the game, by the football team, band, and drill team, who all clearly demonstrated their quality, spirit, and showmanship. The *Massachusetts Collegian* mentioned that there was a great deal of Harvard contempt for the

The Redmen Band and Precisionettes form an L in honor of the university's new president, John Lederle.

The 1960 Redmen Band and Precisionettes form a UM.

The 1961 Redmen Band.

marching band and the Precisionettes, who were referred to as "hayseeds" and "hicks." The Harvard fans also made fun of the band and drill team uniforms, and both were loudly hissed during halftime. However, the *Boston Globe* wrote that the famous Harvard Band got no better than a draw against the Redmen Band, and that the "UMass Precisionettes, an all girl ensemble, stole the show."

The Student Senate continued its support of the University Bands program and provided new jackets for the dance band. In addition, the Senate sent Contino to the College Band Association Conference in Chicago, and the earlier financial controversies were momentarily resolved.

The Varsity Pep Band was revitalized in the fall under the leadership of Ted Souliotis '62, the Redmen Band manager. The group became more active in the basketball program and performed at many of the home games throughout the season. The pep band played marches and pop tunes and was considered by fans to be an enjoyable addition to the basketball atmosphere.

At the inauguration of the university's new president, John W. Lederle, on April 22, 1961, the concert band played "Grand March" to open the program. After Gov. John Volpe invested the new president, the band played "Inaugural Fanfare," a piece specially written for the occasion by Elliot Schwartz, an instructor in the music department. More and more public high school graduates were seeking higher education, and President Lederle's goal for the University of Massachusetts was to have 15,000 students by 1975.

At the outdoor May 14 Pops Concert on the Student Union Terrace, the concert band started a new tradition; instead of wearing the regular band uniforms, students wore suits and ties or dresses. Contino wanted to create a more relaxed atmosphere for the informal concert.

By the fall of 1961, the University Bands had become firmly established as one of the high points of the fall football scene, and many spectators, who were oblivious to the outcome of the football game, looked forward to the combined performances of the Redmen Band and the Precisionettes at halftime. In addition, the sixty-four-member marching band was known for its spirited "oom-pah-pahs" and appeared annually at the Pittsfield Halloween Parade, where it was one of the most impressive marching units.

In the spring of 1962, issues regarding the University Bands' funding resur-

Members of the 1961 Precisionettes execute their traditional salutes.

faced, and campus groups decided they were no longer willing or able to accept financial responsibility for the band. Various organizations declined to sponsor the group, including the Student Senate, the Fine Arts Council, and the athletic department. In April, the Fine Arts Council voted to recommend to the Student Senate that the Redmen Marching Band not be allowed to use student tax money for away trips. The band's proposed trips required an additional $6,000, and the council felt that the needed money should come out of athletic department funds and not from the student tax fund. The controversy continued through the summer.

On July 2, 1962, the Old Chapel bells played a special concert and honored the one hundredth anniversary of the Land Grant Act, which had brought the University of Massachusetts and sixty-seven other state schools into existence. Alviani conducted the concert, which included traditional UMass songs as well as Civil War pieces.

In the fall of 1962, the band's funding controversy came to a full head. Throughout September, the pages of the *Massachusetts Collegian* were full of letters, editorials, and opinions in support of the band or theories on where else the 125-member band and drill team should get its funding. Band members wrote a letter to the editor saying that neither the Fine Arts Council nor athletics would take financial responsibility for the band's away trips. At stake was the September 29 Dartmouth away game. The Student Senate responded and wrote that the student tax fund paid $10,400 to support the band program. Therefore, it and the council decided that the requested $5,000 should come from other sources. Senators met with Lederle to discuss the funding issue, and the Fine Arts Council agreed to review the band's request. The Senate felt that athletics should contribute money to support the band, but athletics did not feel that the band or drill team were under its jurisdiction.

After the Fine Arts Council met and reaffirmed its decision that the band's trips would not be funded by student taxes, the band and drill team resigned themselves to not going to the Dartmouth game. However, at the last minute, the athletic department, dining commons, and Student Union Executive Program Committee joined and gave the groups money for transportation and meals at the Dartmouth game. It was a noble gesture from the coalition, but because Contino and the University Bands thought that they were not being sent to the game, they had not been rehearsing and did not have a show prepared. Since one day was not enough time to prepare a respectable halftime show, they decided not to make the trip. In addition, Contino felt strongly about not accepting temporary aid; he wanted to resolve the ongoing question of whose responsibility it was to pay for the band's transportation to games. After the Dartmouth funding controversy, the Student Senate gave $1,600 for the band to attend the November 10 Villanova game. However, the Senate's funding did not represent a long-term commitment to fund the band's away trips. The struggle over the band's funding continued, and a more permanent solution was not reached until later years.

After the football team defeated Bucknell 21–20 on October 6, the band welcomed the team back to campus. Despite the team's late arrival, the band and three hundred students stood in the rain and waited to give the winning team the reception it deserved.

By 1963, the ROTC Band was phased out.

Although the Redmen Band and Precisionettes were operating under numerous financial restrictions, they continued to perform with dedication on the football field. Various sources commended the groups for their outstanding performance at the school's Centennial Homecoming on October 13, which added to the enjoyment of the 10,000 alumni and fans as UMass beat archrival UConn 16–6. In honor of their state college history, during the halftime show, the Precisionettes formed an "M," and the Redmen Band spelled out "S" and "C."

In May 1963, a time-honored school tradition ended when the ROTC cadets at the University of Massachusetts marched in their last mandatory spring review. It was the school's ninety-sixth review since 1867, and these reviews were one of the main reasons that the battalion drum corps, the ancestor of the Minuteman Band, came into existence. Starting with the fall of 1963, male students were no longer required to take military classes, and ROTC became a voluntary organization at UMass. Although the ROTC Band traditionally performed in reviews, this last year, the Air Force Drum and Bugle Corps played instead, and the ROTC Band was phased out.

The Redmen Band era ended as well. After thirteen years as band director at the University of Massachusetts, Contino resigned his post and became more involved in the music department's woodwind and orchestral ensembles.

THE MICHIGAN INFLUENCE
AT UMASS
1963–1977

In *Academia's Golden Age: Universities in Massachusetts*, Richard Freeland wrote that in the 1960s, the forces that had traditionally retarded the development of the University of Massachusetts were finally overcome, and state authorities began providing the kind of financial support for which previous presidents had pleaded. Between 1960 and 1970, enrollment at the school grew from 6,500 to 18,400, and President Lederle was credited as a man who sought to achieve his ends through conciliation and quiet persuasion. He told state officials in cordial tones there was no reason that Massachusetts could not have a state university as eminent as its outstanding private schools or the great public universities of the West. In 1962, Lederle brought about fiscal autonomy for the University of Massachusetts, which led to the school's transformation into a modern state university.

When Lederle came to the University of Massachusetts in 1960, he had strong visions of what a public state university should be and of what a state university's marching band should be. Having seen the bands of Michigan's legendary band director William D. Revelli, he wanted to re-create the same at the

John A. Jenkins

John A. Jenkins, a graduate of the University of Michigan, was a cornet soloist in the Michigan Band. He studied under William D. Revelli and taught for a number of years in the Ann Arbor, Michigan public school system.

In 1963, Jenkins became the band director at the University of Massachusetts and brought the Michigan Band vision to UMass. He also created the symphony band and wind ensemble programs and brought contemporary band music to UMass students.

Jenkins, who was known by his band as "JJ" and "Dad," explained the musicality of marching bands, saying, "A marching band is a musical organization for its own sake. Its primary concern is sound—big, forceful and precise—never sacrificed to the routine of marching."

Jenkins, a former tank commander in the Army's Sixth Armored Cavalry, continued as the UMass Marching Band director until 1977, when he assumed administrative duties for the university.

John Jenkins brought the Michigan style to UMass.

University of Massachusetts. Revelli had influenced more band directors in the United States than any teacher before him, and he inspired his band members with "a combination of terror and musicianship." Lederle began to lay the foundation for rebuilding the Redmen Band in the Michigan Band mold. He wanted growth and quality, and "more than anything else I want the band to walk across the campus and have everyone be proud of them." He assigned William Venman, assistant to the provost and a former band director in Michigan, to oversee the transition and to secure a new director for the band program. Venman found John A. Jenkins. Jenkins had spent his college years in the Michigan Band, and he brought with him a wealth of knowledge and experience.

In the fall of 1963, Jenkins instituted a variety of changes as he set about re-creating the Michigan experience at the University of Massachusetts. His first mandate was to produce a marching band that reflected the quality of the university, and Lederle showed his support by sending a letter to all instrumental musicians encouraging them to join the marching band. "I earnestly agree that our marching band should and will become the best sounding and best marching band that devoted and enthusiastic leadership, vitally interested students, and the full support of the administration of the University can make possible." To Jenkins, it was clear that Lederle would supply anything he needed, but that it was critical to work within the established system.

Recruiting was a challenge, and although there were at least 150 incoming freshmen who played instruments, there were only fifty students in the marching band. At the time, the music department was also small with only five or six music majors, none of whom came out for the band. However, Jenkins found that various school personalities, such as the football coach, Vic Fusia, and the athletic director, Warren McGuirk, were interested in having the band take the next step forward. Fusia especially wanted the band to sit behind the team and play as often as possible during the game to support the team. In addition, the band received a generous amount of publicity, and it was apparent to Jenkins that the campus community was working together to create a different university marching band.

One of Jenkins' first priorities was to determine who was in charge of the band. The University Bands had a faculty adviser who also functioned as the director of bands, but the student band staff was in charge of making all of the group's decisions. Jenkins fired the entire band staff and, after sharing his vision of how the new band would be, invited them to reapply for their old positions if they were still interested. All of the students reapplied and were accepted.

Of all the changes that the band underwent, perhaps the most profound was the introduction of Band Camp. Band members returned to campus one week before fall classes began to learn music, drill, and the Michigan "high step" or "stop step" marching style. Band Camp also included playing and marching auditions, and typical drills consisted of students high stepping eight steps per five yards for one hundred yards, resting for thirty seconds, and then repeating to build up endurance.

One of Jenkins' main goals during Band Camp was to amaze everyone by turning out a group of freshmen who sounded so much better than anything before. To achieve this, he hired former Michigan bandmate Gerald

Student Band Staff

Students have always had a role in running the bands at the University of Massachusetts. When John Jenkins arrived at UMass in 1963, he remodeled the Massachusetts Band staff in the style of the Michigan Band's.

The student administrative staff offers band members the opportunity to gain practical experience dealing with the logistics of keeping a 320-member college band running. The "ad staff" includes the band manager and assistant managers, as well as managers and staff for the publicity, equipment, uniform, and library departments.

The field staff positions include drum majors, drill instructors, and rank leaders. These band members are responsible for the band's day-to-day operation on the rehearsal field, and they ensure that their fellow students are properly prepared and attired for game days.

John Jenkins teaches the Michigan high step at the first band camp.

Bilik, one of the foremost arrangers in the marching band world, to write arrangements for the band. Bilik's trademark style, which guaranteed the biggest musical impact, made the most of sound by pouring it onto a limited number of lines. He wrote the famous "Block M March" while he was still a sophomore at Michigan, which quickly became a best-selling piece, and he arranged a variety of music for the Michigan Band.

One of Bilik's first tasks for the band was to write new arrangements of "When Twilight Shadows Deepen" and "Fight Massachusetts," which made an enormous difference in how the band sounded. After the freshmen and band staff demonstrated the new arrangements and power sound concept during Band Camp, amazed upperclassmen could not believe how great such a small group could be. Jenkins recalled that when Bilik came out for a surprise visit during Band Camp, it was clear that the students had "bought into" the new style.

Metawampe continued as the school's mascot until 1972.

Although the band was undergoing fundamental changes, it had not lost its humor. Since all freshmen were required to wear beanies, drum major Bruce Cutter '66 gave one to freshman professor Jenkins to wear, which he accepted with a smile. Additional band innovations included expanding rehearsal time to eighty minutes a day. The new drum major uniform was modeled on the style of the Big Ten marching bands, and the Metawampe drum major was no more. However, a student dressed as the Native American chief still appeared at football games and served as the official UMass mascot.

After Band Camp, the renamed Massachusetts Band was ready for its first challenge. On September 28, 1963, in Harvard Stadium, the 110-member UMass Band and Precisionettes presented the "High Lights in Hi-Fi" halftime show for the football audience. Bilik arranged the music for the first show, which concluded with a portion of Bach's "Toccata and Fugue in D minor." Controversy occurred during the game when the band was prevented from using its own announcer for pregame, and only the Harvard announcer was allowed to speak. Jenkins came from the Big Ten background, where there was never a question of who was in charge during pregame—without question, it was the college marching band. The announcer told Jenkins that he could handle the timing of the band's pregame show, and Jenkins retorted that the announcer did not even know what timing was. When the slow-speaking announcer finally made it through "Ladies and Gentlemen, please welcome the University of Massachusetts Marching Band," the band was already halfway through pregame. Afterward, Harvard's president interceded and allowed a one-time exception for the band to use its own announcer during the halftime performance. The band members put on an enjoyable show to the delight of the UMass fans.

John Jenkins runs band rehearsal.

However, after the Harvard game, the Precisionettes were not satisfied with their part during halftime, and after an emotional meeting, decided to disband. As the question of where the Precisionettes belonged arose, the military department stepped in, agreed to sponsor the drill team, and absorbed it into the ROTC program. The Precisionettes soon marched at the head of the Homecoming Float Parade and were no longer part of the university's marching band. In the future, the drill team performed independently at the fall and spring military reviews, in parades, and at some football games. After the Precisionettes left the band program, Jenkins rewrote the marching band's drill for a block of fifty-five band members, and the band presented differently themed shows for each game.

The Massachusetts Band's first home show was a tremendous success. Soon, a contagious enthusiasm developed, and fans looked forward to the group's next football performance. Jenkins and Bilik wrote the halftime shows together, often on Bilik's sailboat, and their main concept revolved around creating subtle shows that would appeal to thoughtful and observant people. The *Massachusetts Collegian* noticed and commented on "the quality of the show and its intelligence," with high hopes that the trend would continue.

Homecoming Weekend 1963 was a memorable time, and the band played at the Campus Pond tailgate picnic while nearly 2,000 alumni basked in the sun. During the October 19 game, the band ushered in the Homecoming queen and her court during halftime with "The Land of the Arabian Nights." The UMass cheerleaders instituted a new policy for all home football games— they did pushups after every touchdown or field goal for every point that the UMass football team had on the scoreboard. Game casualties that Homecoming afternoon included the cheerleaders, whose arms were sore after UMass defeated Rhode Island 57–0.

The good relations between the band and football team continued to grow. For the November 9 game against American International College, the band honored coach Fusia by playing "Fight Massachusetts," spelling out "VIC" on the field, and performing "Mr. Touchdown, USA." Fusia acknowledged the compliments later by climbing up the band's rehearsal tower and presenting Jenkins with a football cap.

Additional fall highlights included the band's performances in the North Amherst and Pittsfield Halloween Parades. The cheerleaders and band had their end-of-season banquet together on November 17, 1963, and turned the Lord Jeffrey Inn into "John A. Jenkins Night," where Jenkins was honored with a plaque inscribed "Presented to John A. Jenkins, Best Marching Band Conductor in the East."

There were additional innovations in the winter, and in February 1964, Jenkins revitalized the UMass Pep Band. On May 17, the concert band performed at the dedication of the Frank L. Boyden Physical

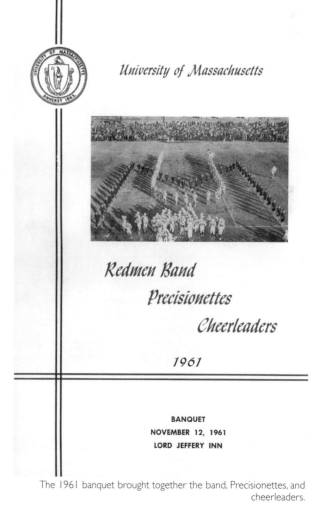

University of Massachusetts

Redmen Band
Precisionettes
Cheerleaders

1961

BANQUET
NOVEMBER 12, 1961
LORD JEFFERY INN

The 1961 banquet brought together the band, Precisionettes, and cheerleaders.

The concert band performs at the New York World's Fair.

Gov. Endicott Peabody and John Jenkins enjoy a football game.

Education Building and gave a concert for Gov. Endicott Peabody, President Lederle, and the assembled audience before the ceremonies began.

With the growth and success of the university's band program under Jenkins and based on the recommendation of Governor Peabody, the University Concert Band was selected to represent Massachusetts at the New York World's Fair. Thousands of visitors enjoyed the Massachusetts Day opening ceremony on June 27, where the concert band greeted listeners with "Fight Massachusetts." The band gave three additional concerts throughout the day at the crowded New England States Pavilion. After the successful performances at the World's Fair, Governor Peabody wrote Jenkins thanking him for the band's spectacular work.

Students soon began to be directly involved with band recruiting. Esther Eisenberg '65 approached Jenkins and told him, "If you hire me for the summer, I'll double the size of the band." Jenkins accepted and Eisenberg was hired for three hundred dollars as the band's first summer recruiter. The fall 1964 semester started with a five-day Band Camp, and for the first time, the Massachusetts Band grew to nearly one hundred students; Jenkins and Eisenberg had doubled the size of the band in less than a year. President Lederle continued his support, writing to Jenkins that the success of the UMass Band lay close to his heart.

Additional innovations occurred this fall when the Massachusetts Band received new uniforms, completing the group's recasting in the Michigan mold. The uniform consisted of a black tuxedo, a white overlay with a red "M" emblazoned on it, and red-and-white hats with red plumes. Mainly because of Bilik's arrangements, the band also sounded fuller and stronger than ever before. Bilik, a professor of music theory at the University of Michigan, was commissioned to write "Roll Down the Field," a new march for the band.

The Massachusetts Band soon added its own announcer. Since the band and chorale shared the auditorium in Old Chapel, the chorale's manager, Peter Ward, overheard the announcing auditions and was less than impressed. Eisenberg, the band's first female band manager, retorted, "If you're so darned good, come down here and announce!" One thing led to another, and Ward became the marching band's announcer. He and Jenkins wrote scripts for pregame and halftime shows for years to come.

Financial issues, which had plagued previous band directors, were temporarily resolved. Jenkins attributed part of the band's success to the fact that the Student Senate and administration were sharing financial responsibility for the group. In addition, student band leaders like Eisenberg facilitated friendly relations with the Student Senate by inviting senators to go along with the band during its tours.

The newly remodeled marching band captured the attention and imagination of the UMass community, and students were impressed by the group's sound and appearance. The band was considered "big-time" and looked "sharp" in its new uniforms, as members ran onto the field in high stepping fashion. At games, alumni were completely "bowled over" by the precision and quality of the band's presentations, and the Alumni Association's president commended Lederle for his direct role in bringing about the creation of the "incredible band." The combination of a strong football team and a great band created the image of a capable and solid university, and alumni were immensely proud.

Reflecting changing times in national politics, the band members were politically active. At the October 31 Vermont away game, the band received a standing ovation for its "Election" show. The show outlined the difficulties of voting and, according to audience response, the band marched and put an "X" on two large "ballots." To the strains of "Donkey Serenade" and "Baby Elephant Walk," fans decided whether to vote Democrat or Republican, and the highly popular halftime show ended with a presentation of Bilik's arrangement of "I Love Paris." "I Love Paris" soon became the unofficial theme song of the Massachusetts Band.

The band members enjoyed playing Bilik's musical arrangements and decided to honor him at the University of New Hampshire football game on November 14. For the halftime show, "A History of Hootenanny," the band danced to "Alexander's Ragtime Band" in a tribute to the early 1900s when ragtime was king. Additional music included "April Showers," "Oh Suzanna," "Red River Valley," and "Joshua Fit de Battle of Jericho." The group also cre-

The Massachusetts Band low brass section demonstrates the high step.

Massachusetts Band drum majors.

The tubas perform "Baby Elephant Walk."

ated a forty-five-yard-long banjo to hold a hoedown and ended the show with "Rhapsody in Blue." On Sunday night, Bilik was the guest of honor at the band and cheerleader banquet.

In December, the University of Massachusetts and its band reached a milestone when the 1964 Redmen football team was crowned Yankee Conference Champions. For the first time in history, the team was invited to a postseason bowl game and was scheduled to appear in Orlando, Florida, at the Tangerine Bowl, later known as the Florida Citrus Bowl.

The entire UMass campus went "Tangerine Wild," and the *Massachusetts Collegian* printed a complete issue in orange. Tangerine became the most popular color at UMass, and tangerine trees were sold for one dollar to benefit the band. The Student Senate led the fundraising drive to send the band and cheerleaders to the bowl game and swamped the campus with tangerine pins that sold for twenty-five cents each. A football "Highlights Night" was also organized to raise the $12,000 needed for the trip. The fundraising was successful, and on December 8, the band and cheerleaders sent off the football team for the game. Several hundred UMass alumni and fans followed the Redmen on charter flights, and for the first time, the Massachusetts Band flew in an airplane. During an unscheduled stop, Jenkins rehearsed the band on the airport runway, before the group arrived in Florida and stayed in the Angebilt Hotel.

At the December 12 Tangerine Bowl, the first half ended with the Redmen leading the Pirates of East Carolina College 7–0. After the halftime show, Angebilt Hotel manager Louie Mueller announced that, having seen all nineteen Tangerine Bowl games, he could say the University of Massachusetts Marching Band was the finest band ever to appear in the bowl. The band received well-deserved standing ovations, and it generated a spirit that was a credit to the university. After halftime, the Pirates won 14–13 on a two-point conversion that the Redmen could not overturn in the last few minutes. Although Massachusetts lost the game, it was an exciting time for the campus community.

During the winter, Jenkins created a new music department ensemble, the University Symphony Band. Band members continued playing in both the marching band and the symphony band, and beginning in January 1965, the symphony band undertook the annual spring tour through Massachusetts. The concert band was temporarily disbanded.

By the spring of 1965, a major change was in place regarding how the band program's finances were handled. The chair of the music department, Philip Bezanson, felt it was inappropriate to have his faculty members go before the Student Senate to ask for funding. At his request, the Senate was removed from the financial equation, and President Lederle reorganized the Fine Arts Council to take over distributing funds for the band. However, although the council was reorganized specifically to fund the band program, council members voted at their first meeting that the band was not part of their campus arts vision and took steps to remove the group's funding. The financial struggle continued.

Marching band membership continued to grow rapidly and, during Band Camp 1965, reached 140. Just two years earlier, the band had numbered fifty-five. In addition, under the course catalog listing "Applied Music—Band," students received one credit for two semesters' participation in the band. The music department also underwent rapid growth as Bezanson brought in a number of new faculty members, and musical ensembles, once considered extracurricular activities, were now official music department courses.

After two busy years, the marching band had a light schedule. The previous season's travel itinerary had been demanding on the members' studies, and Jenkins felt a less strenuous season would help students with their academics. In addition, the physical exertion of the Michigan step sometimes resulted in band "casualties," and Jenkins explained that pulled tendons and strained legs had been an issue that year. However, these injuries allowed the band's alternates, who practiced alongside the regular band members at rehearsals, a greater chance of performing at games.

The new Alumni Football Stadium was dedicated during Homecoming Weekend on October 16, 1965. The band led an antique-car parade for pregame, and during halftime, a crowd of 20,000 watched it perform "I Love Paris." The rest of the band's halftime show recounted the history of stadiums from the time of the Roman Colosseum to the present. President Lederle and Gov. John Volpe dedicated the new $1.4 million football arena, and the band sealed the ceremony by playing the alma mater. The Redmen football team beat the University of Rhode Island 30–0, rounding out the day's successes.

In the fall of 1966, incoming freshmen brought the band's membership to 150, the largest ever at the school. Jenkins was credited with the rare ability to inspire others, which allowed him to produce a "fine band." "With his own determination and spirit, he instilled the band members with the desire to be the

Closeup of a Massachusetts Band trombonist.

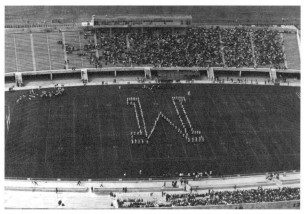

The Massachusetts Band forms an M in the new Alumni Football Stadium.

John Jenkins oversees the Massachusetts Band before pregame.

The Massachusetts Band tuba section is known for its spirited performances.

best." He could have taken the band anywhere, and the dedicated students would have followed with enthusiasm.

Joining the group that fall was the new assistant conductor of the band program, Larry Weed. Weed had a bachelor's of music from Oklahoma City University and a master's of music from the Eastman School of Music. He had been director of bands at Temple University and music department chair of the North Syracuse Central School System in New York. With the Massachusetts Band, Weed handled the group's logistics and wrote some of the halftime shows.

The marching season focused on new music and a spirited, disciplined band. The group began using more staff-written musical arrangements and drills, and the shows grew in complexity. Jenkins also added a student props crew, which rehearsed with the band on the field and created everything from propellers to signs to forty-foot-long strands of balloons. Crew members dressed in band uniforms for the performances and marched along with regular band members.

That fall, the Massachusetts Band came closest to mastering the difficult Michigan marching style. Students were trained to march with precision and, when they pointed their toes and slammed their feet into the ground, their

Francis Kennedy, the center trombonist, created the first Homecoming Alumni Band in 1966.

heads stayed level. The band's spirit and determination increased with the difficulty of the marching style, and the accomplishment fostered high morale and esprit de corps. Jenkins recalled that band members were so dedicated and determined that they once accidentally, without blinking, marched through the entire football team.

After demonstrating the demanding Michigan high step, Jenkins convinced officials that marching in the band counted as a physical activity, although the head of the physical education department did not agree. Awarding academic credit was necessary for recruiting and retaining students for the band, so freshmen and sophomore band members were excused from required physical education classes during football season. In a major innovation, music majors, for the first time, were required to be in the marching band. The renamed music department course, Marching Band 181, offered one credit for two semesters' participation, with a maximum of four credits allowed for nonmusic majors.

One of the Massachusetts Band's favorite traditions began that fall, when Francis (Ducky) Kennedy '24 created the University of Massachusetts Alumni

Alumni Band

Band Alumni return to celebrate George Parks' 20th year as band director in 1997.

The Alumni Band made its first appearance when alumni and regular band members gave a joint concert in June 1939. The combined band also played in the Commencement Parade.

A later incarnation of the Alumni Band occurred for Homecoming 1966, when Francis "Ducky" Kennedy '24 organized the first alumni marching band, which performed pregame with the Massachusetts Band. Each year since then, the Alumni Band gathers for Homecoming festivities. In 2002, over 250 alumni returned to march during Homecoming, honoring George N. Parks' twenty-fifth year as director of the Minuteman Marching Band.

Band. At the October 22 Homecoming game against Boston University, the Alumni Band took the field with the UMass Marching Band, and together the two groups performed the pregame show. The event was considered a great success. That fall also saw the founding of the University of Massachusetts Band Alumni Association.

The band's reputation was growing, and on Sunday, October 30, it performed at its first professional football game. The group was invited by the Boston Patriots to perform during halftime of the Oakland Raiders game. Radio listeners from coast to coast were impressed, and Massachusetts residents proudly stated, "This is our band." The band also gave a short concert outside Fenway Park and played "Rhapsody in Blue." It was a truly memorable event, and one fan wrote that the band played the piece like Gershwin himself would have wanted it played. After the game, various Patriots fans wrote university officials praising the band's performance, saying how refreshing it was to have such a high caliber organization on the East Coast instead of having to look to other parts of the country.

Later in the season, the University Concert Band, dormant since the formation of the symphony band, was reactivated under the direction of Weed. All marching band members were accepted without needing to audition, and membership among the marching, concert, and symphony bands overlapped. In addition, that year the symphony band began rehearsing during the fall semester.

In the fall of 1967, the marching band continued to gather accolades for its performances and made its debut on ABC. The televised halftime show for the September 30 UMass-Dartmouth game included "Ach Du Lieber Augustine," after which the band formed a hand-carved German cuckoo clock complete with a cuckoo bird, moving hands, and a swinging pendulum. The finale included pieces from *The Sound of Music*.

Nancy Deneault May '71 recalled the props crew worked many hours to create the eight-foot-tall, yellow, papier-mâche cuckoo for the halftime show. The well-constructed cuckoo, who lived in Old Chapel, became the band's mascot for a number of years. Occasionally, the cuckoo appeared on the porches and roofs of the houses of newly appointed professors and made additional guest appearances throughout its life. Eventually, the beloved prop disintegrated and was retired.

The second annual Alumni Band convened for the October 21 Homecoming game against Rhode Island. Alumni had a rehearsal on Friday, marched in the

The 1966 Massachusetts Band forms the Block M.

The band marches into Holy Cross Stadium.

John Jenkins and assistant director Larry Weed.

The Massachusetts Band often presented politically-themed halftime shows.

Homecoming Parade that evening, and then met for cocktails afterward. On Saturday, the Alumni Band performed in the pregame show with the Massachusetts Band. For halftime, the Massachusetts Band played music from *Cabaret*, and the Precisionettes made a special guest appearance and once again performed with the band. Fans enjoyed seeing band members dance on the field for the first time, while the Precisionettes marched drill formations during the percussion feature.

For the November 11 Rutgers game, the band presented its "South of the Border" show, which included "Toreador" and "La Virgen de la Macarena," and featured the newly appointed trumpet professor, Walter Chesnut. Chesnut, another Michigan Band alumnus, was a strong friend of the Massachusetts Band program.

By 1968, the band was swept up in the political changes overtaking the country, and during the Vietnam era, there was clear student interest in everything political. One fall, the band went to the away game at Harvard Stadium. In an interesting turn of events, due to drum major error, the band ended up playing its politically-themed show, "Happy Days Are Here Again," in front of the Harvard students who were sitting on the thirty-five-yard line. The students went wild for the Massachusetts Band, since the group had apparently snubbed the wealthy donors who sat on the fifty-yard line. The band received a number of commendations for playing to the students and for making highly political statements with its show.

That fall, the band was planning to perform a political show at an upcoming home game, when Air Force General Curtis LeMay, an advocate of strategic nuclear warfare, entered the political scene as presidential candidate George Wallace's running mate. In addition, at the Chicago Democratic Convention, police had beaten up protesters at Mayor Richard Daley's request. With the national political turmoil, Bilik called Jenkins and said that the band had to rewrite its show in order to make a statement. Bilik asked him, "How much of a risk do you want to take?" The band's lighthearted approach to politics was no longer appropriate. The Vietnam War was overshadowing daily life, and students were asking hard questions about their nation's involvement in Southeast Asia.

Bilik and Jenkins rewrote the band show and premiered "A New Look at Politics" for halftime at the October 26 Homecoming game against UConn. Pregame opened with Harry Ellis Dickson, assistant conductor for the Boston Pops, directing "The Star-Spangled Banner." Then Francis Kennedy conducted his "Band Alumni March," and former Redmen Band director Joseph Contino led "When Twilight Shadows Deepen." For halftime, the revamped show opened as the band played two versions of "America." One version was played by a five-member brass band in the center of the field, symbolic of the more traditional era of American politics. Then the rest of the band, playing "America" from *West Side Story*, marched through the brass band and obliterated it. After a "B-25 bomber" drill formation flew through the band and crashed into the sideline, students, dressed up as Keystone Kops, ran down from the football stands, representing Mayor Daley's Chicago police officers. In the midst of the musical confusion, the show ended with "The Battle Hymn of the Republic," as the band formed the well-known "Peace" symbol on the field. Since university policy forbade anyone to use the peace symbol officially, the band's controversial show was the perfect place to make a political statement. The band overwhelmed the audience with its immensely successful halftime show.

After a strong fall season, the Massachusetts Band's funding became critically unstable in the spring of 1969. Part of the financial problem was that the band had multiple identities on campus, and no one was sure who had financial responsibility for the band program. The band was a registered student organization and therefore received university funding. However, students who participated in band also received one academic credit from the music department, and all music majors were required to be in the marching band for three years. The question lingered—was the band a music department ensemble, a registered student organization, an athletic pro-

The Massachusetts Band forms the controversial peace symbol.

gram, or something else? Before 1969, Jenkins had been successful in convincing the Student Senate to continue funding the band program voluntarily. In addition, he had convinced the athletic and music departments to increase their financial support. However, the joint funding was an unusual and inherently unstable arrangement. The organizations felt that they were paying too much to support the band, and the coalition collapsed.

Kappa Kappa Psi and Tau Beta Sigma

On May 16, 1969, John Jenkins sponsored the formation of the Epsilon Nu chapter of Kappa Kappa Psi and the Delta Delta chapter of Tau Beta Sigma. The Sisters of TBS and the Brothers of KKΨ each strive to promote the university band program through fundraising, membership, and service. These national honorary band fraternity and sorority organizations hold a variety of activities including social functions, concert receptions, Saturday morning wake-up calls for band members, the end-of-year band banquets, and Old Chapel and Fine Arts Center clean-ups. The organizations also helped produce CDs of UMass ensembles such as the University Jazz Ensemble, the Wind Ensemble, the Minuteman Marching Band, and the Hoop Band.

By April 1969, the Senate was resistant to the idea of funding the band because it was not an extracurricular student organization and removed the group's registered student organization status. Finding that the band's budget had vanished, Jenkins played a dangerous game and told the campus community that there would not be a marching band if there was no funding. Stanley Rosenberg '77 and the band staff circulated a petition requesting that the Arts Council continue funding the band program. Although the petition garnered wide student support, the council refused to reinstate the band's funds. At the last minute, President Lederle stepped in and temporarily solved the financial crisis. Although Jenkins was told to recruit for the fall 1969 season, there was still no permanent solution.

Throughout this financial turmoil, the Massachusetts Band continued to perform with enthusiasm, dedication, and determination. UMass was said to have "The Best Band in the East," and the group became known for its trademark display of showmanship and musicianship. In the fall of 1969, the marching band had its finest season under Jenkins. The Michigan marching style was crisp and sharp, and the group had a strong and powerful sound.

Homecoming was one of the season's highlights. The combined Massachusetts and Alumni Bands played "The Intervention March," first performed on campus in 1921, which was composed and conducted by former Massachusetts State College Band leader Ray Swift. The halftime show consisted of music from *Hair* and ended with "The Age of Aquarius." In addition, the tuba section performed a special dance that was choreographed by assistant director Weed.

The band also played host to the Delaware Band when it came up for the October 4 game. Afterward, the Delaware Band sent a letter to its hosts, signed by all band members, thanking the Massachusetts Band for its hospitality. It was the beginning of a long and warm friendship between the two college bands.

The previous fall's "Simon and Garfunkel Show," which included "The Sounds of Silence," "Mrs. Robinson," and "Scarborough Fair," received such an overwhelming response that the band decided to repeat it for the 1969 season. The band also honored the one hundredth anniversary of college football by performing the "Space Show." Created by Weed, with musical arrangements by John Anderson, the show included "Also Sprach Zarathustra," "Up, Up, and Away," and "Fly Me to the Moon."

"Noah's Ark" formation during halftime.

Although the band had a successful fall season, financial difficulties continued to plague it in the spring. In February 1970, the assistant dean of administration, William Venman, wrote to Chancellor Oswald Tippo and President Lederle saying that although no one felt strongly about having a marching band, no one wanted to dissolve the program, either. Venman argued that the university's reputation would decline if it disbanded the group, and that it was time to stabilize the band's budget. He felt the University of Massachusetts was beyond fielding a fun-and-games band that rehearsed once or twice before each show. In spite of Venman's support, in May, the marching band was nearly dissolved due to lack of funding. However, Lederle again resolved the impasse, and the band was fielded for the fall semester.

In the fall of 1970, after bringing the University of Massachusetts to new heights, President Lederle resigned. During his years at the school, student enrollment tripled, faculty numbers grew from 400 to 1,100, and more than forty new buildings were added to the campus. Thanks to his efforts, the Commonwealth of Massachusetts now had a fine state university.

The band program also underwent a leadership change, when Jenkins took a sabbatical to work on

"Octubafest" was a popular musical event at the university in the late 1970s.

his doctorate at the University of Michigan. Larry Weed became the director of bands and during his tenure, a number of changes took place. After Vietnam, students no longer wanted to be regimented, and the marching band became a more laid back organization. The group also developed a new musical style and used a faster marching technique.

Homecoming festivities for the October 24, 1970, weekend included the traditional float and pep rally, and the UMass Band's halftime presentation was the lighthearted "Clown Show." The band's mascot, "Cuckoo," laid eggs that were presented to Connecticut during the football game.

In March 1971, the University Pep Band held a rally for the underdog UMass basketball team before its March 20 game against the twelfth-ranked North Carolina Tarheels. Although UMass lost to North Carolina, its high scorer was "Dr J"— Julius Erving. The next few years of UMass basketball were exciting ones for the campus and pep band members.

In the fall of 1971, the marching band began to move away from its traditional political shows and toward more Broadway-style entertainment. For pregame that fall, Weed also introduced an inverted block M that reversed itself during the show. The UMass Band began to use more humor during performances; for one football show, the group lined up in the north end zone and marched onto the field spelling out "HELLO." However, the letters were mixed up, and the formation ended up reading "O HELL." The band announcer informed the band members of the "error," and the "O" ran through the rest of the group and reformed on the other side, amidst appreciative cheers from the audience.

On August 19, 1972, the UMass Band played host to "The Super Music Bowl," a drum and bugle corps competition benefit to aid the mentally handicapped children at the Belchertown State School. The band hosted four consecutive Super Music Bowls until August 23, 1975.

The band forms UMASS for pregame.

During Jenkins' sabbatical, a number of academic policies regarding the marching band were changed. For one, the music department revoked the requirement that all music majors be in the marching band. In addition, the physical education department decided that participation in marching band was no longer a valid exemption from the one-year physical education requirement, and band members again needed to take gym classes. The group's financial situation took a turn for the worse as well, and for the 1972–73 season, academic funds to support the program were no longer available.

Jenkins returned to the University of Massachusetts in the fall of 1972, and coming back after two years let him see the band in two separate eras. The 1960s band had fewer music majors, but students were willing to commit to the program. After Vietnam, although there were more music majors in the band, it was more difficult to get the total commitment of students. In addition, the student staff was again in control of the band, and the group had little student support in the stands or in the Senate. Jenkins succeeded in reinstating the physical education credit for marching band but was unable to re-establish the music major requirement.

Joseph Duchi, fresh out of college, became the new assistant director of bands and marching band director. Duchi, whose "Robert Redford goodlooks" were appreciated by female band members, brought new ideas in show

Block M Formations

The Redmen Band and Precisionettes form M for Massachusetts.

During pregame, the Minuteman Band marches onto the field in a block formation and forms the traditional M for Massachusetts. Over the years, the M formation used for football games has undergone various changes. The first picture of the band in an M formation dates back to 1927, when the group formed on the parade ground by Old Chapel to pose for a photograph. In the 1930s, the Mass State College Band often spelled out MSC on the field.

During the 1950s and 1960s, the Redmen Band often formed a UM on the field with the Precisionettes. In 1963, when Jenkins brought the Michigan Band concept to UMass, the Massachusetts Band began to form larger Ms. These were modified throughout the years to accommodate the growing size of the band, but the block M formation remains one of the most visible and solid traditions of the Minuteman Band.

design to the Massachusetts Band program. He created such classics as the "Cartoon Show," which was based on popular Saturday morning cartoons.

At this time, Native Americans were requesting equal treatment from the federal government. They asked University of Massachusetts officials to change the school's mascot from Redmen to a name that did not reflect Native roots, and the Minuteman, who was considered more appropriate and historically accurate, became the school's new mascot. The Acton Minutemen, a historical re-enactment group, were selected to appear at the October 14 UMass-Boston University football game, where the official name-changing ceremony took place at halftime. After school officials spoke, the fans gave a loud ovation, and the University of Massachusetts Minuteman Marching Band sealed the ceremony by playing "Variations on a Patriotic Theme" and other spirited songs. The day ended on a high note for the Minutemen football team as well, as it dominated the game and defeated Boston University 44–14.

Fans from opposing teams were sometimes less than courteous when the marching band traveled to away games. Assistant drum major Bob Lloyd '77 recalled impolite treatment after the Holy Cross game on November 9, when the Holy Cross fans blocked the band and refused to let it leave the stadium safely. To remedy the situation, Duchi moved the tubas to the front of the band and had them swing their bells forward, allowing the group to march through the hostile crowd with the tubas plowing the way. Although sometimes faced with discourteous treatment, band members typically responded with humor, and students later created a brochure on how to use musical instruments as defensive weapons.

After being crowned Atlantic-10 Conference Champions, the football team was invited to participate in the December 9, 1972, Boardwalk Bowl in the Atlantic City Convention Hall. At first, UMass was scheduled to play against Delaware, but the Blue Hens refused because Massachusetts was not "commensurate with [their] national ranking." Ironically, marching in the University of Delaware Band that fall was a sophomore, George Parks, who was to become the University of Massachusetts' next band director. After Delaware bowed out, the new opponent for UMass was the University of California at Davis.

Jim Kierstead '92 recalled that, after rehearsing in the aftermath of an Amherst ice storm and carving yard lines into the ice, the band took a six-hour bus ride to New Jersey; band members arrived in the afternoon, had two hours of drill rehearsal, and stayed overnight in a Holiday Inn. At the game, the group played songs such as "Conquistador," "Song Sung Blue," "The Beat Goes On," and "Bridge over Troubled Water," forming the Golden Gate Bridge. In addition, twenty non-marching band members held up flags of different countries, symbolically re-creating the United Nations. After a successful halftime show, the UMass football team emerged victorious, 35–14, in its first postseason win. It was first-rate national exposure, and the Massachusetts Band's fine performance saved it in an upcoming financial crisis.

A Massachusetts Band informational brochure.

The marching band financial controversy came to a head during the winter. No academic funds were available to support the marching band for the 1973–74 season, and the Athletic Council also withdrew its support. However, Jenkins was optimistic and felt that both the Student Senate and Alumni Association were valid places to seek the needed funds.

In the spring of 1973, Jenkins and the music department created a noncompetitive musical contest where school bands received constructive feedback from guest artists. Out of this university conference, the Massachusetts Instrumental Conductors Association (MICA) came into existence. In later years, the conference became known as MICCA, the Massachusetts Instrumental and Choral Conductors Association.

The 1976 Massachusetts Band passes through the Southwest Residential area.

In the fall of 1973, after many years of financial problems, the marching band found itself on stronger financial footing than ever before. The September 8 *Springfield Union News* reported that, due to a coalition of the athletic department, alumni, and a band-generated student petition, the band's budget was increased by 50 percent over the previous year. Jenkins attributed the new support to the band's appearance at the Boardwalk Bowl the previous December, where regional TV showed the pregame and halftime shows. He said, "We went to the Bowl with a lot of dedication and got the needed exposure for the UMass administration to fund this marvelous, dedicated group of young people." Jenkins added that although it had looked as if financial problems would mark the end of the UMass Marching Band, the issues had been resolved.

The band added additional innovations as it continued to move away from the traditional Big Ten marching band style and toward a more entertainment-oriented style. Three things that made the UMass Band "fabulous" that fall were former world baton twirling champion Diane Luciani, the percussive cowbell beat, and good-looking marching band director Duchi.

During the Vermont game on November 3, the university held a "Salute to Yogi Berra Day" to honor Berra, a loyal UMass fan and the manager of the

New York Mets, whose son was on the UMass football team. Unbeknownst to Jenkins, the band members planned and rehearsed a Halloween-themed "Monster Show," with music from "The Addams Family" and "The Munsters."

Spirit Squad members Joann Zouranjian '78, Judy McGuire '80, and Sandy Doo '80.

Diane Luciani thrilled audiences with her baton twirling skills.

In addition to forming a haunted house and the Empire State Building, the band played "Night on Bald Mountain," "Purple People Eater," and "Monster Mash." Yogi Berra Day was a great success.

In the fall of 1974, the marching band added its first colorguard rank in the form of an eight-woman swing flag corps. During halftime, the flag routine was coordinated with portions of the show to add to the music, and during pregame, part of the corps presented the colors. In addition, a favorite Minuteman Band show, "Tommy," made its first halftime appearance this fall.

A highlight of the season was the UMass Band's victory over the Boston College football team. The Minutemen faced the BC Eagles on November 23. Throughout the fall, the band's pregame show started with the band members lining up on the visitors' sideline. That day, the BC football team continued practicing and would not leave the field, preventing the band from starting pregame. Jenkins and Duchi went to the referees and asked for the field to be cleared, but the referees took no action, and the football players continued scrimmaging. Taking matters into his own hands, Duchi spoke directly to the BC head coach and received a colorful response. Incensed, Duchi defiantly ordered the drumline to start pregame. The drummers marched onto the field, which was still occupied by the BC team, until the calmer Jenkins ordered them to stop and return to the sideline. They all returned except for Louie Lipomi '78, who was first in line and did not hear the command. He continued to march onto the field and ended up in the middle of the BC football team's offensive and defensive lines, where he was caught in the collision of players. Enraged by the treatment of their comrade, the entire UMass drumline charged to his rescue. Seeing the drumline run onto the field, the remaining BC football players ran out as well and blocked the rest of the band. As the UMass drummers and BC players confronted each other, coaches and managers entered the fray to calm the volatile situation. After everyone calmed down and Lipomi was discovered to be uninjured, officials told the BC football team to "Get the hell off of the field, NOW," and the Massachusetts Band finally performed its pregame show. Although the UMass football team lost to BC 70–8, the *Massachusetts Daily Collegian* reported that at least the UMass Band had won its battle against the BC football team.

In the fall of 1975, after Duchi resigned and became an instructor of trom-

The 1976 Massachusetts Band forms MASS for pregame.

bone at Ohio State University, Wayne Blackwell from the University of Alabama became the new assistant director of bands. In addition, the new Fine Arts Center became operational, and the music department moved into its new quarters; the marching band, however, remained in Old Chapel. Music for the fall included the "Tommy" show, which was performed for the second year in a row, as well as music from the rock group "Chicago."

One of the major innovations this fall was the creation of the highly popular Multibands Concert. After Vietnam, student support for the band program had eroded, and Jenkins, Blackwell, and the band staff felt such a concert would reinvigorate the students. Multibands was modeled on the old-time band concerts, which featured shorter music and a rapid succession of ensembles with little to no time between groups. Jenkins and Blackwell created the musical program, and Rosenberg was charged with filling the Fine Arts Center concert hall for the October 24 show. The night of the performance, the two ushers assigned to the concert hall were met with thousands of audience members. Rosenberg had filled the house. For the concert, Jenkins had been told that he would not be able to march the band onto the concert stage due to lack of space. Undeterred, flanked by red stage lights, the band did its Michigan fast march pregame entrance onto the stage. When the audience recovered from that, the band played the fanfare and "blew them out of the hall."

Band members sometimes played harmless pranks during rehearsals. One such incident occurred during rehearsal of the Dixie Half Time Show, which featured a race between two steamboats, the *Robert E. Lee* and the *Natchez*. Although the *Robert E. Lee* won the historical race, the drill instructors

Band Members show their enthusiasm at a football game.

arranged for the *Natchez* to win that day. Instead of standing in place and marking time, the band members who formed the *Natchez* marched forward, and soundly beat the *Robert E. Lee*. An alarmed Blackwell stood at the race's finish line, which was formed by the colorguard, and shouted "No! No! Stop! Go Back! You're Rewriting History!"

In the fall of 1976, the UMass Marching Band grew to 190 members. Max Culpepper joined as the new assistant director of bands and helped Jenkins with show preparation and instruction of the percussion, flag, and twirler sections.

Strong student leadership has always been a main strength of the University of Massachusetts' band program. Jenkins recalled that the band staffs were phenomenal for many years, and that from 1973 until 1976, strong student leaders emerged, among them a number of women. He said, "It is impossible to conceive of this band running without the student leadership." In a *Massachusetts Daily Collegian* interview, the band's manager, Joanne Brown said, "The whole band gets psyched for the away games. It's a chance to be rowdy with your friends and still put on a good show." Students reported that being a band member required having four essential characteristics: coordination, discipline, determination, and enthusiasm. It also helped to enjoy push-ups, muddy fields, fifteen-minute lunches, and "wet socks squishing in wet shoes." Head football coach Dick MacPherson added, "If the band plays better, we play better and it helps to win, but when we go to the away games without the band, we really miss them."

Another memorable Harvard game took place on September 25. ABC carried the halftime show live from Harvard Stadium and, keeping the rivalry alive, Harvard's band led the crowd in chanting "boring, boring" while the Massachusetts Band opened its halftime show. However, by the end of the show, the capacity crowd stood and gave the band and feature twirler Diane Luciani a one-minute standing ovation. It was rare for any ensemble to receive a standing ovation at Harvard Stadium. Daniel Melley, director of UMass Public Affairs, commended the marching band for its excellent performance and told Jenkins, "The battle of the bands was no contest, you won hands down."

The band also received a standing ovation at the November 6 Holy Cross game after the halftime show of "Get up and Boogie," Elton John's "Island Girl," and the movie theme from *2001*. In a reversal of earlier years, the Holy Cross fans "treated the UMass Band like royalty," and the appreciative crowd did not want the band to leave the field. The band received a thunderous standing ovation and, like the Harvard crowd, the Holy Cross fans wanted to hear the show again. Another halftime show that fall was "The End of an Era," which saluted America's two hundredth birthday. The band took a nostalgic look back with Gerald Bilik's arrangements of "Give My Regards to Broadway," "You're a Grand Old Flag," and "I'm a Yankee Doodle Dandy."

After a number of years of successful growth under Jenkins, the University of Massachusetts Marching Band was ready to take its next step forward.

George N. Parks

George N. Parks was born on May 23, 1953, and grew up in Delaware. Both of his parents were drum majors, and Parks decided to be a band director when he was in the ninth grade. He was drum major of the Christiana High School Viking Band and credited his band director, L. Jerome Rehberg, with having a strong influence on his life.

After marching in the University of Delaware Fightin' Blue Hen Band, Parks transferred to West Chester University, where he became drum major of the three-hundred-member Incomparable Golden Rams Marching Band. James R. Wells, director of the West Chester Band, said he admired Parks because "on the field, he is a real ham, a showman with a definite ego—but off the field, he is one of the most unassuming people you could ever meet." He added, "George Parks is simply the best drum major I've ever seen."

In 1977, Parks was appointed as director of the Minuteman Marching Band at the University of Massachusetts. His enthusiastic and entertaining approach to the marching band resulted in instant success with football fans throughout the Northeast. For over twenty-five years, Parks' boundless energy helped create "The Power and Class of New England."

George Parks became band director in 1977.

Each summer, over 3,000 students from almost every state in the nation attend his Drum Major Academies. Parks is a recipient of the Massachusetts Conductor of the Year Award, the University of Massachusetts Distinguished Teaching Award, and the Chancellor's Medal for Distinguished Service. In September 1993, Parks was inducted into the World Drum Corps Hall of Fame for his work as drum major of the Reading Buccaneers.

THE POWER AND CLASS OF NEW ENGLAND
1977–2003

chapter twelve

n 1977, John Jenkins was appointed associate director of the Fine Arts Center, and it was time to hire a new marching band director. Twenty-four-year-old George N. Parks, fresh out of Northwestern University with a master's degree in tuba performance, interviewed for the position. With videotapes showing him conducting the West Chester State College Band and the Reading Buccaneers Drum and Bugle Corps, Parks convinced the interview committee that he would create a superb marching band. The impressed committee, which included former Massachusetts Band director Doric Alviani, hired Parks that same day. Parks brought with him ideas from the drum corps world that included marching, conducting, and drill-writing styles that differed from those of the traditional, Big Ten-style marching bands. Jenkins continued to supervise the band and gave invaluable advice to its new director.

At Band Camp, Parks taught the band its new marching style, the glide step, which kept the feet rolling smoothly across the field. The step made it easier for students to maintain a good sound without a great deal of physical exertion. It took the band awhile to get used to the change, but a core group

The Minuteman Band's 1977 "Rocky" show.

of students was intrigued by the new style and was willing to give it a try. Parks also introduced drum major Rich Neely to the mace, which was heavier and longer than the smaller majorette twirling batons of earlier years.

Halftime shows that fall included music from *Rocky*, *Star Wars*, the Beatles, Barry Manilow, and *A Chorus Line*. Parks wanted to create musical shows that told a story, and during the "Star Wars" show, the band formed the Death Star on the field, which was "blown up" as students marched out of it in a circle burst.

The question remained as to whether the home audience would adapt to the Minuteman Band's new style. All doubts were put aside after the first home game on September 17, as the group's music and energy captured the audience's attention. Although Parks had been concerned that the show would not pull together, the band gave an outstanding performance. The football fans enjoyed the band's show, giving it an enthusiastic reception, and the campus community also appreciated the remodeled marching band. Parks recalled that one day he received a call from the football staff, asking if the band would perform for the team during the week, since the football players never had the chance to see the group in action. Parks said, "No one ever did that before, and it blew my mind."

The band also made an impression during away games and traveled to Harvard University on September 24 for the annual UMass-Harvard game. With typically malicious humor, Harvard band members scattered birdseed on

By 1988, the Minuteman Band grew to over 300 members. Shown here is the 1981 band.

the UMass Band's practice field, which caused seagulls to swoop down on students while they rehearsed. During the football game, the Harvard Band led cheers of "boring, boring," and "not impressed" when the Minuteman Band performed. Undeterred, the band members gave a solid performance. The group also traveled to the October 22 University of Connecticut game, and although outnumbered and outplayed by the UConn Band, the Connecticut fans noticed the UMass Band and gave it a generous standing ovation.

The "Cold Duck" tradition, originally based on a football cheer, started near the end of the 1977 marching season. Begun as a protest against Parks and the innovations he brought to the university band program, several graduating seniors brought bottles of champagne onto the football field at the end of the final home game. However, what began as a protest eventually evolved into one of the longest-running traditions of the Minuteman Band, and the champagne toast became a way for senior band members to wish a fond farewell to fellow students and directors. Every year since then, seniors receive a bottle of Cold Duck at the final home game and celebrate their graduation from the band.

For Band Camp 1978, ninety freshmen joined the Minuteman Band and brought the group to 168. In addition, during the first week of school, the band set

The Cold Duck tradition.

up a musical "Festival of Sight and Sounds" in front of Old Chapel to recruit additional students. Funding questions, which had hampered the band in previous years, became less of an issue. Alumni donations, through the Alumni Association Trust Fund, made up the bulk of the band's budget and allowed the group to focus on creating memorable shows.

The Reading Buccaneers

First formed in 1957, the Reading Buccaneers rose to prominence as one of the nation's finest senior drum and bugle corps. Minuteman Band director George Parks made his first appearance on the national scene as the Buccaneers' drum major and, with assistant drum major Darrell Weyman, helped lead the corps to two Drum Corps Associates World Championships. Parks received numerous individual honors, including eight DCA Championship Drum Major Awards.

Learning from such professionals as Ralph Pace, Tony Yaklich, and Reds Windsor, Parks brought the drum corps innovations to the University of Massachusetts Minuteman Band. The Minuteman Band soon delighted audiences with its greater emphasis on showmanship. In addition, the band's drum majors were allowed more freedom to be performers and enhanced the halftime shows by throwing maces. Today, the Reading Buccaneer influence is still a part of the Minuteman Band, as the band is known for its exciting performance presence.

George Parks and the Buccaneers present an energetic show.

Music for the 1978 season included pieces chosen to entertain the audience and to display the band's performance style. The first show opened with "Meadowlands," a song imported from the Reading Buccaneers Drum and Bugle Corps, and additional music included selections from Tchaikovsky's "Fourth Symphony."

The fall marked the Minuteman Band's first performances of "Malaguena" and "My Way," two audience favorites. It was also the first time the group performed in Boston at Faneuil Hall and at the Massachusetts Instrumental Conductors Association Marching Band Festival. At the MICA Festival, the band performed in exhibition for the state's finest high school marching bands. When the band opened with "Festive Overture," Parks recalled that the music "seemed to echo for days," and the audience went wild. The group set a milestone that evening, and the MICA exhibition became one of many recruiting tools that were used to draw students to the University of Massachusetts and the Minuteman Band.

During the fall, a mural appeared in the men's bathroom in Old Chapel, depicting a mouse with one paw raised in an obscene gesture at the eagle that was swooping down on it. The mouse, wearing part of the UMass Band uniform, represented the band, and the eagle, with bright red hair, was the band director, Parks. The caption under the painting read, "The last appropriate gesture in defiance of hopelessness." Although some band members did not accept the direction the band was heading in, enough students were onboard to drive the program forward. In later years, Parks preserved the mural by covering it with plexiglass, and to this day, the eagle and mouse remain in Old Chapel.

When the Morgan State Band came to Amherst for the October 7 football game, the fans enjoyed the high-energy swaying and dancing band. That day, the Minuteman Band learned about what it meant to create a more entertaining show, and Parks recalled that it was the first and last time the *Massachusetts Daily Collegian* ran an article asking, "Why can't our band be as good as other bands?" As a result, the group began making changes to its show designs.

In the fall of 1979, the band began a new unofficial tradition: sleeping on gym floors during overnight trips. Since the band's budget was limited, it was not possible for students to stay in hotels, and saving on these costs allowed the group to take trips that otherwise would have been impossible.

The Minuteman Band traveled to the September 29 Harvard game and gave a short concert for UMass alumni afterward. After a concert at Faneuil Hall, the band marched in Saugus' three hundredth anniversary parade and ended the day on a high school gym floor. Jane Bolton '81 recalled that the

The mouse and eagle mural remains in Old Chapel.

band's photographer, Sid Russell, brought along a print of that year's hit movie *Superman*, and the students watched the movie before falling asleep in a giant "slumber party."

Ever since coming to the University of Massachusetts, Parks had wanted to give the Minuteman Band a new nickname. The Ohio State Band was known as "The Best Damn Band in the Land," and Syracuse University had its "Pride of the Orange." "The Pride of New England" was an idea, but that title had already been claimed by the University of Rhode Island Marching Band. At that season's Harvard game, Parks watched the Minuteman Band play the opening of the "Superman" show against the jeers and boos of the Harvard fans and band members. Although surrounded by ridicule, band

My Way

And now, the end is near;

And so I face the final curtain.

My friend(s), I'll say it clear,

I'll state my case, of which I'm certain.

I've lived a life that's full.

I've traveled each and ev'ry highway;

(And) more, much more than this,

I did it my way.

2003 band members sing "My Way" after the postgame concert.

The Minuteman Band first performed Frank Sinatra's classic "My Way" in 1978, and the song soon became the group's traditional closer. The song, one of the band's most beloved traditions, originally started as a warm-up for the Minuteman Band. To help with intonation, Parks had the band members sing their parts, and "My Way" soon became an indispensable part of the group's performance. Band members strive to "live a life that's full" and to have no regrets by the time they "face the final curtain."

members were not intimidated and played with a powerful sound. Parks watched the group from the sideline and thought, "This band has a lot of power, but we also have class." Soon thereafter, the University of Massachusetts Marching Band became known as "The Power and Class of New England."

Although the group had a new nickname, it was still not as strong as the University of Connecticut's band, which Parks recalled was "the band to catch." On a bitterly cold day, the Minuteman Band traveled to the October 27 UMass-UConn game and gave a good halftime show, but it was clear that UConn still had the better band.

In the fall of 1980, the Minuteman Band became known for its flowing drill patterns that resulted in constantly changing formations, and the group developed a solid, musical sound. In addition, Parks' energetic teaching style brought band member enthusiasm to new levels. Eric Snoek '83 said, "Enthusiasm is infectious, and Mr. Parks is full of it," and Ann Turomsha '81 added, "The charisma of the man is incredible."

That season, graduate assistant Thomas P. Hannum joined the band as the new percussion instructor. Parks and Hannum had marched together in the West Chester University Band, where Parks had been Hannum's drum major. Hannum, a former snare captain for the Golden Rams Band, was a strong addition to the UMass Band's instructional staff.

The group added another innovation that fall. Since the halftime show "Godspell" was based on a musical, it was appropriate to have band members sing during performance. It created a dramatic effect, and during one rehearsal, as the band sang part of "Long Live God," the skies darkened, and clouds formed so low that they covered the top of the stadium. In the eerie pale half-light, the hovering clouds gave an otherworldly quality to the music, and the band remained in a respectful silence after the song ended. The "Godspell" show was a great success.

In the early 1980s, the band experimented with a number of performance effects that "simply weren't done" at the time in the marching band world. Besides singing during performances, the group began "crashing the stands." For the song "Alexander's Ragtime Band," students performed a simple drill, ran to the stands, and played the final bars within feet of the surprised fans, who were overwhelmed and gave an enthusiastic response. The concept of "crashing the stands" was unheard of, and the practice was one of the reasons that the Minuteman Band became known for its exciting performances.

The university's chancellor, Henry Koffler, was a great friend and strong supporter of the band program. After performing at the October 11 Homecoming game against Delaware, the band was invited to entertain Koffler and the Second Century Club at the chancellor's home. Koffler said of the game, "We may have lost the football game, but our band is Number One."

As the band's reputation spread, the University of Massachusetts was selected to play host to the first annual Northeast Regional Music Bowl, sponsored by Beatrice Foods. In October, 18 high school marching bands competed for top honors, after which the Minuteman Band gave a night exhibition under the lights in Alumni Stadium. The music bowl competition drew public attention to the university and in later years, the band re-created the bowl experience by starting its own Band Day.

The band also traveled to Boston for the October

George Parks conducts the Minuteman Band.

The band released records of its halftime shows.

The Minuteman Band presents a powerful and classy performance.

143

25 UMass-Boston University game, which was broadcast on ABC. During "The BU Monsoon," the group performed in a torrential downpour with winds gusting up to fifty miles per hour; tuba players were nearly blown over, and band members recalled that the rain was coming at them sideways. However, they played their "hearts out and truly impressed the ABC announcers." The band managed to deliver a "sterling, although slightly damp performance," and the announcers remarked, "Well, they call themselves the Power and the Class, and they certainly deserve that title."

After a memorable performance at the 1980 MICA Festival, tuba player Greg Penglis '81 put into words what Parks and the band students were feeling: "This band put forth a show tonight, with more guts and more power than anything that has ever walked across this campus. These people, they are the best, and I wouldn't trade them for anything. And we are going to do it year after year after year, and that is all I have to say." His words embody the ideals of the Minuteman Band: to perform with excellence, surrounded by dedicated people who love being in the band. Twenty-three years later, the Minuteman Band continues to uphold

Band members are known for their enthusiasm.

How Are Your Feet?

This Minuteman Band tradition was first introduced by John Jenkins in the 1960s. When George Parks became the band director in 1977, he added the "Eyes—With Pride" section at the end. At the end of each rehearsal or performance, Parks calls the group to attention. He begins, "How are Your Feet?" and the band members shout back, "Together!" The words help the students to remember a solid marching posture and provide a fitting closure for the day's events.

Through Parks' work with the George N. Parks Drum Major Academy and the Bands of America Summer Symposium, thousands of high school drum majors and band leaders have brought this cheer back to their bands. Over the years, "How are Your Feet?" has become nationally recognized and is used by groups across the country.

How are Your Feet?   Together!
Stomach?   In!
Chest?   Out!
Shoulders?   Back!
Elbows?   Frozen!
Chin?   Up!
Eyes?   With Pride!

Who's got the Best Band anywhere?
UMASS!

these traditions and consistently performs for its audiences with intensity, power, and class.

With classic college humor, members of the UMass Band played a prank on Connecticut's mascot for the November 1 UMass-UConn game. Over thirty students were involved in a plan to obtain the Husky uniform. Yale students had been caught in the act of taking the Husky, but the UMass conspirators came up with a foolproof scheme. Led by Penglis, the students contacted the UConn mascot, convinced him they were from Harvard University with a letter written on Harvard University stationery, and deceived him into thinking that he was taking part in a scientific study about mascots. Band members interviewed the mascot and videotaped him walking through Storrs in costume, shaking hands with passersby. Afterward, they had the mascot put his Husky outfit in their car as they went out for drinks, and Nancy Wyllie '81 drove the costume back to Amherst. Back in the Connecticut bar, the assembled band members took off their sweatshirts to reveal the "Massachusetts" T-shirts underneath, told the shocked mascot he had been deceived, and that his outfit was in Massachusetts. The next day, Minuteman Band member Mike Krivitsky '82 wore the UConn Husky uniform for the first half of the game, and whenever UMass scored a touchdown, the "UMass Husky" did push-ups. Although the UConn fans were upset to see their mascot dancing with UMass band members, and a riot nearly broke out in the Connecticut Band, the Husky was returned to UConn before halftime. The Connecticut mascot, who had watched the game from the Connecticut stands, reappeared as the real Husky by halftime, and the UMass football team went on to win the game 39–21.

Additional fall trips found the band marching in Boston's Jubilee 350th Grand Parade even, as a hundred years earlier, the Morris Drum Corps marched in Boston's 250th Anniversary Parade. The band, funded by $1,600 raised in the annual Alumni Fund Drive, also performed during halftime at the November 16 New England Patriots-Los Angeles Rams game.

Deciding that the Minuteman Band was ready for

Band members obtained UConn's mascot outfit and displayed it at the UMass–UConn game.

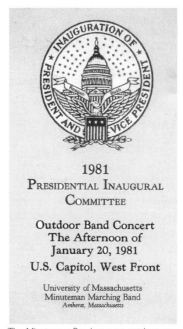

1981
PRESIDENTIAL INAUGURAL COMMITTEE

Outdoor Band Concert
The Afternoon of
January 20, 1981
U.S. Capitol, West Front

University of Massachusetts
Minuteman Marching Band
Amherst, Massachusetts

The Minuteman Band gave an outdoor concert on the steps of the Capitol Building during the 1981 Inaugural Ceremonies.

bigger challenges, Parks applied to have the group march in the 1981 Presidential Inaugural Parade. He told his students, "Well band, I applied for the Inaugural, and the competition was just too intense. They only accepted seven college bands." He named off the first six bands, and when he named the seventh, the University of Massachusetts Minuteman Marching Band, "the students went wild with pure intensity and enthusiasm," as they realized that they would be traveling to Washington, D.C. to perform for the president of the United States. Suddenly the Minuteman Band was on the national stage.

In January, the Minuteman Band arrived in the nation's capital, gave a concert at a local high school, and spent the evening in a hotel, which was a luxury after sleeping on gym floors. The next day, the band assembled for the January 21 Inaugural Parade, which was delayed for several hours due to intense negotiations to resolve the Iranian hostage crisis. The parade eventually stepped off, and as the band turned onto Pennsylvania Avenue and prepared to pass the reviewing stands, the television cameras pulled away for a breaking headline story. The American hostages were being released, and the Iranian hostage crisis was resolved.

Although the Minuteman Band missed its chance to appear on national television, the band represented the university and the Commonwealth of Massachusetts in grand style and, after the parade, was one of only three groups chosen to play a concert on the steps of the Capitol Building. After the band played "Alexander's Ragtime Band," Master of Ceremonies Willard Scott, nationally known for his role as weatherman on "The Today Show," enjoyed what he heard and said, "That has to be the best damn band I've ever seen!" After the successful parade and concert in Washington, the students watched a fireworks display and ended the evening by playing "My Way" on the steps of the Capitol Building. Sen. Ted Kennedy sent his personal congratulations to Chancellor Koffler, commending band members "on their outstanding performance during the Inaugural Festivities and Parade. The Minuteman Band brought unique honor and distinction to the University and to our Commonwealth. I watched

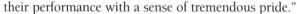

their performance with a sense of tremendous pride."

Although the 1981 Inaugural Parade was a highlight for the UMass Band, it was also a time of reflection, as it was the last time that the Michigan-style band uniforms were worn. Thanks to a donation from the annual Alumni Fund Drive and Athletics, the band would have new uniforms for the fall semester. In addition to strong financial support from the Alumni Association, the group also received additional backing from the chancellor's office. Koffler's continued support was invaluable, and in May 1981, he sent a letter expressing his "personal pride and thanks for the outstanding per-

The Minuteman Band marched in the 1981 Presidential Inaugural Parade.

The colorguard displays the band's new red uniforms.

formance of the Band during the last year. You are a credit to the University and bring much enjoyment to thousands of people."

A new era dawned in the fall of 1981 when the marching band received $40,000 worth of new red uniforms. Wanting to move the band away from the overlay-style uniform look, Parks borrowed design ideas from various top marching groups: the long red uniform coat from the Santa Clara Vanguard Drum and Bugle Corps, the cape from the Phantom Regiment Drum Corps, the shako from the Blue Devils Drum Corps, and the sash from the University of Illinois Band. The rest of the uniform consisted of black pants with a red stripe, a white "UMASS" sash, a white citation cord, white gauntlets, white gloves, and a black-and-white shako with a long, red plume. Although the new red uniforms were a combination of other successful design concepts, the overall look was unique to UMass. The changeover from the older, darker look to the stunning red had a profound effect. From now on, in addition to garnering attention for its exciting musical performances, the Minuteman Band presented a powerful visual presence as well. The new uniforms had their debut in Alumni Stadium for the September 19 Holy Cross game, which the Minutemen won 13–10. Halftime music for the fall included "Coronation March," the opening from Shostakovich's "Fifth Symphony," and "Big Noise from Winnetka."

Although the Alumni Association and its president, Ruth Levins, were instrumental in supporting the band's activities, Parks needed additional funding to continue taking the group on tour. In order to supplement the band's budget, students began fundraising on campus. Over the years, student

Colorguard

In 1974, the Minuteman Band's first colorguard unit was created in the form of an eight-woman swing flag corps that took the field with the musicians. Over the years, the flags grew to a full thirty-two member visual ensemble, and a number of outstanding students, such as Leanna Kelley and Melody Essex, taught the guard.

In 1981, Kristen O'Melia, a graduate teaching assistant, was added as the Minuteman Band's first colorguard instructor. Tina Sochia ran the guard from 1982–83, and the colorguard received new silks to replace the older "M" flags. In 1984, the instructor, Joe Perednia, added a number of innovations, and the guard received uniforms that were different from those of the regular Minuteman Band members. In addition, the group began using a wider variety of colored flags. Spitfire, a competitive winterguard, was created in 1984 by Perednia, and in 1985, the group won the National Judges Association Circuit in Wildwood, New Jersey. Spitfire was disbanded in 1990.

In 1988, David Hautanen took over instructing the colorguard from Leanne Riley, who taught from 1986–87. When Christine McHugh became the new instructor in 1990, Hautanen continued as the colorguard coordinator and advisor. McHugh placed a greater emphasis on body movement, and the group wore white dress uniforms with black tops. Erica Jacob (1996–97) added larger equipment and took the guard to a higher level of technical proficiency, and Joyce Landers (1998–99) added gray tops to the uniforms. With Cecil York (2000–01), the guard wore red sweater tops and black bottoms. In 2001, when the Minuteman Band received its maroon-and-white uniforms, the colorguard received new color-block tops of burgundy, black, and gold. Hautanen resumed instructing the colorguard for the fall of 2002, and during the "Gladiator" show, the group used multicolor costumes. For the 2003 season, Jessica Adame, the new instructor, brought a greater variety of bodywork and silk colors to the ensemble. The band also added one of its first twirling instructors, Kristi Kupras.

Over the years, the versatile colorguard has used a variety of equipment, including sabers, rifles, four- to seven-foot flagpoles, Spanish sabers, expandable globes, swing flags, streamers, split flags, Can-Can panels, Island Magic scepters, and gladiator shields. The colorguard adds a rich dimension to the Minuteman Band's musical performance.

fundraising allowed the band to give a variety of off-campus performances that would otherwise not have been possible and brought the group greater national exposure.

With the additional funds, for the first time, the Minuteman Band traveled to the October 10 away game at the University of Delaware. For Parks, who had grown up in Delaware and performed with the University of Delaware Fightin' Blue Hen Band, it was "like going home." Whenever the band performed in a new stadium, it was important to have music in place that would excite the audience, and "Alexander's Ragtime Band," a favorite of both the band and the audience, was brought back as a crowd-pleaser. At halftime, the Minuteman Band performed in front of 22,000 Delaware fans, and after the postgame show was over, the excited football audience blocked the exits and would not let the band leave the field until it played the entire show again. The fans also enjoyed the band's rendition of "New York, New York." After the repeated postgame show, the Delaware fans were so pleased with the band's

The Minuteman Band is known for its exciting performances.

performance that they gave out free food and drinks to band members. Even Delaware's governor, Pierre S. DuPont, appreciated the show and wrote to Parks, "I was very impressed with the performance of your band and have never seen such personality and spirit. Everyone stayed and raved about the entertainment, and you should be most proud. I have never enjoyed halftime so much. All of your students were a true credit to your fine University." With such an overwhelming response, the Minuteman Band made its mark in Delaware Stadium. After the successful game, the entire band took part in a mass square dance, given by a friend of Parks' mother, Vesta.

In the fall of 1982, the Minuteman Band embarked on a "Quest for Excellence" and sought to become the best band in the Northeast. At the October 30 UMass-UConn game in Connecticut, the group performed its halftime show of "Jubilant Prelude," "Still," and "Let's Groove," the band's first major dance routine. After the energetic performance, band members felt that they possibly edged out the mighty UConn Band and arguably took the title of "Best Band in New England." Nevertheless, both groups showed their good spirit and combined to perform "Ice Castles" to end the halftime show, receiving standing ovations from the football crowd.

Additional performances for the Minuteman Band included the extravagant Woburn Halloween Parade and halftime for the New England Patriots-

The Minuteman Band performs "The 1812 Overture" for the New England Patriots.

New York Jets football game. The band also traveled to the Harvard game, and with Harvard's overly enthusiastic students and fans, the trip was always one of the most challenging for the group.

A notorious event, dubbed "Banned in Boston," took place this fall. Although the Minuteman Band planned to give its traditional Faneuil Hall Concert, scheduling conflicts prevented it from playing in its usual spot. The band instead performed at Government Center, and afterward, the drumline marched the group back to the buses on rim-taps. A nearby Faneuil Hall security officer said the drum taps were disturbing the peace and told Parks to accompany him to sign a trespass warrant, which would have barred the UMass Band from ever returning to Faneuil Hall. The officer offered to handcuff Parks if he did not come with him immediately. Parks, whose first priority was to see the band safely to the buses, insisted that he had to stay with his students. The officer saw it differently and handcuffed Parks, taking him to security. Meanwhile, the band returned to the loading area to the cadence of "My Sharona," singing the words "Banned in Boston!" Back at security, a band parent came up and began to argue with the officer. When the officer began to threaten the parent, Parks signed the warrant to end the matter, and the band returned to Amherst. However, later that week, Parks heard a rumor that the warrant he signed had vanished, and nothing more was made of the matter.

The Minuteman Band had an active traveling season in the fall of 1983 and made trips to Harvard University, UConn, and the University of New Hampshire.

Thomas P. Hannum

Thomas P. Hannum was born on June 14, 1957, in Chester, Pennsylvania. He received his bachelor's degree in music from West Chester University and a master's degree from the University of Massachusetts.

In 1983, Hannum began working with the Garfield Cadets Drum and Bugle Corps, and in 1984, he became the assistant director of the Minuteman Band. Hannum, one of the nation's foremost percussion clinicians, has presented numerous seminars and workshops throughout the United States, Canada, Europe, and Southeast Asia. In addition, he is a product consultant and clinician for the Pearl Corporation, Avedis Zildjian Cymbal Company, Vic Firth Sticks and Mallets, and Evans Drum Heads.

A member of the Drum Corps International Hall of Fame, Hannum is best known for his work with the DCI World Champion Cadets of Bergen County and Star of Indiana. He is currently on the design team for the theatrical productions *Blast!* and *Shockwave* and directs the Minuteman Hoop Band as it cheers on the UMass basketball team. His marching percussion ensembles continue to be the finest in the country, and students come from all over to be part of the Minuteman Band's percussion section.

Thomas Hannum's marching percussion ensembles have won national and international recognition.

Music for the fall's halftime shows included "Mambo" from *West Side Story*, "Let's Groove," "The Stars and Stripes Forever," and "New York, New York." The band returned to Delaware for the October 8 game and presented music from *Godspell*. After the show, band members received "a standing ovation that wouldn't end."

By the fall of 1984, although the band had made great strides, Parks felt the group needed a stronger percussion section, and Thom Hannum was the best choice to be the band's new assistant director. After Linda Paul convinced Parks it was possible to persuade the university to hire another staff member for the marching band, he and Gerry Grady approached the interim music chair, Al Huetteman. Huetteman agreed and recommended the hiring to Murray Schwartz, dean of the faculty of humanities and fine arts. With the dean's permission, Jon Hite, director of alumni relations, worked to convince Chancellor Joseph Duffey. Parks had band members write letters

The 1988 snare line performs during the percussion feature.

George Parks and Thom Hannum.

Drum major Linda Paul plays a trumpet solo.

to Duffey telling him how important Hannum was to the Minuteman Band program. Duffey was convinced, and in the fall of 1984, the band had two teaching professionals assigned to it for the first time.

The Minuteman Band's professional leaders were in place. The *Massachusetts Daily Collegian* reported that Parks, who was well liked and respected by band members, was a major reason for the success of the 220-member Minuteman Band, and that his charismatic leadership was why many students joined the program. Students also played in the band for the sheer fun, enjoyment, and performance opportunities that the group provided.

The band had a smooth season and a great sound, and head drum major Neil Freebern '89 said, "This year we've pushed for musical perfection more than others, and the band has improved 100 percent." For the first time, band favorite "The 1812 Overture" was performed as part of a halftime show.

In addition, the band's front ensemble began to take shape. In earlier years, the band had a bell player and xylophone player, both of whom marched on the field. In 1984, Hannum brought small xylophones from the Garfield Cadets Drum and Bugle Corps, and with four old timpani, the "Pit" percussion section was born. Over the years, the Pit's musical contributions have grown. At the time of this writing, the ensemble has electronic instruments, such as a keyboard and bass guitar, which allow for musical versatility within the marching band.

That fall, the Minuteman Band performed in exhibition at a Friday night West Chester University game, and although it was not yet as strong as the Incomparable Golden Rams Band, it was invaluable experience for the UMass Band members. Before John Calipari came to UMass with his "anyone, anywhere, anytime" motto for the basketball program, the Minuteman Band understood that it was important to see and emulate the best bands in the area. Over the years, Parks brought the group into the stadiums of the best bands in the Northeast and Mid-Atlantic, which provided the UMass Band with a standard for measurement. After the West Chester exhibition, the band traveled to Delaware Stadium for the November 10 UMass-Delaware game and combined with the Delaware Band to perform "The 1812 Overture," complete with cannons.

The Minuteman Band forms UMASS for pregame.

Although Parks applied to have the group march in President Ronald Reagan's Inaugural Parade in January 1985, the band was instead invited to perform as a sit-down ensemble along the parade route. As the students gathered in Amherst during winter break and began rehearsing, it became apparent that it would be a challenging trip. Due to heavy snows, band members arrived all throughout the day amid accidents and delays. When the band arrived in Washington, the hotel rooms were not ready. The group was scheduled to perform for Ronald Reagan's Friday evening Pre-Inaugural Ceremony Concert, and at the last minute, presidential security moved the reporting time up by two hours. Band staff scrambled to buy cheeseburgers and drinks and handed them out hurriedly as the 220 band members were told they had five minutes to eat and change into uniform. On arriving at the concert, Parks was startled when he was asked to report to White House security, but luckily it was only to retrieve his lost briefcase. The next morning was brutally cold, and the band left to record a clip for the "Good Morning America" show, but since no one had woken the band's truck driver, the percussion section did not have drums for the performance. Without drums and with frozen valves, Parks recalled that the band had "a special sound" that morning. After the band played as best as it could, Parks announced, "This is the Minuteman Marching Band, and we'd love to wish you a happy morning." The producer reminded him that the name of the show was "Good Morning America." After various takes, the band was told that the cameras had frozen, and none of the

George Parks leads the Minuteman Band in "My Way."

morning's footage made it onto the air. Due to the subzero temperatures, the Inaugural Parade was also canceled. Later on, Parks convinced officials to let the group give an additional performance at the Old Post Office Pavilion, promising that the 220-member marching band would not drown out the 16-member jazz band that was playing nearby, since the jazz band had electronic amplification. After the Minuteman Band began playing "Malaguena" and "The 1812 Overture," Parks recalled, "The poor jazz band didn't know what hit them." The next day, the band arrived at a restaurant for its scheduled breakfast, but the pipes at the eatery had frozen, and no food was available. The students left for Amherst and returned after a long trip at 2 a.m., only to discover that UMass security had towed all the band members' cars. It truly was "The trip from hell."

Band Day

Band Day typically draws 4,000 high school students each year.

Since its inception in 1985, Band Day has brought thousands of students to the University of Massachusetts to experience the thrill of being in a college band and watching a college football game. The philosophy behind Band Day is to encourage high school musicians to feel good about playing in a school band, and each year, between 3,000 and 4,000 high school band members attend the UMass Band Day. Students from sixty to eighty high school bands throughout New England, New York, and New Jersey spend the morning rehearsing music and learning a massed block drill. During halftime, after the Minuteman Band plays a short selection, the high school students march onto the field, in full uniform, and play a variety of popular selections. Band Day is one of the most effective recruiting tools not only for the Minuteman Marching Band, but also for the University of Massachusetts.

The fall of 1985 was a less active travel season and the band stayed close to home. Halftime shows included selections from the movie *The Right Stuff,* "Alexander's Ragtime Band," "The 1812 Overture," and "Russian Sailor's Dance." Highlights for the Minuteman Band's season included a performance at the Fine Arts Center's tenth anniversary, concerts at the Eastern States Exposition and at Faneuil Hall, and halftime shows at Harvard and New England Patriots football games. During the fall, the band rehearsed in the middle of Hurricane Gloria, which hit Massachusetts on September 27. Although the rest of the campus had closed, band rehearsal went on as usual.

Students often played pranks on their band directors, and one memorable story was entitled "The Great Pumpkin Caper." Heidi Sarver '88G recalled that several band members pulled off the road at a pumpkin patch outside campus and began picking pumpkins for Halloween. When the car was loaded, it became apparent that they had picked more pumpkins than they would ever need. They hit on the idea that the best place to drop the extra pumpkins was the lawn of Parks' house. At night, the band members arrived and stealthily carried pumpkins from the car to the front yard, and in a short while, the lawn was covered with pumpkins. Suddenly Parks' dog, Ralphie, began to bark, and the students froze to await the worst. The driveway light came on, and someone peered from behind a curtain to see what the dog was barking at. Finally, the light went out, and the students rapidly finished their task. The yard was filled, and the next day at rehearsal, the students grinned when Parks commented to the band about the "sea of pumpkins" on his lawn.

In the fall of 1986, music for the Minuteman Band was headlined by *West Side Story,* and additional songs for the season included "Twist and Shout" and "Echano." In addition, graduate assistant Michael J. Klesch joined the band staff as the brass arranger and worked with the wind instruments.

On October 11, the Delaware Band came to Amherst for the UMass-Delaware Homecoming foot-

George Parks and future University of Delaware Band director Heidi Sarver.

Band Banquet

Each year after the marching season, the Minuteman Band holds its traditional banquet to celebrate the group's accomplishments. One of the earliest banquets took place at Amherst's Drake Hotel on November 22, 1949. The event was hosted by the music department to honor the work of the marching band, drill team, concert band, and cheerleaders. The band banquet now takes place on campus in either the Campus Center Auditorium or the Student Union Ballroom, and usually five hundred band members, friends, and honored guests take part.

ball game. In a *Massachusetts Daily Collegian* interview, Parks noted that the UMass Band and fans had a reputation of being supportive of visiting bands, and the Delaware and UMass Bands combined to play "America the Beautiful" for the appreciative audience. Other Minuteman Band appearances that fall included performing at halftime during the October 5 Patriots-Dolphins game in Sullivan Stadium.

Drum major Therese Murray '87 leads the band onto the field.

Band trombones with red-and-black slide covers.

The Harvard game, always a challenge, was especially colorful this year. The band traveled to Harvard for the November 8 game and spent the morning rehearsing in the rain. Although the band requested a spot indoors where they could dry off and eat lunch, university officials said "No" and asked the band to stay on the buses. By the time the game began, band members were cold and wet, at which point the Harvard Band began to shout insults over the field at the Minuteman Band. One of Harvard's insults was a cheer, directed at the University of Massachusetts in general, of "Safety School!" A more creative taunt was, "Why do you call yourself UMASS?—is it because you can't spell University or you can't spell Massachusetts?" to which the Minuteman Band responded, "NO—it's because we can't spell 'of'!"

During the game, the Harvard athletic director spoke to Parks and told him that the Minuteman Band would not be allowed to perform during halftime, since the band would supposedly damage the field. The band was offered two choices: play the halftime show in the stands or line up in the end zone and play it there. Parks walked through the stands and told the band members that if they stepped on the field at halftime, they would be arrested. After a long day of being wet and enduring the Harvard Band's insults, drum major Jeff Poulton '87 and the drumline's section leader Joel Gittle '89 decided there was a third option. They formed a simple plan: as soon as Poulton blew his whistle during the halftime show, the band would charge out of the end zone and take the field. Before halftime, the 230 band members lined up in the end zone, and ten Harvard University police officers lined up along the goal line to keep them there. The band played its first few numbers, Poulton blew his whistle, and the Minuteman Band charged. Both sides of the stadium cheered as the band crashed through the police line and played its closer, "The Stars and Stripes Forever." After halftime and the band's spirited antics, the festivities between the Minuteman Band and Harvard Band contin-

Dr. Tim

Dr. Tim Lautzenheiser is an inspiring and nationally known teacher. His association with the Minuteman Marching Band began in 1987, when he and Parks started teaching band leadership clinics together. Soon, Lautzenheiser's ideals of leadership and attitude had an impact on the UMass Band members, and the group went through a number of positive changes.

The current Band Camp tradition of upperclassmen welcoming band freshmen is a strong example of Lautzenheiser's teachings. Drum major Jen Boltz '90, fresh from a leadership seminar at the Bands of America Summer Symposium, felt that greeting the freshmen and carrying their luggage to their Band Camp dorm rooms would make their first day less intimidating. The Minuteman Band's student staff met the freshmen and their parents in the parking lot, welcomed them with loud cheering, and carried their gear to their rooms. The new students immediately felt "at home." Dr. Tim's positive leadership is a hallmark of the Minuteman Band, and student leaders strive to create memorable experiences for underclassmen.

Dr. Tim Lautzenheiser is a nationally known motivational speaker.

ued. After regrouping in the stands, UMass Band members shouted over to the Harvard fans, "Hey Harvard, have Daddy buy you a new field!" Parks later recalled that the highlight of the game was the comments from Massachusetts football coach Jim Reid. UMass was losing the game at the half, and everyone in the Massachusetts contingent, including Reid, was aware that the Minuteman Band had been denied the opportunity to perform at halftime. The UMass locker room was right off the field and as Reid later told at sports luncheons, he heard the Minuteman Band playing, opened the doors, and saw the band charging the field and doing the show against Harvard's orders. Reid looked at his team and said, "If the band can go out there and kick their (. . .), then you can go out there and kick their (. . .)! The Massachusetts football team came back from defeat and beat Harvard 17–7.

For the November 22 UMass-UConn game, the band performed a take-off from the movie *Ferris Bueller's Day Off* and added an innovation, as David Soreff '88 sang "Twist and Shout" through the long

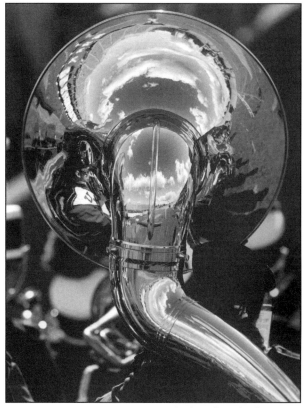

A tuba reflects the days events.

Band Camp

The Minuteman Band prepares for its Band Camp performance.

First created by John Jenkins in August 1963, Band Camp quickly became a Minuteman Band tradition. Each year, hundreds of band members gather together the week before classes start. In addition to learning the basics of marching, students learn music and drill for the first game, and by the end of Band Camp, band members typically memorize seventy pages of marching drill and four songs. The group's camaraderie is strengthened by its time on the field in the blazing sun, and many students make lifelong friends in the Minuteman Band.

ranger amplification system. Soreff's performance was well-received by the audience, as the band used a singer for the first time to add a new dimension to its field show. It was a major developmental moment for the Minuteman Band, which over the years has used a number of singers to enhance its half-time shows.

For the fall of 1987, the 235-member Minuteman Band learned the entire drill to the song "Silverado" and was marching and performing the piece by the end of Band Camp. Before this, students spent most of the week learning marching basics, and often, only one day was spent working on drill. However, as the band matured, it was possible to teach basics faster, and more time was available to rehearse music. Additional songs for the fall included "America the Beautiful" and the band favorite "Canto Del Viento," written by the Reading Buccaneers' brass arranger, Tony Yaklich.

Another innovation included the addition of the Fine Arts Center's director James Mac-Rostie as the band's announcer. MacRostie became known as "the voice of the Minuteman Band," and his work included reading texts for shows such as "Mermaid," "Phantom," and Shakespeare's "Henry V."

One of the highlights of the season occurred after the band's trip to the November 14 University of New Hampshire game. Although Parks had warned members that band funds were running at a deficit and that students would have to bring their own money for dinner, the band buses drove into Newick's Lobster House. It turned out that the band had a budget surplus that year; to their great surprise and pleasure, the students each received seven dollars to spend on dinner, instead of the usual "three dollar limit." The band's administrative staff table alone was overflowing with lobster shells. However, with the group's continued growth and an increase in Band Camp costs, it was the last time the group had a surplus.

The Minuteman Hoop Band was active throughout this time as well. A memorable event took place at the February 20 UMass-Duquesne basketball game, where university officials honored Julius "Dr J" Erving for his contributions to UMass basketball. In honor of "Dr J," the Hoop Band played

"Thanks for the Memories," arranged by "Dr." Rob Hammerton '88. Hammerton had been writing music for the Hoop Band since 1986, and his arrangements were important in helping the band develop an identity. He brought to the Hoop Band such classics as "Blues Brothers Opener," "Gospel John," "Hip to be Square," "Night Train," "One" from *A Chorus Line*, and "Perfect World," as well as a variety of ESPN SportsCenter songs. For the marching band, his arrangements of "Bandstand Boogie," "Bill Bailey," "Hook," "Blue Rondo a La Turk," and a Phil Collins medley made him one of the Minuteman Band's most prolific arrangers.

In the spring of 1988, the University of Massachusetts basketball program began its climb to unprecedented heights, and the Hoop Band, under the direction of Thom Hannum, was there to cheer the players on. John Calipari became UMass' newest coach, and soon the turnaround of UMass basketball was considered "one of the greatest building jobs in college basketball history."

A new era dawned for the Minuteman Marching Band in the fall of 1988, after summer band manager Jocelyn Fein Steinberg '89 recruited 340 students to report for Band Camp. It was the first time that the band had more than three hundred members, and a

The 1988 Minuteman Band performed with a new intensity.

new vitality energized the band program. The group had a record forty-eight trumpets that fall, which brought a power and intensity to the music. In addition, George Zingali, nationally renowned drill writer for the Cadets of Bergen County and the 27th Lancers Drum and Bugle Corps, was brought in to work with the band. A leading innovator in drill design, Zingali visited Amherst during the fall.

Selections for the 1988 season included "Festive Overture," which started in a tight drill block that expanded until the entire field was filled with band members. Additional halftime pieces included "The 1812 Overture" and the "Can Can," which was first performed during the 1987 season. For "Can Can," which was complete with a kick line of band members and tuba player Sean Kennan '89 riding a unicycle, students dropped a kitchen sink on the field. The piece truly had everything in it "including the kitchen sink."

With the marching band's larger membership, fundraising became more important than ever, and Parks found that the budget was stretched thin. Since Band Camp costs were rising and the group remained level-funded, after 1988, fundraising became critical in supporting the band's day-to-day

Tom Savage '84 and Therese Murray dance at Homecoming 1982.

Southwest and Postgame Concerts

On game days, it is a Minuteman Band tradition to stop in the Southwest Residential Area as the group passes through on its way to McGuirk Alumni Stadium. There, the band gives a short concert and rouses sleeping students in anticipation of the day's football game.

During John Jenkins' tenure, the Massachusetts Band, in the style of the Michigan Band, gave a traditional block band concert at the end of each football game. When George Parks became director, the postgame concert was styled after that of the West Chester University Band's, and the tradition continues to the present day. At the end of each home football game, the band plays its complete halftime show and ends with "My Way." The concert is unofficially known as the "Fifth Quarter" of the football game, and hundreds of loyal fans and alumni stay to watch the performance.

operations. In September, after receiving a promise from Parks that he would swim in the Campus Pond if they raised $30,000, band members sold enough magazines to meet their goals. To the delight of his students, Parks donned a scuba suit and, with an inflatable raft, swam in the murky pond.

A great rivalry ended that fall. On September 24, after years of combat both on and off the gridiron, the University of Massachusetts and Harvard University met for the last time in Harvard Stadium. David Mark, editorial writer of the *Massachusetts Daily Collegian*, wrote that his favorite feature of the game was the Minuteman Band, which was also one of the best things about the University of Massachusetts, especially in the wake of Harvard's "snobbery." UMass won the last game 45–28.

The band also gave halftime performances at two New England Patriots football games: the October 2 game against the Indianapolis Colts and the October 30 game against the Chicago Bears. For the Bears game, the band performed its infamous "Pontiac" show, having been hired by the automaker to perform the "Pontiac Is Excitement" theme for halftime. Although band members were adept at learning drill, they only rehearsed shaping "PONTIAC" on the field twice before the game, and during halftime, Steve Robinson '89 recalled that the "a" and "c" blended together in a less than precise formation. Although the Minuteman Band did not generate its usual excitement, the Patriots did and beat the Chicago Bears 30–7.

With the end of the marching season, the Minuteman Hoop Band geared up for operation. Relations between the basketball team and the Hoop Band were growing, and in April 1989, Hannum received a note from Calipari reading, "You and the pep band did a great job last season of helping to continue the Rage in the Cage. Keep up the good work."

The Minuteman Band's main halftime show for the fall of 1989 was "Batman," complete with a costumed Caped Crusader. At the MICA show, band members used fire extinguishers to lay down mist on the field, which allowed Batman, played by Chris Gardiner '90, to emerge mysteriously, creating a stunning effect. Additional music for the season included "El Boro," "Elks Parade," "Russian Christmas Music," and the "Curly Shuffle."

The University of Massachusetts was faced with severe budget cuts that fall, and it was a difficult year for the Minuteman Band. In addition, the group was smaller that year, although a large number of incoming freshmen kept numbers from falling too low. In an effort to save the university from the cuts, students traveled to Boston and rallied at the State House. The band attended, lending its music to the strong and vibrant rally. Afterward, the group gave its traditional Faneuil Hall Concert.

The fall marked the one hundredth anniversary of the Clark Cadet Band and the band program at the university. To celebrate the event, the Band Alumni Association, along with the University Archives, held an exhibit entitled "History of the UMass Band Program," created by senior archives assistant Michael Milewski.

By March 1990, the UMass basketball team made its first appearance at the Atlantic-10 Championship game, and the Minuteman Hoop Band had the opportunity to travel to Temple University to support the team. Suddenly, the band found itself on the national stage, and band members assembled an impromptu uniform of V-neck maroon sweaters, black pants, black shoes, and white shirts. Although the team played hard, it lost to Temple 53–51.

In the spring, Parks' work with the Minuteman Band was recognized, and he received one of the highest honors bestowed by the University of Massachusetts. Nominated by his students, he was awarded the Distinguished Teaching Award for his dedication and teaching excellence.

One of the band's most memorable shows, "The Phantom of the Opera," took place in the fall of 1990. The show featured Tony Lechner '93 as the Phantom, and throughout the season, Lechner and the Minuteman Band often had audience members in tears during the last chords of "The Music of the Night." However, due to rain, the show debuted late

Mike Wadness performs with the Pit ensemble.

George Parks and the Minuteman Band delight the audience.

George Parks leads the concert band.

The beloved 1990 Phantom Show was highly successful.

The Minuteman Band often performs at professional football games.

and was performed only once in its entirety. In this "Year of Rain," it was common for band members to lose shoes, pieces of instruments, and other equipment in the mud of the football field. Additional music for the season included "St. Louis Blues," "Canto del Viento," and the percussion feature, "Bandstand Boogie."

In October, there was another budget crisis and the band found itself without any funds. At the time, 80 percent of the budget came from alumni funds, and the group's trip to perform at the Delaware and New York Giants football games was in jeopardy. However, band members circumvented the pitfall and raised $15,000. With additional support from the Alumni Association, the Minuteman Band made the trip to Delaware.

In Delaware, Kappa Kappa Psi brothers built a special magic chair on a tall wooden box, which allowed the Phantom to "vanish." During the final moments of the "Phantom" show, the Phantom sat down in the chair and sang softly, "It's over now, the music of the night," while being covered with a black cloth. As the band resolved the final chord, the cloth was pulled away. The Phantom had vanished, and only his mask and the last strains of music remained. Lisa Morrow '92 recalled that after the band finished the show, she looked up and saw the 22,000-strong Delaware crowd on their feet cheering for the band, tears in their eyes. Band members stood at attention on the field, tears running down their cheeks as well. After the highly successful Delaware show, the Minuteman Band performed during halftime of the October 21 Giants game and entertained 65,000 fans and millions more on national TV.

There was a similar response at the November 11 University of New Hampshire away game. Parks remembered "a man, beer in one hand and wife in the other," who was misty-eyed when the Phantom vanished. As the final chords faded, a silence descended on the field. Then the UNH fans cheered nonstop, and the Minuteman Band played every piece of music in its repertoire for the pleased fans, from the "Phantom" show to "St. Louis Blues" to the UMass fight songs.

Part of what made the band's shows successful was that the group did more than play music; it focused on creating something special and magical. "Phantom" was one of the Minuteman Band's most beloved and effective shows.

The UMass basketball team continued to excel, and by March 1991, it advanced to the National Invitational Tournament's Final Four. For the first time, the Hoop Band received funding to travel with the team to New York's Madison Square Garden. The team played well before losing to Stanford and Colorado.

The fall of 1991 was a challenging season for the Minuteman Band. The second show was based on music from Disney's *The Little Mermaid*, and although various band members remained unconvinced of the music's validity, football audiences enjoyed the show. "Mermaid," which was complete with a walking red lobster and a singing mermaid, also proved successful on television and was well-received when the band performed at halftime during the Patriots-Minnesota Vikings game.

A 1990 football program highlights Band Day.

It was also a difficult season due to budget limitations. During the fall, funds were extremely limited, and the marching band survived entirely as a result of band members' fundraising. It was the first year that money from the magazine drive was used to buy instruments and other necessities. In addition, Chancellor Richard O'Brien gave special funding to the marching band, which enabled the group to attend that season's away game at Boston University. Parks said, "Of course funds are tight, but the band members are great. They are selling magazines and we all sleep on gym floors on overnight trips to save on hotel bills." One of the main reasons the Minuteman Band continued to grow through the 1990s was the students' selling efforts; these funds allowed the group to circumvent earlier pitfalls that had hampered the band programs at the school in the past.

Although the fall was a challenging time for Parks, he did not completely lose his sense of humor. During the Friday rehearsal for the annual Multibands Concert, Parks was tired of listening to band members complain about muddy practice field conditions. Jeff Hirsch '96 recalled that Parks, who was wearing white pants, climbed down the tower, jumped knees first into the mud, and asked if band members had anything else to complain about. After several trombone players followed their director's lead, rehearsal resumed with muddier band members and no more complaints.

Additional music for the season included selections from the movie *Robin*

163

Merry Maple

Another favorite Minuteman Band tradition is participating in the town of Amherst's Merry Maple holiday celebration. One of the earliest Merry Maples took place in December 1947, when the brass choir of the band played carols in Amherst center on a Friday evening.

The full Minuteman Band's first Merry Maple performance took place in December 1978. In early December each year, the entire band parades to the Amherst Common and plays holiday carols for the assembled audience. Band members often light their instruments with Christmas lights or Menorahs, and the colorguard members hand out candy canes to the gathered children.

Hood, "An American in Paris" and "Brass Machine." In addition, the band marched in Brattleboro, Vermont's anniversary parade and afterward gave an exhibition for local residents. The band also marched in the Woburn Parade, and the season ended with the annual Merry Maple festivities in Amherst center.

In January 1992, due to the growth of the UMass basketball program, the Minuteman Hoop Band began playing during winter break games. The athletic department gave the band funds to buy new uniforms, and the group's new look consisted of maroon-and-white rugby shirts, blue jeans, and sneakers. The Hoop Band now presented a classy image on TV. In addition, the all-time leading scorer, guard Jim McCoy, mentioned that the basketball team liked hearing the band play songs such as "NBA on CBS" and "Road to the Final Four," because it made the team members feel like they were "big-time."

UMass played a number of outstanding games during the 1991–92 basketball season and on February 16 faced off against Temple, whom the Minutemen had never beaten. In an exciting game, UMass finally defeated the Owls 67–52. After UMass won its first regular season Atlantic-10 title, the Hoop Band traveled to Philadelphia and supported the team as it won its first Atlantic-10 Tournament Championship. UMass was invited to the NCAA Tournament as the third seed in the East, and the band traveled to Worcester, where the team beat Fordham and Syracuse. The team made it to the Sweet Sixteen, and the band traveled to Philadelphia, where UMass' season ended in a heartbreaking 87–77 loss to Kentucky, after a controversial technical foul was called on Calipari. Back in Amherst, praise for the Hoop Band came from all sides, and the group played at TV 22's tribute to the basketball team. Chancellor O'Brien sent Hannum a telegram saying, "Thanks to you and your wonderful band for the great support you give to our outstanding team." In addition, columnist Joe Calabrese wrote of the group, "The UMass Band is the best in the league. Not only are they good and loud, but they are creative." Calipari added, "The band is great."

The basketball team brought a tremendous amount of publicity to the University of Massachusetts. Before Calipari came to campus, no one referred to the university as "UMass" because that term sounded too much like "ZooMass," which carried negative connotations from the university's party-school image of the 1970s. However, "UMass" was now the preferred name, and Commonwealth pride in the Minuteman team and the University of Massachusetts began to grow.

In the fall of 1992, the Minuteman Band's first show included music from the movie *Batman Returns*, which featured Batman, played by John Thomson '96, as well as Catwoman, Joker, and the Penguin. The band's second show was entitled "Won't You Join in Our Crusade?" based on music from Broadway's *Les Miserables*.

The band opened its season on September 12 at the away UMass-Delaware game. The next day, the group traveled to the Meadowlands and played at halftime for the New York Giants-Dallas Cowboys game. To supplement the vitally important band member fundraising, that fall Parks started up "The Halftime Club," which reached out to band alumni and gathered contributions to keep the band program operating.

The Minuteman Band continued to delight audiences and began distracting sports announcers at away games. At the September 19 Holy Cross game, during the halftime finale of "Part of Your World," former Boston College football coach Jack Bicknell became so engrossed in the band's "Mermaid" finale that he wasn't able to finish his commentary. TV sportscaster Bob Lobel, after trying to pry Bicknell's attention away from the band, eventually gave up, and both men watched the rest of the show.

During halftime of the October 17 UConn game, the band honored its great friend, trumpet professor Walter Chesnut, for his continued support. An additional fall performance for the band included the Woonsocket, Rhode Island, Columbus Day Parade, after which the band gave an exhibition for the town on a baseball field.

The Hoop Band had a busy season, and in January 1993 played at both the UMass-Cincinnati game at the Springfield Civic Center and the UMass-DePaul game at the Worcester Centrum. In February, its local reputation growing, the band performed in "The Really Big Show" at the Northampton Academy of Music, and posters proclaimed, "Providing music throughout the show will be the legendary UMass Hoop Band."

Calipari's "Refuse to Lose" became UMass' fight-

George Parks is known for his energetic style.

Former drum major Linda Paul and trumpet professor Walter Chesnut.

ing slogan, and back in the Curry Hicks Cage, the building shook with "Minutemen Mania." At the highly emotional Temple game, the Minutemen came back to beat the Owls 52–50, and Hannum nearly earned a technical foul after arguing with one of the referees. Hannum, who often became involved in basketball games, apparently stepped onto the court, which was less than a foot from the cramped bleachers where the Hoop Band sat. The referees heard some of the comments that he was making about the officiating in general and threatened him with a technical to quiet him down.

On January 29, the Minutemen played their final game in the Cage, beating Southwestern Louisiana 84–74. After the Minutemen won the Atlantic-10 regular season title, the Hoop Band traveled to Philadelphia for the tournament. The championship game returned to Amherst, where UMass beat Temple 69–61 in the Mullins Center to win the A-10 Championship. The campus went wild. The NCAA Tournament was next, and Parks took the Hoop Band to Syracuse with UMass as the third seed in the East. In the Carrier Dome, the Minutemen beat Pennsylvania before losing to Virginia 71–56, and the season ended. However, band members were excited to cheer on the team and enjoyed experiencing the "big-time" NCAA Tournament atmosphere.

The fall of 1993 marked one of the biggest opportunities ever for the

Minuteman Marching Band, as it spent the fall preparing to perform at the Bands of America Grand National Championships (BOA) in Indianapolis, Indiana. BOA was the major event for marching bands in the United States, and each fall, eighty of the nation's outstanding high school marching bands competed for top honors. In this venue, the Minuteman Band was slated to perform as the college exhibition band in front of the most knowledgeable and critical marching band audience in the country. Parks said of the BOA performance, "We were chosen as the exhibition band, and we will be featured as the entertainment. It's the biggest thing in the history of the band. This is an amazing challenge for us." An additional challenge was that the 1993 band was one of the smallest in years because a large number of seniors had graduated. During the first week of school, there were only 230 students in the band, and the BOA drill had fifteen holes.

BOA preparations included changes to the band's uniforms, as the white uniform accents were replaced by black highlights. The white citation cords and gauntlets were removed from the uniform entirely, and the white gloves and "UMASS" sashes were replaced by black gloves and sashes. Music chosen for the national stage was "The Wind and the Lion," an original composition entitled "Georgeassic Parks" written by music professor Jeff Holmes, percussion feature "Bill Bailey," and a complete show based on themes from the movie *Hook*. After extensive recruiting throughout the fall, the drill holes were finally filled, and on November 11, the band left for BOA, stopping for a rehearsal and an overnight in Ohio. In Indianapolis, the band rehearsed in the Indianapolis Hoosier Dome, and the drum majors taped college hash marks onto the Astroturf with silver duct tape.

The next day, the band performed in front of 30,000 marching band fans, and eight-year-old Mary Elizabeth Geehern, niece of band member Anne Trotman '94, stole the show when she sang "When You're All Alone" during the "Hook" show. After ending with percussion feature "Bill Bailey," complete with vocalists and a stage band, an appreciative audience applauded for the band. The Minuteman Band made its mark in the marching band world. Afterward, Parks said, "It was one of the most gratifying performances in the seventeen years I've been at UMass. The entire band represented UMass in grand style."

During the fall, the Mussari-Loftus film producers set about creating a documentary about the Minuteman Band and recorded how the group prepared for the BOA trip. Anthony Mussari and Kitch Loftus first created a band-related documentary in 1992 entitled *Leader of the Band*, which chronicled Parks and Dr. Tim Lautzenheiser teaching high school students to be positive leaders and role models. Mussari referred to Parks as an "incredibly impressive miracle man who uses music to help people develop leadership skills," and the new documentary focused on how the band built character in band members. Building character is an important aspect of the Minuteman Band, which is often highlighted by the way in which band members deal with crisis. That

Tony Mussari films *Building Power and Class* while Michael Coogan directs the stage band.

season, as the band left to perform at the New England Patriots-Detroit Lions game, the drumline bus broke down right outside campus. Within twenty minutes, students and equipment were redistributed among the remaining five buses, and the group continued its trip to Foxboro Stadium. The band arrived on time and played a halftime show of "The Wind and the Lion" and "Bill Bailey" to the pleased football audience.

In March 1994, after an exciting fall season, the Minuteman Hoop Band traveled to the A-10 Tournament at the Philadelphia Palestra. After winning in Philadelphia, the team returned to Amherst to face the Temple Owls in the championship game. UMass Band alumna Heidi Sarver, now the Temple University band director, brought up the Temple Hoop Band, and the two hoop bands enjoyed playing across the arena to each other. During the hard fought game, it became apparent to Parks that the UMass students might rush onto the court if UMass beat Temple, and he arranged to get Sarver and the Temple Band safely out of the Mullins Center. When UMass defeated Temple 70–59 to take the A-10 Championship title, students crashed the court, and although the Temple Band was safely evacuated, Parks was trampled by the celebrating students and had his foot broken.

After winning the tournament, UMass was awarded the second seed in the Midwest Regional for the NCAA Tournament, and thirty members of the Hoop Band flew to Wichita, Kansas. In the second round, after defeating Southwest Texas State, UMass faced Maryland and lost 95–87. It was a strong run for the UMass basketball team. Additional season highlights for the Hoop Band included playing at the wedding reception of the university's president Michael Hooker and State Rep. Carmen Buell, performing at the Basketball Banquet in April, and playing for Massachusetts legislators at the State House in Boston.

George Parks and Thom Hannum receive the key to Wilkes-Barre, Pennsylvania.

After many years of dedicated service to the university, the Minuteman Band and its director were honored for their accomplishments. On April 25, 1994, Chancellor O'Brien, a strong supporter and good friend of the band, presented the Chancellor's Medal for Distinguished Service to George N. Parks and the band during the University Concert Band Concert. It was the university's highest honor and was "bestowed on those who rendered exemplary and extraordinary service to the University."

The fall 1994 band season was considered by many to be the "perfect year," since there was no rain or mud during any of the football games, and the weather stayed agreeable throughout the fall. Halftime shows consisted of themes from *Henry V*, "Non Nobis Domine" with vocalist Greg Silverman, percussion feature "Blue Rondo a la Turk," a Gloria Estefan medley with vocalist Beth Ayn Curtis '92, and "The Stars and Stripes Forever."

At Band Camp, an old tradition was revived, and the band held a post-Band Camp barbeque for band members, family, and friends. The Minuteman Band gave its first performance and afterward nearly 1,000 people gathered for a cookout sponsored by the band's service organizations, Tau Beta Sigma and Kappa Kappa Psi.

A new tradition started with the creation of the Colonial Honor Guard. Dressed in authentic period uniforms, the guard marched at the head of the Minuteman Band, and along with the ROTC colorguard, presented the colors during pregame. Although no longer an active sponsor of the band

Drum major Richard Johnson and young band fans at the Wilkes-Barre exhibition.

Tony Mussari joins in with the Minuteman Band while Kerstin Becker '96 conducts.

A brochure for *Building Power and Class.*

program, the military department and band continued to honor their long history together.

At President Hooker's request, the band traveled to Boston to kick off the "Americorps" program and played for various dignitaries, including Sen. Ted Kennedy. The band also traveled to the October 22 Delaware game and stopped off at the Six Flags Great Adventure amusement park in New Jersey on the way home. In November, after the band sold $25,000 worth of magazines, Parks took his last swim in the Campus Pond. After losing a bet made with band members, he said, "The University takes good care of us, but you can never get all the funding you need."

One of the highlights for the season was the Minuteman Band's trip to King's College in Wilkes-Barre, Pennsylvania, for the screening of the Mussari-Loftus documentary *Building Power and Class.* After the documentary received a standing ovation from hundreds of viewers, the mayor of Wilkes-Barre gave Parks the key to the city, and the Minuteman Band gave a command performance in the center of town. The concert ended with "The Stars and Stripes Forever" and "My Way," as band members pulled filmmakers Tony Mussari and Kitch Loftus into their ranks.

At the end of the marching band season, it became tradition for the senior band members to "kidnap" the director and associate director and take them to dinner. This fall's kidnapping surpassed all previous years', as Parks and Hannum were flown off the field in a waiting helicopter. As an added gift for the directors, who were watching from high above, the band members performed "Rocky Point Holiday."

Basketball season began, and Calipari praised the Hoop Band, saying that it contributed to the home court advantage. He added, "We've got the number one fans in America, and as far as I'm concerned, we've got the number one Hoop Band as well. They energize both our players and our fans." Other sources agreed about the Hoop Band's energetic performances. A February *Massachusetts Daily Collegian* article stated that the Hoop Band promoted audience support and played a wider variety of music than just the school and fight songs. Due to the basketball team's success, Hannum was able to recruit a larger number of jazz musicians from the music department, which allowed the band to play standards and songs like "In the Mood," "Jumpin' at the Woodside," CBS's "Road to the Final Four," and "Sanford and Son." Hannum added, "My goal is to build the best hoop band in the country. Taking that approach lets us keep up with the basketball team. When people in the audience see the band, they see the University and I think we do a good job. We try to have the best hoop band in the country."

In March 1995, after UMass beat Temple 63–44 to win the A-10 Championship four years in a row, the Hoop Band traveled to Albany, New York, for the NCAA Tournament. UMass beat St. Peter's and Stanford in the first and second rounds and headed to the Meadowlands in New Jersey for the third and fourth rounds. UMass defeated Tulsa to join the Elite Eight, and after a strong run, the Minutemen bowed out of the tournament, losing to Oklahoma State 68–54. It was an exciting season for both the team and its band.

A new addition to the Minuteman Band's professional staff was Hermie Malone, who was hired as the band's new secretary in the late spring. Malone was responsible for bookkeeping and general finances, and she recalled that there is "always an air of activity in the band office, especially in the two hours before band rehearsal, when drill needs to be copied, as well as music, and there are people running around getting things ready."

In the fall of 1995, Michael J. Klesch, who had arranged music for the band for a number of years, also joined the band's professional staff and became the new assistant band director. It was the first time that the school's band had three teaching professionals assigned to it. During their undergraduate years, all three Minuteman Band directors had been part of the West Chester University "Incomparable" Golden Rams Marching Band, under the direction of James R. Wells.

Music for the Minuteman Band season included "El Boro," a Phil Collins medley, themes from *E.T.*, and "The Circle of Life" with the student group "A Cafellas" as guest soloists. The Minuteman Band also released its first CD, entitled *Dreams from Neverland*, which featured music from the 1991 through the 1994 marching seasons.

On November 5, the band traveled to Boston and performed at the opening of the Reggie Lewis Center, where President Hooker presided over the festivities. The band also performed at a United States Scholastic Band

Michael J. Klesch

Michael J. Klesch was born on February 6, 1962, in Johnstown, Pennsylvania. In 1986, he graduated from West Chester University and joined the Minuteman Band as a graduate teaching assistant. After receiving his master's degree, he became the fine arts director for Nazareth Academy in Rochester, New York. In 1995, he returned to UMass and became the Minuteman Band's assistant director.

Klesch, who serves in the role of music arranger, is one of the band's most prolific writers. For the Minuteman Band, he arranged music from *Les Miserables, The Phantom of the Opera, Henry V, Hook, E.T., The Wind and the Lion, Silverado, West Side Story*, and The Who's *Tommy*. In addition to arranging music for the Minuteman Band, Klesch has also written for the Cadets of Bergen County and the Crossmen Drum and Bugle Corps.

The Minuteman Band's marching percussion section is known for its excellence.

Association show at the Meadowlands in New Jersey, and after a night on a gym floor, the group left for Boston for the November 11 UMass-Boston University game. After the equipment truck lost its way, the band was delayed. The group arrived at the game right before halftime, and band members got off the buses in full uniform and performed their halftime show.

The Hoop Band geared up for a tremendously exciting basketball season. On December 9, UMass and Boston College met at Boston's Fleet Center for the Commonwealth Classic game, and the band traveled in near-blizzard conditions to cheer on the team. The game was broadcast nationally on CBS, and a crowd of nearly 19,000 watched live as UMass defeated the BC Eagles 65–57.

In March 1996, the Minutemen traveled to Philadelphia's Civic Center for the Atlantic-10 Tournament, where the Hoop Band cheered the team on to win the A-10 Tournament Championship. Next was the NCAA Tournament, which had the Minutemen as the number one seed in the East. For the first two rounds of the NCAA Tournament, the band traveled to Rhode Island, where the team defeated Central Florida and Stanford at the Providence Civic Center. The next two rounds took the team and band to Georgia, and band members were excited to fly to Atlanta, where they stayed in a beautiful atrium-style downtown hotel. After defeating Arkansas and Georgetown, UMass advanced to the Final Four for the first time. The campus went wild with "Minutemania."

There was "sheer electricity" surrounding the March 30 UMass-Kentucky Final Four game in the Meadowlands. Marty Dobrow, in his book *Going Bigtime*, wrote that the UMass section was filled with dignitaries including

Minuteman Hoop Band

The earliest recorded appearance of the Minuteman Hoop Band occurred in December 1921, when band members created a group to play for winter basketball games. By 1942, the Massachusetts State College Band was playing at basketball games and was credited with generating "much morale." After several years of inactivity, in 1954, the Varsity Pep Band was revitalized. In 1958, the pep band became an officially recognized student organization and played at basketball games.

Throughout the 1970s, the pep band was a vital force in supporting the basketball team. Coach Jack Leaman said, "A large percent of school spirit in the basketball program is accomplished with the help of the pep band. The crowd, aided by the band, really gets into the game. And because of it, my players get their adrenaline pumping a little faster, making them concentrate more on the game." In the spring of 1973, the pep band supported the team in the National Invitational Tournament in New York City. The University Pep Band was also active in the spring of 1977 and went to the tournament at the Philadelphia Spectrum, where the UMass basketball team beat Rutgers. Afterward, the band faded for a few years.

In 1980, the Minuteman Hoop Band was revitalized under the direction of George Parks. When Thom Hannum was hired in 1984, one of his new responsibilities was to direct the Hoop Band. Before the Mullins Center was built, the Hoop Band performed in the Curry Hicks Cage, and when the cheering became particularly intense, the paint from the Cage's ceiling would flake off and fall onto the basketball court.

One of the highlights of the Hoop Band's career was during the early 1990s, when John Calipari's team and the "Refuse to Lose" attitude swept through the UMass campus. Before it was over, the Minutemen had won several Atlantic-10 tournaments, received various bids to the NCAA Tournament, and had been ranked number one in the nation. In 1996, UMass made it to the Final Four of the NCAA Tournament, before falling to Kentucky.

The current Hoop Band uses a jazz band set-up with saxophones, trumpets, trombones, and a rhythm section, performing standard big band jazz arrangements as well as rip-roaring crowd pleasers such as "Hey!" Other favorite songs include the band's theme song "Big Noise from Winnetka," "Road to the Final Four," "Sanford and Son," "Blues Brothers Opener," "ESPN College Hoops," "Gimme Some Lovin'," and "Slammin'." In 1996, the Hoop Band released a CD entitled *Refuse to Lose*, with popular tracks featuring jazz, rock, and fight song favorites.

Julius Erving '72, university president William Bulger, former President Hooker, State Sen. Stan Rosenberg, Sen. Ted Kennedy, and national security adviser Anthony Lake. After an overwhelming and emotionally draining game, where band members and UMass fans cheered themselves hoarse, the UMass Minutemen fell to the Kentucky Wildcats 81–74. On the court, the players hugged each other, as did Calipari and his mentor, former UMass point guard and Kentucky coach, Rick Pitino. A drained Calipari said of the UMass team, "We refused to lose. We never stopped playing. We played right down to the end. And I'm proud of them." It was the most successful year for basketball at the University of Massachusetts.

Later in the spring, in a show of appreciation for the Minuteman Band program and its support of the football and basketball programs, Chancellor David Scott invited all 320 band members to have lunch at the chancellor's house on campus. Scott, a great friend of the Minuteman Band, often visited rehearsals to watch the group in action and was an avid and vibrant supporter.

Over the summer, Calipari and basketball star Marcus Camby left UMass. Calipari accepted the position of coach for the New Jersey Nets, and Camby, surrounded by controversy resulting from his accepting gifts from agents, turned pro and was chosen by the NBA Toronto Raptors. The basketball glory years of "Coach Cal" ended.

The fall of 1996 found the Minuteman Band preparing for the first annual

Steve Pollino, David Purdy, and Mike Verrastro warm up for a performance.

College Marching Band Exhibition in Allentown, Pennsylvania, hosted by West Chester University's band. To make a strong statement and to have the right music in place, the Minuteman Band brought back past successes "Gloria," "Silverado," "The Stars and Stripes Forever," and "Canto del Viento." In September, marching bands from the Northeast and the Mid-Atlantic states performed at the Allentown exhibition, including those from the University of Delaware, West Chester University, Boston University, and the University of Massachusetts. The Minuteman Band performed last and gave a truly outstanding performance that had thousands of marching band fans on their feet. It was one of the group's finest shows.

In designing a marching band show, it is critical to choose the right music because it is the "little things" that make shows special and magical. Minuteman Band favorites such as "Alexander's Ragtime Band" and "Gloria" were brought back when no other music fit or to bolster a weakness in the current show. Parks said, "As a supplement to outstanding band performance, I will incorporate amplification, vocalists, guitars, cartoon characters in costume, sword fighters, pretty little eight-year-old nieces singing about Peter Pan, masks, balloons, word formations, disappearing chair acts, fire extinguishers, shields printed with "Massachusetts" and "The Right Stuff," Can Can dancers, cannons, New York skylines, Dance Steps (the same ones . . . year after year, if necessary), recorders, and even tuba players riding unicycles. Anything, if it will get someone to sit up, stop talking, notice a band performance, and feel something."

A highlight of the fall season was the band's November 3 performance for President Bill Clinton in Springfield, Massachusetts. At the request of the White House, the band played at the Clinton-Kerry rally before Election Day. After the Secret Service inspected instruments and equipment, the band gave a short concert for President Clinton, Sen. John Kerry, Rep. John Olver, and 25,000 rally supporters. *The Worcester Telegram* reported that Kerry "drew a roar from the University of Massachusetts Marching Band" as he said, "I've decided to borrow the motto of UMass and Refuse to Lose." In addition, Timothy Volpe '00 recalled that President Clinton honored the band by saying, "And finally, I'd like to thank the Minuteman Marching Band. I'll tell you what, these are the best sound effects I've ever seen. If I had another plane I'd take them with me."

On November 16, after fifty years of history, the final game of the Yankee Conference took place between UMass and UConn. In a game entitled "The Miracle at McGuirk," a last-minute touchdown pass pushed UMass to a 39–38 victory in the greatest comeback the school had ever had. In the history of the Yankee Conference, the UMass football team won more league titles (17) and games (160) than any other conference member.

The Minuteman Band performs for President Clinton.

In the spring of 1997, the Minuteman Band received devastating news. The bell tower of Old Chapel was on the brink of collapse, and the band needed to vacate the building immediately so that repairs could begin. Over the course of a few days, students and directors moved more than forty years of band history out of the building and into storage containers. It was a heart-breaking time. Old Chapel had been home to the Massachusetts Band since the 1960s, and the band was its longest tenant. Without the building as a base of operations, everything was in disarray, including uniforms, which had to be moved to off-campus storage units.

After the loss of Old Chapel, the fall of 1997 was slated to be one of the Minuteman Band's most difficult seasons. However, band manager Joel Whalen '98, echoing the determination of the band members, said, "This year's season poses some interesting challenges. But as usual the band will rise to the occasion and, as always, put on a great show for the

The Old Chapel Home of the Minuteman Band

Old Chapel, the band's beloved home.

fans." The band members met the challenge, and the fall was one of the marching band's most successful seasons. After five days of Band Camp, band members surpassed all expectations and learned eighty pages of drill in addition to five pieces of music.

Parks felt that it was time for the Minuteman Band to see one of the best bands in the country. The schedule had UMass playing James Madison University on September 20, and the JMU Band was considered one of the top four marching groups in the country. No one took a band into the JMU stadium and attempted to match the 440-member Royal Dukes Band. The Minuteman Band arrived at the night game, and five minutes before halftime,

Old Chapel

12-A   1918

Old Chapel in 1918.

Old Chapel, one of the most striking features of the University of Massachusetts' campus, "has character like nowhere else on campus." The building, first known as the "new stone chapel" and later as the chapel-library, has long been a vibrant and essential center for student activities.

Construction started in 1884, and for many years, Chapel served as both a student meeting space and a library. In the 1910s, baseball games were held on the Varsity Field, with third base in front of Chapel's front door. The building was renovated in the 1930s, and by 1932, the chapel-library contained over 90,000 volumes. When the new Goodell Library opened in 1935, Old Chapel, the building's new name, became the headquarters for the Division of Social Sciences. Two bronze plaques in the lower hall of Old Chapel told that the clock was a gift of the class of 1892. The illumination of the clock was a gift of the class of

1910, and the chime was a gift of Bernard H. Smith.

Although Old Chapel was no longer a library, the October 1937 *Alumni Bulletin* wrote, "The grand old building mirrored in the pond continued to be the most beautiful and characteristic feature of the campus." By 1956, the growing music department, which was housed in Memorial Hall, was out of room and needed a new building. East Experiment Station was considered, as was Clark Hall, but Doric Alviani thought that Old Chapel, as a traditional building with the historical practice of "bells in the belfry," would be a more appropriate home. When Bartlett Hall was built for the English department, it moved and vacated Chapel in 1960, and the music department moved in to await construction of the new Fine Arts Center. Helen Perry, music department secretary, recalled that in 1964, the music department moved into trailers by the library and later into Machmer Hall. However, due to lack of space, the marching band remained in Old Chapel. When the Fine Arts Center opened in 1975, the music department moved into its new headquarters. However, the department had grown too large, so various groups, including the marching band, found that there wasn't enough space for them in the new center.

From 1960 until 1997, Old Chapel was the home of the University of Massachusetts Marching Band. Over the entry doors, one could once read the words, "Through These Doors Walk the Power and Class of New England." For nearly four decades, thousands of students put on the maroon-and-white or the red-and-black uniform of the UMass Band. A number of band members spent more time in Old Chapel than in their dorms, and many found, upon graduating, that it was harder to walk away from Old Chapel than it was to leave the university. In the spring of 1997, the Minuteman Band was

The drill hall, Old Chapel, and the bandstand, c. 1890s.

An ivy-covered Old Chapel forms the backdrop for the school's songs.

forced to vacate its home. Old Chapel, the site of so much vibrancy in the past, now sits alone, dark and deserted.

The Delaware Connection

The Minuteman and Delaware Bands share a great friendship.

The marching bands of the University of Massachusetts and the University of Delaware share a special bond. It began in the 1970s, when Minuteman Band director George Parks made his debut as a high school drum major at Delaware's Band Day. He later marched in the Delaware Band, and his first and last performances as drum major of the West Chester University Marching Band were in Delaware Stadium. Parks recalled that over the years, many of the Minuteman Bands' most memorable shows have taken place in Delaware Stadium.

During the fall of 1994, University of Delaware president David Roselle made a monumental decision and gave his full support to developing the Delaware Marching Band Program. Soon thereafter, Temple University band director Heidi Sarver, a former Minuteman Band drum major, became the new director of the University of Delaware Fightin' Blue Hen Band. Jim Ancona, a percussionist and UMass Band alumnus, became the group's assistant director. The Delaware Band soon grew from less than 120 students to over three hundred. Even after becoming director of the Delaware Band, Sarver continued her involvement with the UMass Band, writing the drill for such classic Minuteman Band shows as "Silverado," "Batman," "Robin Hood," "Bill Bailey," "The Wind and the Lion," "Henry V," "West Side Story," and "Tommy."

Today, the Fightin' Blue Hens have one of the nation's newest and fastest growing marching bands. The Minuteman Band and the Delaware Band are great friends, sharing a strong camaraderie and often visiting each other's stadiums during the football season.

it rained heavily. The brand new sound system was out of commission, and vocalists Nate Altimari and Greg Silverman sang "Pinball Wizard" through a bullhorn. In the soft opening of the "Tommy" show, the James Madison fans shouted loudly, "We can't hear you!" However, when the Minuteman Band played the opening chord, the fans took notice, and after the postgame show, gave the band a respectable standing ovation.

For the October 25 Delaware game, Heidi Sarver, now director of the University of Delaware Fightin' Blue Hen Band, brought her group to Amherst. Both bands, numbering over six hundred red-and-black and blue-and-gold members, combined to perform "Pictures at an Exhibition," as Sarver played the trumpet solo.

After the loss of Old Chapel, the university remodeled Grinnell Arena for the Minuteman Band. At the Grinnell dedication ceremonies on December

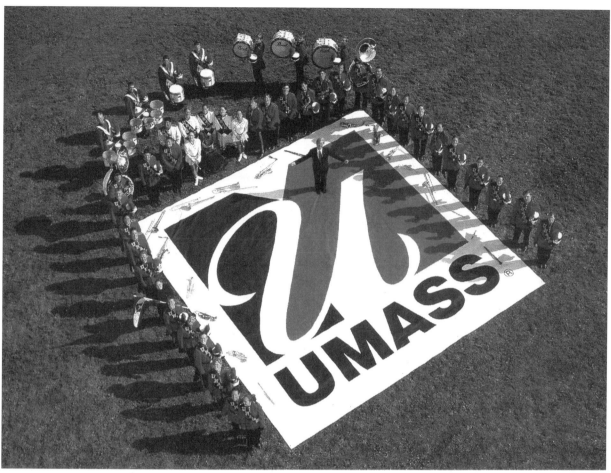

The Minuteman Band unveils the university's new logo.

21, 1997, Parks surprised the assembled students, faculty, and administration with the news that the Minuteman Band had just won the highest honor in the college marching band world. The group had been selected to receive the coveted Sudler Trophy, and he said, "For now and forever more, you are part of one of the greatest marching bands of all time." Stan Rosenberg, a Massachusetts state senator since 1991 and a former Massachusetts Band tuba player, added, "The people of this Commonwealth should be proud to have this jewel in its crown." Although the band had lost Old Chapel, it was now recognized as one of the nation's most outstanding college marching bands.

For the spring of 1998, both the UMass men's and women's basketball teams were invited to participate in the NCAA Tournament, and two hoop bands were formed to accompany the teams. Hannum took one band to the men's tournament in Atlanta, and Parks took the second band to the women's tournament in Iowa City. Although both teams played well, the UMass men lost to St. Louis, and the UMass women lost to Iowa.

Band Camp 1998 was off to a strong start as 140 freshmen tried out for the Minuteman Band, and music for the season included selections from *West*

Joseph Contino, George Parks, William Bulger, and John Jenkins look on as Col. John Bourgeois awards the Sudler Trophy to the Minuteman Band.

Side Story and the rock group Chicago. The band was honored when it was chosen to unveil the new University logo and was featured on the cover of *UMass Magazine*. The group also embarked on its first international performance, when the Canadian Football League's Montreal Alouettes invited the group to perform during halftime for the September 13 Montreal-Hamilton game. In McGill University's Molson Stadium, more than 350 band members performed for 18,000 enthusiastic Canadian football fans.

The annual Delaware game took place during Band Camp, so the UMass Band was not able to take its customary trip to see the Delaware Band. However, Sarver and the Delaware Band invited the UMass Band to come to Newark, and the bands shared halftime during Delaware's October 3 game with Northeastern University. The solid friendship between the two groups was evident.

On October 10, Band Day, the Minuteman Band received its highest honor. William Bulger, president of UMass, and Col. John Bourgeois, former director of the "President's Own" Marine Band and president of the John Philip Sousa Foundation, awarded the Sudler Trophy to director George N. Parks, associate director Thomas P. Hannum, and assistant director Michael J. Klesch. Eighty high school bands, hundreds of band alumni, and 14,000 fans were in attendance as the Minuteman Marching Band took its place among the top groups of the college marching band world. The tremendous honor spoke to over 125 years of college band excellence at the university. Colonel Bourgeois commented that the Minuteman Band "exhibits a great deal in practice, dedication, and in maintaining a great spirit, which adds a lot to the atmosphere of the college," and the Sudler Trophy presentation committee added that the group was one of the best bands they had heard.

Past and present band directors received Sudler Trophy plaques. Joseph Contino, Redmen Band director from 1950 to 1963, commented, "I think it's a tribute to the improvement of the band to this level of excellence in both sound and spectacle. The students go out and rehearse like crazy for which they don't get very much tangible credit, and this award is something they've really deserved." Parks added, "We have great respect for the contributions of all our athletic teams, and we're happy to contribute to the great quality that is going on there. I'm just so proud of the whole band and the contributions of the alumni who came back, for all of them really made the program what it really is. These kids will sleep on gym floors, eat stale donuts, and do anything they can to make a great band. These are the most dedicated and most committed students anyone could ask for."

After the Band Day game and presentation, nearly one thousand band alumni and friends met in the Mullins Center for the Sudler Trophy Celebration Banquet. In addition, Chancellor Scott announced his intention to create a chancellor's task force to look at continued support for the Minuteman Band program. Preliminary plans were unveiled for an addition to Grinnell Arena that would include a rehearsal hall, practice rooms, offices, and a band music library, at an estimated cost of $3 million.

The UMass football team also had a strong season and was crowned Atlantic-10 Champion. The team went on to the playoffs, and after beating McNeese State, Lehigh, and Northwestern State, the Minutemen advanced to the NCAA Division I-AA Championship Game against Georgia Southern University. Although Parks had been told that the band would be able to go with the team for postseason play, he received a phone call telling him that there was no funding available. Rob Luhrs '99, who was at Parks' house when the "no-go" call came in, felt that after the band's and team's outstanding seasons, something had to be done. He drove to Chancellor Scott's house and knocked on his door. After Luhrs and Scott talked, the chancellor decided that it was only right for the band to accompany the team to the playoffs.

Sudler Trophy

The Louis C. Sudler Trophy.

One of the Minuteman Band's greatest honors came in 1998, when it was awarded the Sudler Trophy in recognition of its ranking as the best college marching band in the nation.

"The purpose of the Sudler Trophy is to identify and recognize collegiate marching bands of particular excellence which have made outstanding contributions to the American way of life. The Sudler Trophy is awarded annually to a college or university marching band which has demonstrated the highest of musical standards and innovative marching routines and ideas, and which has made important contributions to the advancement of the performance standards of college marching bands over a period of several years."

The trophy is given out annually by the John Philip Sousa Foundation, and only sixteen other university bands, including those from the University of Michigan and Ohio State University, have previously won this award.

1982 University of Michigan
1983 University of Illinois
1984 Ohio State University
1985 Florida A&M University
1986 University of Texas
1987 University of Oklahoma
1988 Michigan State University
1989 University of Kansas
1990 University of Iowa
1991 Arizona State University
1992 Northwestern University
1993 UCLA
1994 James Madison University
1995 Purdue University
1996 University of Nebraska
1997 West Virginia University
1998 University of Massachusetts

The next day, Parks received a call saying that the Minuteman Band was cleared to go to the December 19 game in Chattanooga, Tennessee. It was the marching band's first plane trip since the 1964 Tangerine Bowl, and the students flew overnight and landed early in the morning. After one-and-one-half-hours of sleep, the Minuteman Band arrived at Finley Stadium, where the six hundred-member UMass contingent was heckled by a full crowd of 20,000 with classic cheers like "Yankees Go Home," to which the band responded once with "Who Won the War?" before being quieted by Parks. Head football coach Mark Whipple recalled that at first the UMass team felt a little uneasy and overwhelmed in the foreign stadium, until the bright red, 320-member Minuteman Band entered the stadium and sparked up the team. The band members cheered their hearts out. When the game ended, the UMass football team had defeated the top-rated Georgia Southern University Eagles 55–43 and became the NCAA Division I-AA National Champions. It was a tremendous accomplishment. Afterward, the band flew back to Amherst, where the football goal posts had been torn down by celebrating students and dragged through campus. The entire Tennessee band trip occurred in less than twenty-four hours, and the campus now possessed not only the year's top college band, but also a group of NCAA football champions.

In the fall of 1999, President Bulger made the announcement that he planned to give the Minuteman Band $140,000 for new band uniforms. Robert Connolly, vice-president of the university, said that the Minuteman Band is "the number one band in the nation and their hard work and achievement deserves to be recognized." Parks added that the current uniforms were nearly twenty years old, older than many of the freshmen and sophomores currently marching in the band. With the help of Bob Goodhue from the President's office, work on the new uniform design began.

The band's halftime show that season centered on music from the movie *Zorro*, complete with a duel between the hero and his evil counterpart. Additional pieces included "In the Stone" and "Mambo Swing." On band trips, the 320-member band performed at a USSBA show in Giants Stadium and at the Allentown Exhibition.

In December, after two years of work, Old Chapel's steeple was successfully restored. At first this appeared to be good news for the band, but because the license to occupy the building had expired, Old Chapel was now considered "condemned." In order for it to be reoccupied, issues such as fire codes, handicapped accessibility, the obsolete heating system, and roof replacement had to be addressed. The band was heartbroken when it found out it would not be allowed to move back into Old Chapel. Instead, the group was moved into the University Apartments complex, another condemned section of buildings. With the band's instruments, uniforms, and other equipment, Grinnell Arena was inadequate for storage and was too small to house the full band.

On campus, the question of what to do with Old Chapel continued, and the first of three forums on the future of the building was held in February 2000. Some in attendance felt that the building was a historic campus fixture and should be preserved. Assistant director Michael Klesch mentioned that, except for the Minuteman Band, all other Chapel occupants had moved from the building to better quarters. The band, however, had "simply been evicted." The forums and debates continued, and the Minuteman Band remained without a home.

In the fall of 2000, music for the season included band standards such as "Malaguena," "The 1812 Overture," and "The Wind and the Lion." Following the November 4 Homecoming game against Villanova, the band performed in front of Old Chapel at the Time Capsule 2000 internment ceremony. The capsule was sealed in the Old Chapel crypt until 2100, and it was the first time that most current band members were allowed inside Old Chapel.

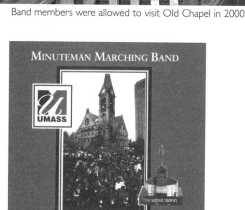

Band members were allowed to visit Old Chapel in 2000.

Somewhere . . . and Other Favorites band CD.

The Delaware Band visited for the November 11 UMass-Delaware game, which happened to fall on Veterans' Day. In a show of intercollegiate friendship, the two bands put together a combined Veterans' Day show, consisting of "Salute to the Armed Forces," "The Stars and Stripes Forever," and "God Bless the USA," sung by soloist Heather Ikonen. Parks recalled that a week after the band performed the Veterans' Show, complete with vocalists and amplification, a member of the campus community came to him and, with great emotion, thanked Parks and the band. His wife's father was killed in the Pacific during World War II, and she had never had the opportunity to meet him. After watching the Veterans' Day halftime performance, she spoke to him for the first time about having never met her father. The Veterans' show and "God Bless the USA" became staples in the Minuteman Band's repertoire for the next few years.

The band released its second CD in December. Produced by Grammy-nominated recording engineer Jeff Harrison, *Somewhere . . . and Other Favorites* featured a variety of band music from recent seasons and included "The Stars and Stripes Forever," "The 1812 Overture," "West Side Story," and "Tommy."

Continuing its tradition of performing at presidential ceremonies, the Minuteman Band was invited to march in the January 20, 2001, Inaugural Parade. State support for the band was strong, and Massachusetts' governor Paul Cellucci said, "We are proud that the UMass Minuteman Marching Band will represent the University and the Commonwealth in the Presidential

Inaugural Parade." The cost of the Inaugural trip was estimated at over $80,000. $40,000 was provided by President Bulger's office, and the remaining cost was covered by the Alumni Association, athletics, and gift funds from the campus.

Parks recalled that in getting the Minuteman Band ready for the parade, "We worked one of our best miracles." The band members returned to campus during winter break on January 17, had one day to prepare, and left the next day for Washington. On January 18, the band gave a concert at Baltimore's Harborplace Amphitheater. Susan Mattei '84G, alumni relations director, recalled that when the band played "The 1812 Overture," naval officer Richard Slingluff '00 had the guns of the *USS Constellation*, anchored in the harbor, fire in time to the music's cannon shots. Another concert, which was attended by Massachusetts' senator John Kerry, took place the next day in Washington's Farragut Square. After the band performed "The 1812 Overture" and "The Wind and the Lion," Senator Kerry thanked the group for its proud representation of Massachusetts.

The day of the Inaugural Parade dawned cold and rainy, and the band made a 7 a.m. security check at the Pentagon before stepping off at 3 p.m. During the parade, Kerstin Becker '96 recalled that the sea of red uniforms coming down Pennsylvania Avenue with the Capitol Building behind the band was "a sight to behold." The day before the parade, Parks had stepped off the distance to ensure that "God Bless the USA" would be playing as the Minuteman Band approached the reviewing stand. During the parade, the timing worked out perfectly, and as the band passed in review, both President George Bush and Vice President Dick Cheney rose. Although the UMass Band was not the biggest group in the parade, alumni felt it had a presence and sound that some of the bigger bands seemed to lack. The *Boston Globe* reported that the Minuteman Band "did the state proud." The band received additional coverage in the *Boston Herald* and the *Washington Post*, as well as on the "Today Show," C-SPAN, and CNN. UMass news director Barbara Pitoniak said, "You could never put a price tag on this kind of positive publicity for the campus. We're delighted that the band's participation in the Inaugural Parade generated so much interest across the state and even across the nation." In addition, the band was presented with a certificate of appreciation by Rep. John Olver's chief of staff, Hunter Ridgway, and Olver entered the group in the *Congressional Record* on January 30.

After the highly successful and celebrated Inaugural Parade, Chancellor Scott stated that the band was important not only to the Department of Music and Dance and the College of Humanities and Fine Arts, but also to athletics in general and to an array of outreach and ambassadorial activities for the entire university. He added, "In the light of the past and recent successes and of the visibility of the marching band under the leadership of director George Parks and his staff, this is an appropriate time to conduct a study on the future." Parks felt that the time had come to show that the Minuteman Marching Band was clearly deserving of stable university funding, since the band was currently at a crossroads. Whatever happened, the band would not remain the same. In February 2001, a chancellor's task force was convened to report on the band's future, with a wide range of issues on the table, including funding, facilities, admissions, and recruitment.

In the spring, the band's new maroon-and-white uniforms arrived, remodeled in the university's traditional colors. The old uniform's shako, sash, and cape were maintained as part of the new look. The new white coats were accented by maroon-and-gold highlights, and new maroon sashes kept the traditional "UMASS" lettering. The black pants had maroon stripes on either side and were held up with suspenders. In addition, the maroon-and-white shakos came with two plumes, a white feathered one for sunny weather and a white plastic one for rainy days. The uniform was designed on two levels. From the viewing stands, the outfit presented a sharp and simple appearance. Up close, a myriad of details were visible, from the gold braid and the UMass lettering to the "Power and Class" logo on the sleeve. The final touch was the two lapel pins, similar to those found on a military uniform. The first pin read, "Energy—Enthusiasm—Excellence. UMMB. Minuteman Marching Band." The second pin read, "Eyes With Pride—Sudler 1998" with Old Chapel in the center. Parks recalled that a great deal of thought went into designing the new look.

The tuba section traditionally blocks traffic as the Minuteman Band parades to the stadium on game days.

In July, the chancellor's task force report was released, and it was a welcome show of university financial support for the band. One of the main elements of the report involved the creation of a new band building, since Old Chapel would not be habitable in the near future. Phase one of the building project called for the expansion of Grinnell Arena; after three building phases were complete, the band would have space in excess of 13,000 square feet. To aid with recruiting and membership retention for the band program, the report also recommended that the band be given ten leadership-based and fifty talent-based Chancellor's Talent Awards. In addition, the band's budget, facilities, and general university-wide mission were reassigned from the music department to the chancellor's office. However, although the task force report attempted to put the school's band on solid footing, due to budget cuts at the university and other obstacles, the report has yet to be put into full effect.

The fall of 2001 marked a strong start for the Minuteman Band. In a September 9 e-mail to band alumni, Parks wrote, "I am happy to say that the most important thing is that the band is off to one of the best starts ever. In the midst of all potential concerns that this program always seems to have,

Power and Class

In the fall of 1981, Parks wanted to take the Minuteman Band to the University of Delaware away game, so band members supplemented the travel budget by selling bumper stickers. Since the group needed a logo for the stickers, a mascot was created for various band items, and drum major Linda Paul '82 came up with the band's beloved "Herman." Over the years, Herman, a saluting figure who wore the group's red uniform, grew into the Minuteman Band's beloved icon.

With the arrival of the band's new uniforms in 2001, Herman was renamed Norman, in honor of Parks' father, and took to wearing the new maroon-and-white marching band uniform.

funding, facilities, departmental and university politics, and any number of other issues that seem to come up from time to time, the most important concern—the only one really—is always creating a great experience for those who are in the mud and heat from 4:40–6:00 every day throughout the fall, selling magazines, sleeping on gym floors and creating the finest college band performances in the region."

The first home football game, and the debut of the Minuteman Band's new uniforms, was scheduled for the night of September 15. Then the world changed on September 11. The game was canceled, and students and faculty members struggled for answers after the World Trade Center collapse. The band instead traveled to the University of Delaware for the weekend of September 21–23 and performed with the Delaware Band at its Band Day. The Minuteman Band's new uniforms had their debut in Delaware Stadium. At the end of the game, the two bands combined, and the six hundred-member maroon-and-white and blue-and-gold band played "God Bless the USA" for the 22,000-member audience. It was an overwhelming moment for the entire stadium as the crowd rose en masse and sang along with the bands.

After the Delaware trip, the Minuteman Band traveled to Indiana in November and performed at the Bands of America Grand National Championships as one of the exhibition bands. The highly popular 1997 "Tommy" show, which was ready to be performed by the end of Band Camp, was revived for the performance because "it would work for the BOA audience." In the RCA Hoosier Dome, during a spectacular performance, the band received five standing ovations from a highly knowledgeable group of 30,000 marching band enthusiasts. "The UMass Minuteman Marching Band is truly one of the finest marching bands in the nation," said the executive director of Bands of America, Scott McCormick. "I have rarely seen such an overwhelming reaction to a band by the band students and families in the audience as I saw and heard at Grand Nationals during the UMass Band's performance." Parks added, "It was a remarkable achievement for the band and a feather in the UMass cap."

Heather Ikonen and the Minuteman Band perform on the *Marching for Freedom* CDs.

After September 11, a number of college bands came together to create music to remember the tragedy. Parks announced in April 2002 that the Minuteman Band was included on the first of a series of compact discs entitled *Marching for Freedom: Music of the American Spirit*, honoring those lost on September 11. All net profits of the CDs, which were produced by Jeff Harvey of Emphatic Music, an independent record label in Valley Forge, Pennsylvania, were donated to the Salvation Army. By November, three volumes of *Marching for Freedom: Music of the American Sprit* were released, and the Minuteman Band was featured on all three, performing "God Bless the USA" on volume 1, "The 1812 Overture" on volume 2, and "El Boro" and "Cool" from *West Side Story* on volume 3.

In the fall of 2002, music from the movie *Gladiator* was the band's main halftime show, complete with Roman soldiers, gladiators, an evil emperor, and a singing empress. The "Gladiator" show, with its blend of music, movement, actors, visuals, and singers, came closest to the ideal show concept that the band was trying to achieve.

Parks reached a milestone that fall and celebrated his twenty-fifth year as

The band performs music from *Gladiator.*

Pregame starts in a block band formation.

Closeup of 2002 Minuteman Band trumpets.

director of the Minuteman Marching Band. At the October 12 Homecoming halftime show, the Band Alumni Association and former Massachusetts Band director John Jenkins presented Parks with an engraved silver cup, honoring him for his outstanding work and dedication. 250 band alumni performed during halftime, and the university's new chancellor, John Lombardi, marched along in the clarinet section. Later that evening, State Senator Rosenberg, Chancellor Lombardi, and Jenkins spoke at a reception held in Parks' honor. Rosenberg presented Parks with a citation issued by the Massachusetts legislature, and the gathered alumni, administrators, and friends applauded Parks nonstop for his many years of excellence.

In an additional season highlight, Patrick Sheridan, world-renowned tuba virtuoso and former soloist with the Marine Band, performed with the Minuteman Band during the October 19 Band Day. Sheridan thrilled the audience by playing the piccolo solo from "The Stars and Stripes Forever" on his tuba.

On November 2, the University of Delaware Band came to Amherst for the UMass-Delaware game. It was Delaware's dress rehearsal before performing at the Bands of America Grand National Championships in Indiana, where the Delaware Band, following the Minuteman Band's example, gave a command performance of its "Evita" show.

The Minuteman Band also traveled to Montreal and performed for 65,000 fans at the November 17 Montreal Alouettes-Toronto Argonauts football game. In the Montreal Olympic Stadium, the band crashed the stands for pregame, and the Canadians went wild. The band also played during the opening ceremonies for the Basketball Hall of Fame in Springfield, MA.

The fall 2003 season was one of the Minuteman Band's smoothest seasons. Musical selections included "Birdland," "The Legend of the One-Eyed Sailor," "El Boro," "Adagio" from Rodrigo's *Concierto de Aranjuez,* performed on english horn, Elton John's "Your Song," and "Y Tu Oye," a percussion feature based on Gloria Estefan songs.

On September 20, the band performed in exhibition at the Piscataway Superchief Marching Band Festival in New Jersey, before traveling to take part in the Allentown Intercollegiate Festival the following day. On September 27, Patrick Sheridan again entertained the Band Day audience when, dressed as a black-and-yellow bumblebee, he played "Flight of the Bumblebee" on tuba.

The UMass Band traveled to Delaware for the November 15 UMass-Delaware game, and after the game went into triple overtime, the Minutemen lost the hard-fought contest 51–45. Afterward, the Minuteman and Delaware Bands each presented their postgame shows before combining to play "God Bless the USA" for the assembled crowd.

The football team (10–2) finished its outstanding season and faced Colgate in the first round of NCAA I–AA playoffs. On November 29, Parks and a Minuteman Pep Band traveled to Hamilton, NY, to lend musical support to the team. Although the Minutemen fought bravely, the near-blizzard conditions shut down their offense, and UMass lost 19–7.

The 2003 Minuteman Band season ended with the traditional Merry Maple Celebration, and for the first time in years, there was snow on the ground.

Top left: Clarinetist Regina Shotwell '07 models the Minuteman Band's current uniform.
Center: The cheerleaders and football team charge into the stadium as the band plays.
Bottom right: Closeup of a 2002 Minuteman Band trumpet player.

INTO THE TWENTY-FIRST CENTURY

2003–

*ince the founding of Massachusetts Agricultural College in 1863, the drum corps and bands of the University of Massachusetts have performed and cheered for their fellow students and athletic teams, and they will continue to do so.

Fundraising for the Minuteman Band continues to be a concern, especially in these changing times, with public higher education in Massachusetts under intense scrutiny yet again. The chancellor's task force on the marching band created some improvements, including planning a state-of-the-art building for the band finally to call home. Since 1997, when Old Chapel was closed for renovations, the Minuteman Band, one of the most effective ambassadors of the University of Massachusetts, has been without a permanent headquarters.

chapter thirteen

Nevertheless, the marching band at the University of Massachusetts has traveled far, from its beginnings as an eleven-member drum corps to a full-fledged, 320-member nationally respected marching band. Whatever challenges lie in the future, one can be sure that the University of Massachusetts Minuteman Marching Band will rise to meet them.

Minuteman Band drum majors salute by Campus Pond.

"The essential elements of everything we do are choice, love, and passion." —George Parks

Over the past 27 years, I have had so many proud and extraordinary moments with the Minuteman Marching Band. Many of the most obvious center around performances of the band: our first "Rocky" at UConn's Stadium, the look on Michael Jendrysik's face during the opening notes of "Festive Overture" at our first MICCA, the audience blocking Linda Paul's path at Delaware Stadium because they wanted to hear more, the fireworks at the '81 Inaugural, the mysterious cloud covering the stadium during "Godspell," and Harvard Band members' jaws dropping during the opening of "Festive Overture." In addition, who can forget "Phantom!," Mary Elizabeth's solo at BOA '93, Tony Mussari's *Building Power and Class* premiere at King's College, the performance for President Clinton in Springfield, David Scott's assistance in obtaining a little plane ride for the band to Tennessee, the 2001 Inaugural and BOA performances, the crowd-roaring response from 60,000 in Montreal, and so many, many more. Of course, there are quite a few non-performance moments as well: "Banned in Boston," Jeff Poulton and Joel Gittle leading the band past the police line in Harvard Stadium, Newick's Lobster

House, The DC trip from H__L, exploding pumpkins, and swimming in the campus pond.

But some of the most important memories deal with the personal impact that we, that you who are former members, have had on others: the exciting moment when Gerry Grady received his band jacket, the look on Dick O'Brien's face as he conducted the Minuteman Band, and the induction of Bob Bertram into the UMMB Hall of Fame. I will never forget being on the field, about to receive the Sudler Trophy and speaking with President Bulger, when a small 8th grade trombonist approached me: "Sir, do you know where I belong? Can you help me?" President Bulger chuckled as I found the exact spot, among the 3500 others, where this young lad belonged.

Among my most treasured memories are those times when we brought back John Jenkins and Joe Contino to conduct the Minuteman and Alumni Bands. It was their band—their tradition—that I, along with Thom, Michael, Heidi, Dave and others, had the honor of continuing. And as the years have passed, the importance of this has continued to grow. It meant a great deal to me to get a picture of the three of us, representing the leadership of this band that has now stretched to over 50 years. I began to think that we had to somehow document the work of the band and of those individuals. Sadly, a few years later we lost Joe, and I felt an increasing urgency to somehow tell this history before it was lost forever. Of course, we all have so many dreams and goals that are never realized. But this one has become a reality, because of the remarkable work of one determined individual.

Thank you Kerstin, for your incredible dedication to this project. Thank you for telling the story of so many who have given so much to this great organization. It was a project I always dreamed about and yet, in honesty, never thought could really happen.

Finally, thank you to those who created the story that has been told. Kerstin states that she knew instantly upon her arrival on campus that there was something special about this organization. She was right. For those who have marched in the mud and the rain, who braved the slippery hill on the way to the practice field, who sold the magazines, who carried the freshmen suitcases at Band Camp, who slept on the gym floors, who endured the $3.00 limit at McDonalds' for over a decade, who loaded the truck up and down Chapel's stairs, who marched in blistering heat and freezing cold, who helped the thousands of Band Day students find their spots, who shared the "cold duck experience" or to those who gave your all for one or two seasons, unable to march that senior show: You are what is special about this band. Even during the most challenging and difficult times, the development of this program has never failed to amaze me. To those who walked "Through These Doors" and sadly for those in recent history who have not, you have built an organization that went far beyond any reasonable expectation. Thank you. May you always "live a life that's full."

George N. Parks

eneral sources
www.cfbdatawarehouse.com/data/div_iaa/atlantic10/massachusetts/index.php
www.politicalgraveyard.com/index.html
www.umass.edu
www.umass.edu/pastchancellors
www.umassathletics.com
www.readingbuccaneers.org
Unless otherwise noted, cited works may be found in Special Collections and Archives, University of Massachusetts at Amherst.

Chapter One

Index: vol. 1.
Index: 1870, 1871, 1873, 1875.
Cary, Harold Whiting. *The University of Massachusetts; A History of One Hundred Years.* Amherst: University of Massachusetts, 1962.
Caswell, Lilley B. *Brief History of the Massachusetts Agricultural College.* Springfield: F.A.Bassette Co, 1917.
Rand, Frank Prentice. *Yesterdays at Massachusetts State College.* Amherst: Massachusetts State College, c. 1933.

Chapter Two

Index: vol. XII, vol. XIII, vol. XIV, vol. XV, vol. XVI, vol. XVII.
Index: 1880, 1881, 1900.

Caswell, Lilley B. *Brief History of the Massachusetts Agricultural College.* Springfield: F.A. Bassette Co, 1917.

Peters, Austin. "In Memory of Charles Louis Flint." *College and Alumni News* September 1904.

"Expenses." *Eighteenth Annual Report of the Massachusetts Agricultural College* January 1881.

Chapter Three

Index: 1891, 1892, 1893, 1894, 1895, 1896, 1897, 1898, 1899, 1900, 1901.

Cornish, Lester W. "Report of Military Department." *Twenty-Seventh Annual Report of the Massachusetts Agricultural College* January 1890.

Cornish, Lester W. "Military Department." *Twenty-Eight Annual Report of the Massachusetts Agricultural College* January 1891.

Untitled. *Aggie Life* October 1, 1890.

"Our Musicians." *Aggie Life* October 29, 1890.

"Gleanings." *Aggie Life* January 14, 1891.

"Gleanings." *Aggie Life* February 11, 1891.

Cornish, Lester W. "Military Department." *Twenty-Ninth Annual Report of the Massachusetts Agricultural College* January 1892.

Dickinson, Walter M. "Military Department." *Thirtieth Annual Report of the Massachusetts Agricultural College* January 1893.

Rand, Frank Prentice. *Yesterdays at Massachusetts State College* Amherst: Massachusetts State College, c. 1933.

"The New Band Stand." *Aggie Life* April 27, 1892.

"College Notes." *Aggie Life* May 25, 1892.

Wright, Wm. Mason. "Military Department." *Thirty-Fourth Annual Report of the Massachusetts Agricultural College* January 1897.

"College Notes." *Aggie Life* March 17, 1897.

"Military Appointments." *Aggie Life* June 22, 1897.

Wright, Wm. Mason. "Military Department." *Thirty-Fifth Annual Report of the Massachusetts Agricultural College* January 1898.

Chapter Four

Index: 1902, 1903, 1904, 1905, 1906, 1907, 1908, 1909, 1910, 1911, 1912.

Anderson, John. "Military Department." *Thirty-Eighth Annual Report of the Massachusetts Agricultural College* January 1901.

Anderson, John. "Military Department." *Thirty-Ninth Annual Report of the Massachusetts Agricultural College* January 1902.

"College Notes." *Aggie Life* October 10, 1900.

"Editorials." *Aggie Life* October 16, 1901.

Rand, Frank Prentice. *Yesterdays at Massachusetts State College* Amherst: Massachusetts State College, c. 1933.

Anderson, John. "Military Department." *Fortieth Annual Report of the Massachusetts Agricultural College* January 1903.

"Band Concert." *College Signal* May 7, 1902.

"Band Concert." *College Signal* May 28, 1902.

"College Notes." *College Signal* October 8, 1902.

Anderson, John. "Military Department." *Forty-First Annual Report of the Massachusetts Agricultural College* January 1904.

"College Notes." *College Signal* February 25, 1903.

"Band Concerts." *College Signal* March 18, 1903.

"Program for the Thirty-third Commencement." *College Signal* June 16, 1903.

"Battalion Roster." *College Signal* June 16, 1903.

"Editorials." *College Signal* November 4, 1903.

"College Notes." *College Signal* May 11, 1904.

Anderson, John. "Military Department." *Forty-Second Annual Report of the Massachusetts Agricultural College* January 1905.

Anderson, John. "Military Department." *Forty-Third Annual Report of the Massachusetts Agricultural College* January 1906.

Martin, George Chipman. "Military Department." *Forty-Fourth Annual Report of the Massachusetts Agricultural College* January 1907.

Martin, George Chipman. "Report of the Military Department." *Forty-Fifth Annual Report of the Massachusetts Agricultural College* January 1908.

"College Notes." *College and Alumni News* September 1905.
"College Notes." *College Signal* April 19, 1905.
"College Notes." *College Signal* May 3, 1905.
"College Notes." *College Signal* January 24, 1906.
"College Notes." *College Signal* June 6, 1906.
"The New Tug of War." *College Signal* September 26, 1906.
Untitled. *College Signal* May 29, 1907.
"Anniversary Celebration." *College Signal* October 16, 1907.
"Editorials." *College Signal* November 25, 1908.
"Assembly." *College Signal* January 18, 1910.
"Concert of the Musical Association." March 9, 1910.
"Assembly." *College Signal* May 17, 1910.
"College Notes." *College Signal* May 31, 1910.
"College Singing." *College Signal* September 27, 1910.
"College Notes." *College Signal* October 18, 1910.

Chapter Five

Index: 1913, 1914, 1915, 1916, 1917, 1918, 1919, 1921.
"Battle of Cushman." *College Signal* May 7, 1912.
"Spring Musical Trip." *College Signal* March 25, 1913.
"High School Day." *College Signal* May 13, 1913.
"Musical Clubs." *College Signal* September 30, 1913.
"Campus Notes." *College Signal* October 7, 1913.
"Campus Notes." *College Signal* October 14, 1913.
"Communications." *College Signal* December 2, 1913.
"Military Demonstration." *College Signal* May 5, 1914.
"Students Supplied Money and Labor for Alumni Field." *Massachusetts Collegian* December 7, 1950.
"Military Appointments." *College Signal* June 16, 1914.
"Campus Notes." *Massachusetts Collegian* May 11, 1915.
"Cadet Appointments." *Massachusetts Collegian* June 15, 1915.
"Team Given Send-off." *Massachusetts Collegian* October 19, 1915.
"Campus Notes." *Massachusetts Collegian* October 26, 1915.
"Enrollment of Entering Class Drops to Low Mark." *Massachusetts Collegian* October 16, 1917.
"Aggie Battalion Will Parade in Northampton." *Massachusetts Collegian* April 16, 1918.
"Battalion is a Feature of Northampton Parade." *Massachusetts Collegian* April 23, 1918.
"S.A.T.C. Unit Established at M.A.C." *Massachusetts Collegian* October 16, 1918.

Chapter Six

Index: 1923, 1926, 1928.
"Alumni Parade for Commencement." *Alumni Bulletin* April 24, 1920.
"Detailed Program for the Parade." *Alumni Bulletin* May 24, 1920.
"The Band." *Massachusetts Collegian* May 26, 1920.
"Alumni Parade to Precede Game Saturday." *Massachusetts Collegian* June 16, 1920.
"Band Organizes." *Massachusetts Collegian* October 13, 1920.
"Once More the Aggie Band Will Lead Us." *Massachusetts Collegian* November 10, 1920.
"Campus Calendar." *Massachusetts Collegian* November 17, 1920.
"Sidelights on the Game." *Massachusetts Collegian* November 17, 1920.
"Commencement Program is Practically Complete." *Massachusetts Collegian* March 16, 1921.
"Semi-Centennial Commencement." *Alumni Bulletin* March 24, 1921.
"Alumni Parade to Amherst Game." *Alumni Bulletin* May 24, 1921.
"Band." *Massachusetts Collegian* November 9, 1921.
"Freshman Drum Corps." *Massachusetts Collegian* April 19, 1922.
Shnyder, Frederick. Memo to Kenyon Butterfield. October 25, 1922.
"Campus Notes." *Massachusetts Collegian* October 25, 1922.
"Campus Notes." *Massachusetts Collegian* November 1, 1922.
"Are You Going?" *Massachusetts Collegian* November 8, 1922.
"Tag Day Monday Nets Goodly Sum for Band." *Massachusetts Collegian* November 15, 1922.
"Side Lights." *Massachusetts Collegian* November 22, 1922.
"Legislature at M.A.C." *Massachusetts Collegian* May 9, 1923.
"Military Unit is Organized." *Massachusetts Collegian* October 1, 1924.

"A Real Band." *Alumni Bulletin*, November 25, 1924.
"Campus Notes." *Massachusetts Collegian* November 19, 1924.
"Cheer, Boys, Cheer." *Massachusetts Collegian* October 21, 1925.
"Down At Pratt Field." *Massachusetts Collegian* November 4, 1925.
"Mass Meeting." *Massachusetts Collegian* November 18, 1925.
"New Officer for R.O.T.C. Unit." *Massachusetts Collegian* October 6, 1926.
"Personals." *Massachusetts Collegian* November 17, 1926.

Chapter Seven

Index: 1933.
"Military Notes." *Massachusetts Collegian* January 12, 1927.
"Military Notes." *Massachusetts Collegian* January 19, 1927.
"Military Notes." *Massachusetts Collegian* January 26, 1927.
"Military Notes." *Massachusetts Collegian* February 2, 1927.
"Military Notes." *Massachusetts Collegian* February 9, 1927.
"Military Notes." *Massachusetts Collegian* March 2, 1927.
"Military Notes." *Massachusetts Collegian* April 13, 1927.
"Military Notes." *Massachusetts Collegian* October 5, 1927.
"Military Notes." *Massachusetts Collegian* October 19, 1927.
"Plan Impressive Inaugural Parade." *Massachusetts Collegian* October 26, 1927.
"Real Pep Shown at Mass Meeting." *Massachusetts Collegian* November 22, 1927.
"Tufts Luck." *Massachusetts Collegian* November 22, 1927.
"Military Notes." *Massachusetts Collegian* January 25, 1928.
"New Course in Music." *Massachusetts Collegian* October 3, 1928.
"Military Notes." *Massachusetts Collegian* October 3, 1928.
"Military Notes." *Massachusetts Collegian* October 10, 1928.
"Support the Band." *Massachusetts Collegian* October 31, 1928.
"Boston Alumni Hold Football Rally." *Alumni Bulletin*, November 25, 1928.
"Military Notes." *Massachusetts Collegian* January 23, 1929.
"Military Notes." *Massachusetts Collegian* March 6, 1929.
"Gridsters Cheered at Mass Meeting." *Massachusetts Collegian* October 9, 1929.
"Outstanding Performance of the Week." *Massachusetts Collegian* October 9, 1929.
"College Band Progressing Under Captain Sumner." *Massachusetts Collegian* February 5, 1930.
"Famed U.S. Army Band to Play Next Week." *Massachusetts Collegian* October 16, 1930.
"New College Song by Capt. E.M. Sumner." *Massachusetts Collegian* November 1, 1930.
"Captain Sumner to Remain Another Year." *Massachusetts Collegian* April 23, 1931.
"Military Men Take Prizes at Hartford." *Massachusetts Collegian* May 13, 1931.
"Capt. Sumner Again Leads College Band." *Massachusetts Collegian* October 7, 1931.
"And the Band Played." *Massachusetts Collegian* November 4, 1931.
"Capt. Sumner Sent to Kansas." *Massachusetts Collegian* April 27, 1932.
"College Band Now an Academic Activity." *Massachusetts Collegian* April 27, 1932.
"Academics: Band." *The Alumni Bulletin* October, 1932.
"New Band Prospects Look Very Favorable." *Massachusetts Collegian* October 13, 1932.
"Singing and Cheering Practiced at Assembly." *Massachusetts Collegian* October 20, 1932.
Academics Board. Memo to ROTC Colonel Romeyn. April 3, 1933.
"Academics News: the Band." *The Alumni Bulletin* May 1933.
"Band to Appear in Inaugural Parade." *Massachusetts Collegian* October 5, 1933.
"Action Taken on Band Dissension." *Massachusetts Collegian* November 9, 1933.
"Band Organization to Play at Tufts Game." *Massachusetts Collegian* November 23, 1933.

Chapter Eight

Index: 1934, 1935, 1938, 1939, 1940, 1941, 1942.
Snow, Samuel P. "To the Editor of the Collegian." *Massachusetts Collegian* September 27, 1934.
"The Band (?)." *Massachusetts Collegian* October 4, 1934.
"Announcements." *Massachusetts Collegian* November 1, 1934.
"Band Practices for Tufts Trip." *Massachusetts Collegian* November 8, 1934.
"Academics: Band." *The Alumni Bulletin* December 1934.
"Outstanding Student Achievements in Campus Affairs." *Massachusetts Collegian* January 4, 1935.
"Campus Calendar." *Massachusetts Collegian* March 21, 1935.
"Maroon and White Band Soon to be a Reality." *Massachusetts Collegian* April 11, 1935.

"Academics: Band." *The Alumni Bulletin* April 1935.

Baker, Hugh P. Memo to Academics Board. October 4, 1935.

"Academics: the Band." *The Alumni Bulletin* October 1935.

President's Office. Memo to William Machmer. October 15, 1935.

"Academics: the Band." *The Alumni Bulletin* January 1936.

"Band to Play at March 26 Convocation." *Massachusetts Collegian* March 19, 1936.

Aplington, Horace. "The Band." *Massachusetts Collegian* June 6, 1936.

"Academics: Band." *The Alumni Bulletin* May 1936.

Thayer, Clark. "From the Academics Mailbag." *The Alumni Bulletin* June 1936.

"Band Lays Plans for Busy Season" *Massachusetts Collegian* September 24, 1936.

"Band Schedules Five Appearances." *Massachusetts Collegian* October 8, 1936.

"College Broadcast on Alumni Night, November 5." *The Alumni Bulletin* November 1936.

"Academics: Band." *The Alumni Bulletin* November 1936.

"Band to Appear in Convocation on February 25." *Massachusetts Collegian* February 18, 1937.

Convocation Concert Program. February 25, 1937.

"Senate Gives New Uniforms for Band." *Massachusetts Collegian* March 4, 1937.

"Band to Broadcast over WBZ Tonight." *Massachusetts Collegian* March 18, 1937.

"Band Seeks for Twirling Co-ed." *Massachusetts Collegian* September 30, 1937.

"Old Chapel to be Occupied by Social Science Divisions." *The Alumni Bulletin* October 1937.

"Two Coeds Remain in Drum Major Contest." *Massachusetts Collegian* October 21, 1937.

"Alumni Broadcast Tonight from Springfield." *Massachusetts Collegian* October 28, 1937.

"The 1892 Clock." *TheAlumni Bulletin* November 1937.

"Academics: Band." *TheAlumni Bulletin* November 1937.

"Band Will be in Combined Parade." *Massachusetts Collegian* November 4, 1937.

"Alumni Night Broadcast." *The Alumni Bulletin* December 1937.

"Academic, Bay State Revue." *The Alumni Bulletin* December 1937.

"R.P.I. and M.S.C. Combine Bands Saturday." *Massachusetts Collegian* November 12, 1937.

"Last Rally of Season Friday." *Massachusetts Collegian* November 18, 1937.

Baker, Hugh. Memo to Frank Rand. November 27, 1937.

"Students Vote 75c on Band and Index Taxes." *Massachusetts Collegian* January 20, 1938.

"First Band Concert of Year is Given on Fifth Reorganization Anniversary." *Massachusetts Collegian* December 15, 1938.

"Academics: Band." *The Alumni Bulletin* December 1939.

"Academics: Band." *The Alumni Bulletin* January 1939.

"Musical Activities of Past Year Outstanding in History of State." *Massachusetts Collegian* May 25, 1939.

"Alumni Day, Saturday, June 10." *The Alumni Bulletin* June 1939.

"Band's Christmas Concert Wed." *Massachusetts Collegian* December 11, 1941.

Christmas Concert Program. December 17, 1941.

"Band Announces New Instrument Purchased." *Massachusetts Collegian* January 29, 1942.

"College Band to be at Next Convocation." *Massachusetts Collegian* February 19, 1942.

"Spring Band Festival Will Meet at Boston U." *Massachusetts Collegian* March 5, 1942.

"Music for Morale to be Theme of Fourth Annual Music Week." *Massachusetts Collegian* April 23, 1942.

"Spring Concert to be Given May 3." *Massachusetts Collegian* April 23, 1942.

"The Cavalry—R.O.T.C.—At Massachusetts State." *The Alumni Bulletin* July 1942.

Chapter Nine

Index: 1943, 1944, 1945, 1946, 1947, 1948, 1949, 1950.

"Band May Include Women Members." *Massachusetts Collegian* October 15, 1942.

"Retreat Formation Starts for Cadets." "Work Of the Band." *Massachusetts Collegian* October 22, 1942.

"Christmas Concert by Band Features Military Numbers." *Massachusetts Collegian* December 17, 1942.

Christmas Concert Program. December 19, 1942.

"Academics: Band." *The Alumni Bulletin* December 1942.

"Many Changes on Campus Noted with Arrival of "Singing Fifty-Eighth." *Massachusetts Collegian* April 8, 1943.

"Coeds Members of 58th CTD Band."*Massachusetts Collegian* October 28, 1943.

Alviani, Doric. Music Department Report. c. 1956.

"Twirlers, Drum Majors, Majorettes, Band Men, Girl Drill Team Chosen." *Massachusetts Collegian* October 9, 1946.

"Homecoming Rally." *Massachusetts Collegian* November 1, 1946.

"Snappy Appearance of Band And Bandettes." *Massachusetts Collegian* November 8, 1946.

"MSC Bandettes Cause Mild Riot at Tufts." *Massachusetts Collegian* November 22, 1946.

"Cadets, Band, Baseball Mark Legislature Day." *Massachusetts Collegian* May 15, 1947.

"Music Groups Join in Xmas Program." *Massachusetts Collegian* December 11, 1947.

"Schabas to Direct UM Marching Band." *Massachusetts Collegian* September 24, 1948.

"1000 Attend Rally, Torchlight Parade." *Massachusetts Collegian* September 30, 1948.

"Joint Concert Planned of Amherst, UM Bands." *Massachusetts Collegian* November 11, 1948.

"Huge Audience Cheers New UM Concert Band." *Massachusetts Collegian* February 10, 1949.

"Mothers Enjoy Play and Band Concert." *Massachusetts Collegian* May 19, 1949.

"Beat Norwich Rally to be Friday Night." *Massachusetts Collegian* September 29, 1949.

"50 Gals a Handful Says Doug Footit." *Massachusetts Collegian* September 29, 1949.

"Enthusiastic Crowd Jams Bowker for First Football Rally of Season." *Massachusetts Collegian* October 6, 1949.

"Girls in Band." *Massachusetts Collegian* October 13, 1949.

"Marching Drill Team and Band Highlight UM-Rochester Game." *Massachusetts Collegian* October 27, 1949.

"Tufts Rally March to Hit Amherst; Floats, Mechanized Band in Parade." *Massachusetts Collegian* November 10, 1949.

"Two Drill Teams, Band Highlight Springfield Game." *Massachusetts Collegian* November 10, 1949.

"Banquet at Drake Honors Drill Team, Band, and Others." *Massachusetts Collegian* December 1, 1949.

"Little is Known of Metawampi, Guardian Spirit of the University." *Massachusetts Collegian* April 20, 1950.

"Band Concert Draws Large Crowd." *Massachusetts Collegian* May 11, 1950.

Chapter Ten

Index: 1951, 1952, 1953, 1954, 1956, 1957, 1958, 1959, 1960, 1961, 1962, 1963.

"UM Bands Expand to Include Coeds." *Massachusetts Collegian* September 28, 1950.

"Metawampe Saved from Embarrassment by Campus Hero." *Massachusetts Collegian* September 28, 1950.

"Coeds Make Fine Showing in Debut with U of M Band." *Massachusetts Collegian* October 5, 1950.

"Gigantic Rally this Friday Night." *Massachusetts Collegian* November 2, 1950.

"Metawampe, Gift of Class of '50 Unveiled, Accepted by Van Meter." *Massachusetts Collegian* February 15, 1951.

"Metawampe—a Tradition." *Massachusetts Collegian* March 27, 1951.

Fox, Bruce "Band Support." *Massachusetts Collegian* March 27, 1951.

"Marching Band Policy Changed." *Massachusetts Collegian* September 28, 1951.

"Bonfire, Concert to be in Parking Lot Friday." *Massachusetts Collegian* October 12, 1951.

"Contino Reveals Marching Band Plan for Short Range Expansion." *Massachusetts Collegian* October 17, 1952.

"Three New Twirlers Join Marching Band." *Massachusetts Collegian* October 21, 1952.

"Band and Drill Team Feature Waltzy Steps." *Massachusetts Collegian* October 24, 1952.

"TV to Carry UM Drill Team and Band at Tufts." *Massachusetts Collegian* November 14, 1952.

"Band Sports New Uniforms this Season." *Massachusetts Collegian* September 21, 1953.

"Senate Appropriates Money to Buy New Band Uniforms." *Massachusetts Collegian* October 2, 1953.

"Marching Band Swings into 1953 Season." *Massachusetts Collegian* October 6, 1953.

"Pep Band." *Massachusetts Collegian* January 15, 1954.

"Student Senate to Buy Uniforms for Drill Team." *Massachusetts Collegian* March 19, 1954.

May, Madeleine. "Rodgers & Hammerstein Receive Honorary Degrees at UM Convo." *Massachusetts Collegian* April 2, 1954.

"WHYN to Televise Concert Band Show." *Massachusetts Collegian* May 18, 1954.

"President Mather Leads Harvard Motorcade." *Massachusetts Collegian* October 1, 1954.

Gordon, Jack. "Entire University Makes Great Showing in First Major Public Appearance as O'Rourkemen Stun Harvard, 13–7." *Massachusetts Collegian* October 5, 1954.

May, Madeleine. "Redmen Warwhoop Heard from Amherst to Boston." *Massachusetts Collegian* October 5, 1954.

"Band and Drill Team Excel." *Massachusetts Collegian* October 5, 1954.

"Univ. Concert Band to Make Campus Appearance Sunday." *Massachusetts Collegian* April 22, 1955.

"Mem Hall Lawn Will be Stage for Pops." *Massachusetts Collegian* May 13, 1955.

"UMass Obituaries." *Massachusetts Collegian* October 4, 1955.

"No Football; Fans Enjoy Precisionettes' Show." *Massachusetts Collegian* October 19, 1956.

"UM Band Completes Spring Concert Tour." Massachusetts *Collegian* March 29, 1957.

"Precisionettes and Three Umie Bands Face Coming School Year's Activities." *Massachusetts Collegian* September 6, 1957.

"And the Band Plays On ..." *Massachusetts Collegian* October 31, 1958.

Bresciani, Dick. "UM Gridders Invade Delaware's Blue Hens." *Massachusetts Collegian* November 7, 1958.

"UMass Concert Musicians Will Perform This Friday." *Massachusetts Collegian* December 3, 1958.

Soucy, Andrew J. and Ira Barr Poretsky. "Contino Quits as Band Director as Senates Votes "No Confidence." *Massachusetts Collegian* May 8, 1959.

Croteau, Don. "Maine Visits Alumni Field; No UMass Band to Play." *Massachusetts Collegian* September 18, 1959.

Witkoski, Donald E., Richard A. Draper, and Shannon McCune. "The Band Controversy; Conflicting Viewpoints." *Massachusetts Collegian* September 18, 1959.

Teran, Lloyd. "School Spirit Is Not Dead." *Massachusetts Collegian* September 28, 1959.

"Band and Precisionettes Set for First Appearance Saturday." *Massachusetts Collegian* September 30, 1959.

Basile, Vin. "Redmen Swamped by Mighty Delaware." *Massachusetts Collegian* October 5, 1959.

Jarvela, Judy. "Precisionettes at R.I. Game." *Massachusetts Collegian* October 20, 1959.

Reseigh, Ann. "Precisionettes and Band Expand with University." *Massachusetts Collegian* November 9, 1959.

"Concert Band Will Play for Tree Lighting In N.Y." *Massachusetts Collegian* December 7, 1959.

University Bands Handbook. c. 1960.

"We Really Showed Them!" *Massachusetts Collegian* October 3, 1960.

"Harvard Band Loses, Too!" reprinted from the *Boston Globe*. *Massachusetts Collegian* October 3, 1960.

"New Senate Sworn In; Dance Band Jackets Okayed." *Massachusetts Collegian* October 7, 1960.

Gallivan, Jacqueline. "Colorful Procession Launches Lederle Inauguration. *Massachusetts Collegian* April 24, 1961.

"Informality Keynotes Spring Pops Concert." *Massachusetts Collegian* May 8, 1961.

Massachusetts Alumnus Fall 1961.

"Money for Spirit." *Massachusetts Collegian* September 21, 1962.

Robicheau, Betsy. "To the Redmen Marching Band." *Massachusetts Collegian* September 21 1962.

"A Common Goal." *Massachusetts Collegian* September 24, 1962.

"Arts Council Turns Down Redmen Band." *Massachusetts Collegian* September 26, 1962.

Miller, Ann. "Offer Made to Band; but Redmen Cannot Go." *Massachusetts Collegian* September 28, 1962.

"Campus Stepchild." *Massachusetts Collegian* September 28, 1962.

"Fans Greet Redmen." *Massachusetts Collegian* October 8, 1962.

Miller, Ann. "Senate Appropriates Funds; Band Will Go to Villanova." *Massachusetts Collegian* October 26, 1962.

"Thee Our Alma Mater." *Massachusetts Collegian* November 28, 1962.

"Redmen Band Members Excused from Phys. Ed." *Massachusetts Collegian* May 8, 1963.

Band Alumni Newsletter Fall 1989.

Chapter Eleven

Index: 1971.

Freeland, Richard M. *Academia's Golden Age: Universities in Massachusetts.* New York: Oxford University Press, 1992.

Massachusetts Band History Scrapbook. c. 1963.

University of Massachusetts Football Programs: 1963–1977.

Haracz, Dave. "Old Redmen Band Sports New Look This Year." *Massachusetts Collegian* September 18, 1963.

McNamara, Elwin. "UMass Precisionettes Future Role in Doubt." *Massachusetts Collegian* September 30, 1963.

"Precisionettes and Band See Rift Widen." *Massachusetts Collegian* October 7, 1963.

McNamara, Elwin. "Precisionettes and Band Still Without Solution." *Massachusetts Collegian* October 9, 1963.

McNamara, Elwin. "Precisionettes Join ROTC, March in Parade Tonight." *Massachusetts Collegian* October 18, 1963.

"Arabian Nights Feature of Marching Band." *Massachusetts Collegian* October 18, 1963.

"Band to Play at Home with Brand New Routine." *Massachusetts Collegian* November 1, 1963.

"Marching Band Honors Fusia." *Massachusetts Collegian* November 6, 1963.

"Newly Appointed Conductor Lauded." *Massachusetts Collegian* December 6, 1963.

"Pep Band Appears at Game." *Massachusetts Collegian* February 12, 1964.

"Band to Introduce Arranger Sat." *Massachusetts Collegian* November 13, 1964.

"Send Band to Bowl." *Massachusetts Collegian* November 18, 1964.

"Orange Tags Aiding Band." *Massachusetts Collegian* December 1, 1964.

"Redmen Head South." *Massachusetts Collegian* December 9, 1964.

"University Symphony Band to Present First Concert of New Season on Sunday." *Massachusetts Collegian* January 6, 1965.

"University Band Ready with New Halftime Show." *Massachusetts Collegian* September 16, 1966.

University of Massachusetts Bulletin Undergraduate Schools 1965–1966, p. 137.

University of Massachusetts Bulletin Undergraduate Catalog 1966–67, p. 179.

Venman, William. Memo to Oswald Tippo and John Lederle. c. February 1970.

Venman, William. Memo to Oswald Tippo and John Lederle. May 27, 1970.

Chapter Twelve

Index: 1992, 1993, 1996.

Dobrow, Marty. *Going Bigtime: The Spectacular Rise of UMass Basketball.* Northampton: Summerset Press, 1996.

Mark, David R. "Music to My Ears." *Massachusetts Daily Collegian* September 27, 1988.

"Marching Band to Perform on National Television Oct. 21." *The Campus Chronicle* October 12, 1990.

"UMass Marching Band Prepares for First Football Game Aug. 30." *The Campus Chronicle* August 29, 1997.

"Minuteman Marching Band chosen tops in U. S." *The Campus Chronicle* January 9, 1998.

Carey, Mary. "Come on and Hear." *UMass Magazine* Fall 1998.

Trenkle, Jason. "Power and Class Honored as Best in Nation." *Massachusetts Daily Collegian* October 13, 1998.

Buchholz, Sarah R. "Capital Day for the Minuteman Band." *The Campus Chronicle* January 26, 2001.

Fitzgibbons, Daniel J. "Panel to Review Marching Band." *The Campus Chronicle* February 23, 2001.

Buchholz, Sarah R. "Marching Band Wins Cheers in Indianapolis." *The Campus Chronicle* January 18, 2002.